Parking Lot Picker's Songbook

MANDOLIN EDITION

By Dix Bruce

Online Audio www.melbay.com/96865BCDEB

A collection of over 200 great Bluegrass, Old Time, Country, and Gospel standards. Melodies are presented with standard notation and tablature along with lyrics and chords. The audio includes recordings of EVERY song in the book with Dix Bruce on guitar, mandolin, and vocals and Bill Evans on banjo and vocals.

Learn to play songs written and recorded by the giants of traditional American music: Bill Monroe, The Stanley Brothers, Flatt & Scruggs, Ralph Stanley, The Osborne Brothers, Jimmy Martin, Doc Watson, and many more.

Also included: Step-by-step instruction on how to transpose any song to any key!

Special thanks to Sherry Shachter, Bob Bergman, and Lorna Swain for their help in preparing this book.
Their kind suggestions improved it greatly.

Cover photos by, clockwise from top: Dix Bruce, Bill Evans, Gene Tortora, Bill Evans and Tom Tworek.

1 2 3 4 5 6 7 8 9 0

Visit us on the Web at www.melbay.com — E-mail us at email@melbay.com

Table of Contents

Introduction

The Parking Lot Picker's Songbook is an all-in-one sourcebook for musicians to help build their bluegrass repertoire and more effectively play with others in jam sessions and in bands.

Bluegrass and old time music is unlike most other types of music. Aside from the obvious differences in sound, bluegrass fans are usually players in addition to being listeners. Bluegrass fans typically bring their instruments to concerts and festivals and spend as much time swapping songs and jamming as they do watching the headline acts. Everybody picks: young and old, male and female, beginners to professionals. It's a wonderfully communal, world-wide group that welcomes like-minded strangers who pack a guitar, banjo, mandolin, fiddle, or a voice to sing with.

The shared repertoire is what brings them all together and it's a powerful phenomenon. You can go to a bluegrass get together in Tokyo, Buenos Aires, Paris, Reykjavik, or anywhere else in the world, and the local players will know the same Bill Monroe and Stanley Brothers songs and fiddle tunes that you know. You'll be able to break musical bread and communicate with strangers no matter what the local language is. *The Parking Lot Picker's Songbook* is my attempt to collect a large number of these songs in one place and present them to you with melody, lyrics, chords, tablature, and a recording of each individual song. *The Parking Lot Picker's Songbook* provides easy access to much of this core repertoire and is a great resource for both the newcomer and the more experienced player who is looking to expand his or her song repertoire.

So, what's a "parking lot picker"?

The term "parking lot picker" grew out of the early bluegrass festivals where fans would stand around in parking lots adjacent to festival or concert sites and jam or "pick." These days you're likely to find assorted groups of parking lot pickers jamming, swapping tunes and licks, and sharing their love of the music at any bluegrass event you attend. Parking lot pickers play music together at every opportunity. If you have an interest in playing and singing bluegrass music with others — no matter what your experience or ability level — then you are a "parking lot picker" and this book is for you!

What songs are included in this book?

Many of the most loved and important songs in traditional American music are collected in the *Parking Lot Picker's Songbook*, including many traditional favorites from gospel music. I love every one of them! I've heard many of them all my life, around home, at school and in church. Every one is special to me. Each represents a favorite theme, artist, or period in the history of American bluegrass, country, gospel, and old time music. It is my hope that you too will love these songs and use this book at jam sessions and performances sharing great music with friends and family.

In compiling this anthology I combed though my LPs and CDs, song books, and set lists. I paid special attention to the works of the pioneers of bluegrass and American old time music: Bill Monroe, the Stanley Brothers, Flatt & Scruggs, Ralph Stanley, the Osborne Brothers, Jimmy Martin, Doc Watson, along with many other important artists. You'll find them strongly represented, both with traditional pieces that were part of their repertoires and with songs they composed themselves. Over 100 years of American music is contained in these pages. From Stephen Foster's tragic "Hard Times" to Dean Webb and Mitch Jayne's "Old Home Place," to the traditional-turned-jam band favorite "I Know You Rider." You're bound to encounter many of your favorites as well as discover new songs that you'll want to add to your repertoire. Of course I had to leave out hundreds more. Maybe someday there'll be a *Parking Lot Picker's Songbook Volume Two*!

Most of these songs have been recorded again and again by bluegrass, country, gospel, and old time artists. I've listed the names of some of them on each song. If I left out your favorite artist, I apologize. My aim was to give you a representative group for each song rather than a comprehensive or all-inclusive list. I did lean toward the pioneers of the styles mentioned above. I also included some personal favorites that I wanted you to know about. I mentioned a few of my own recordings, both solo and with Jim Nunally.

It's important that you seek out and listen to these seminal recordings. I didn't name specific CDs the songs can be found on since collections, titles, and availability are constantly changing. Anything I might have included would likely be out of date within a month or two. Since the advent of box sets, compilations by the great artists are widely available. These days you can also search for instantly downloadable versions of your favorite songs on the internet. iTunes and other downloading services are convenient and reasonably priced and seem to be the wave of the future.

Some of the songs are more obscure and may not have been recorded widely. Still they are special favorites of mine that I hope you will enjoy both in the book and on the accompanying audio recordings. And I couldn't resist putting in a few of my original compositions.

How do I use the Parking Lot Picker's Songbook?

The songs are listed alphabetically and I've designed this book to minimize page turns. Song titles are shown centered at the top of each page. Composer information, if known, is shown on the upper right. Audio and track locations are shown on the upper left under key designation. For example, the recording of "Are You From Dixie?" is on audio number one, track six. Most song titles are shown in the "Notes on Selected Songs" section on page 285 where alternate titles are listed. This section includes any additional information or comments I might have on the individual songs. Following this, you'll find a listing by artist.

Most of these songs are based on traditional sources and as such can be heard with a variety of versions, melodies and lyrics. I went with the versions I was most familiar with. Feel free to do the same and substitute your favorite chords, lyrics, and melodies as the mood strikes you.

Typical performance keys for both male and female voices are shown in the upper left corner of each song. I used my own voice as a starting point. My voice is a fairly typical male voice, not too low, not too high. I have found that if I sing a song in the key of G, a typical female voice will sing the same song in the key of C or D, a fourth or fifth higher than where I sing it. This is reflected in the notation:

M: G
F: C or D

"M" stands for "male voice," which will sing the song in the key of "G," "F" stands for "female voice," which will sing the song in the key of "C" or "D." Of course there will be cases when these suggested keys might not fit your voice, whether you are a male or a female. Never fear, we'll learn to transpose the songs to any key.

Most of the songs are pitched in the keys of G and C. There are several reasons for this. G and C are probably the most popular keys for bluegrass, gospel, and old time music, and many of the "original" recordings of these songs are in G or C. G and C are also relatively easy keys to play in. However, most of the songs fit well into other keys too. Don't be afraid to move songs around. You'll discover all sorts of tonal characteristics unique to different keys.

What's the best way to learn a song?

It's a good idea to listen to the recorded version of the song first to get an idea of how it goes. Audio and track numbers are listed under the key designations on each page. Short representative excerpts of **all** the songs have been recorded with guitar, mandolin, banjo, and vocals on the audio accompanying this book. My friend, banjo player and singer Bill Evans, recorded them with me. I sing and play guitar and mandolin. Bill wrote the banjo version of this book. It's identical to this one and includes chords, lyrics, melodies in standard notation, plus banjo tablature. I also wrote a guitar version of *The Parking Lot Picker's Songbook*. It's just like this mandolin edition except that it includes guitar tablature instead of mandolin tab.

As you listen to a song, follow along with the lyrics, music and tablature. Then play along. Try singing with the recording to determine if the song is pitched in your key.

As I mentioned above, I've found that a typical female range is usually a fourth or fifth musical interval above the male key. Key designations on each song reflect this. Of course everybody's voice is a little different and we're looking at this rule only as a starting point. So, if a song is written here in the key of D, to back up a female voice, you'd start by transposing the chords of the song from the key of D to the key of G or A, a fourth or fifth above the key of D. More about the process of transposing below.

How can I change the key of a song to better fit my voice or instrument?

Let's say the suggested keys don't work for your voice or for how you want to play the mandolin. It's a simple process to transpose the chord progression to other keys. It's a bit more involved to change the melodies and write them out, but the same principles apply. Most of you will probably just need to transpose the chords so you can accompany yourself in a new key.

Let's look at "Amazing Grace" on page 11. It's presented here in the key of G, noted in the upper left hand corner of the page. Again, "M: _G_" means that a typical male voice would sing "Amazing Grace" in the key of G. To accommodate a typical female voice we need to change the chords to a different key, C or D. The *Scale and Transposition Chart* will make the process of transposing easier.

Scale and Transposition Chart

Key	Key signature #/b	Major scale	1	2	3	4	5	6	7	8 (1)
			I	ii	iii	IV	V	vi	vii°	I
C	none	C	C	Dm	Em	F	G	Am	B°	C
F	1 - ♭	F	F	Gm	Am	B♭	C	Dm	E°	F
B♭	2 - ♭	B♭	B♭	Cm	Dm	E♭	F	Gm	A°	B♭
E♭	3 - ♭	E♭	E♭	Fm	Gm	A♭	B♭	Cm	D°	E♭
A♭	4 - ♭	A♭	A♭	B♭m	Cm	D♭	E♭	Fm	G°	A♭
D♭	5 - ♭	D♭	D♭	E♭m	Fm	G♭	A♭	B♭m	C°	D♭
G♭	6 - ♭	G♭	G♭	A♭m	B♭m	C♭	D♭	E♭m	F°	G♭
C♭	7 - ♭	C♭	C♭	D♭m	E♭m	F♭	G♭	A♭m	B♭°	C♭
C♯	7 - ♯	C♯	C♯	D♯m	E♯m	F♯	G♯	A♯m	B♯°	C♯
F♯	6 - ♯	F♯	F♯	G♯m	A♯m	B	C♯	D♯m	E♯°	F♯
B	5 - ♯	B	B	C♯m	D♯m	E	F♯	G♯m	A♯°	B
E	4 - ♯	E	E	F♯m	G♯m	A	B	C♯m	D♯°	E
A	3 - ♯	A	A	Bm	C♯m	D	E	F♯m	G♯°	A
D	2 - ♯	D	D	Em	F♯m	G	A	Bm	C♯°	D
G	1 - ♯	G	G	Am	Bm	C	D	Em	F♯°	G

The chart shows the scales, chords, and key signature (number of sharps or flats) that identify each key. If you look in the key of G line at the bottom of the chart, you'll see in the second column ("key signature") that the key of G has one sharp in its key signature. If you read across to the right you'll see "G Am Bm C D Em F♯°." These are the chords of the key of G and all are made up using only the notes of the G major scale. Songs in the key of G can have other chords as well, like E or A7, but to make these chords we need to use notes from outside of the G major scale. If you remove all the "m" (minor) and "°" (diminished) chord designations, you'll come up with the G scale, which is "G A B C D E F♯." Be sure to leave the sharps and flats shown or the scale changes. So, how do we use this to transpose?

Going back to "Amazing Grace," we see that the chord progression to the first line of the song is G—C—G. Since "Amazing Grace" is written here in the key of G (noted in the upper left hand corner of the page, "M: _G_") let's see where these chords occur in the "key of G" line in the chart. The G chord is in the "I" (upper case Roman numeral one) column. The G chord in the key of G is a "one" chord. The C chord is in the "IV" column and is a "four" chord. We need to know where these chords fit numerically in order to transpose them. All chords are identified by Roman numerals, upper case for majors (I, IV, V) lower case for minors (ii, iii, vi) and the lone diminished chord which has a little circle as part of the chord name (vii°).

Let's transpose "Amazing Grace" from the male key of G to the first suggested female key of C. We'll be transposing it to a higher key, which will be to a key "later" in the musical alphabet (A, B, C, D, E, F, G) like C, D, E, etc. (That might be a little confusing but keep in mind that the musical alphabet continues to the right and left, like a keyboard: A, B, C, D, E, F, G, A, B, C, D, E, F, G, A, B, C, D, E, F, G. If you start in the middle on a G, you can get to an A by going either left or right, "earlier" or "later" in the musical alphabet. For our purposes here, let's say that "later" in the musical alphabet is toward a higher key, "earlier" is toward a lower key.)

Let's start with the first chord of the original key, the G chord, in the "I" column. Follow up in the "I" column to the key of C row. The I chord in the key of C is an C chord. Write a "C" in everywhere you see a G chord on the music to "Amazing Grace." (I suggest that you write in pencil in case your voice changes!)

The next chord in the original key of G version of "Amazing Grace" is a C. The C chord is in the IV column of the key of G row. Follow that column up to the key of C row and you'll find the new chord is an F. Write an "F" in everywhere you see a C chord in the music to "Amazing Grace."

There's one more chord in the key of G version of "Amazing Grace" and that's the D. Once again, find the D in the key of G row. It's in the "V" column and is a "five" chord. Follow up in the V column to the key of C row and you'll find a G chord. Write a "G" in everywhere you see a D chord in the music to "Amazing Grace." Now you've changed every G chord to a C, every C to an F, and every D to a G, transposing the chord progression from the key of G to the key of C.

You may need a key higher than C for "Amazing Grace." If that's the case, go through the same proceedure and try transposing from the key of G to the key of D. In the key of D your new chords will be D, G, and A. What if "Amazing Grace" is pitched too high to sing in the key of G? You will need to transpose it to a lower key, which will be to a key "earlier" in the musical alphabet (A, B, C, D, E, F, G) like F, E, etc. Try transposing "Amazing Grace" to the key of E. Start with the first chord of the original key, the G chord, in the "I" column. Follow up in the "I" column to the key of E row. The I chord in the key of E is an E chord. Write an "E" in everywhere you see a G chord on the music to "Amazing Grace." Do the same proceedure as before. Your new chords in the key of E will be E, A, and B.

Transposing other songs

Some songs are in kind of nebulous keys like "I Know You Rider," "Shady Grove," "Rain and Snow," and "Wayfaring Stranger." The first three are sometimes described as "modal," the last as "minor." In cases like this, it may not be clear to you which key row to use. If you match the number of sharps or flats in the key signature of the song to the second column ("♯/♭") of the chart, you can't go wrong. Just make sure that you follow up or down in the correct column.

There will be times when the exact chord you're transposing can't be found on the chart. In "Wayfaring Stranger" there's an "A7" chord but there's no "A7" in the key of F row, only an "Am" in the "iii" column. **You can still use this column as long as you maintain the original "quality" of the chord as you transpose.** For example, if the original is a seventh, the transposed chord needs to be a seventh. If the original chord is a minor, the transposed chord needs to be a minor also. Let's transpose "Wayfaring Stranger" from the given key of F/Dm up to G/Em. The first chord is a Dm. Find the Dm in the key of F row. It's in the "vi" column. Follow the "vi" column down to the key of G row and you'll find an Em. Pencil in an Em everywhere you see Dm in "Wayfaring Stranger." Find the next chord, the Gm in the key of F row, in the "ii" column. Follow the "ii" column down to the key of G row where you'll see Am. Write Am in the music where you see Gm. The next chord in the original key of F is B♭. Find the B♭ in the "IV" column of the key of F row. Follow this down to the key of G row, where you'll find a C. Pencil it in. Do the same with the original F chord changing it to G. Finally, find the A in the iii column, where it's listed as Am. The original chord is an A7. Follow down in the iii column until you get to the key of G row. There you'll find a Bm, which you'll change to a B7 to preserve the dominant seven quality of the original. That's all there is to it, you've transposed the chords of "Wayfaring Stranger" from the key of F to the key of G.

A similar thing happens in "Little Maggie." It's printed in the key of G and the second chord is an F. However, there's no F chord in the key of G row, only an F♯ in the "vii" column. F♯ is one half step higher in pitch than F natural. All you have to do is take that into account in the transposed key. Let's transpose "Little Maggie" to the key of D. The first chord of the original key is a G. The G chord is in the I column of the key of G row. Follow this up in the I column to the key of D row and our first chord is transposed to a D chord. Now go back to the key of G row and the "vii" column, which is still an F♯. Lower it one half step to get the F chord from the song in the original key of G. Follow up in the vii column to the key of D row. You'll find a C♯. Since we lowered our original F♯ one half step to F natural, we'll need to do the same here and lower the C♯ one half step to C natural. So, the first two chords in the key of D version of "Little Maggie" are D and C. For more about music theory and transposing, check out my *Guide to Capo, Transposing, & the Nashville Numbering System* from Mel Bay. Although the capo section applies to guitarists, the theory will work with any instrument.

More on transposing: why the mandolin is way cooler than the guitar or banjo

The mandolin is tuned in fifths, so the musical interval between two neighboring strings is a perfect fifth. The interval between the E (string one) and the A (string two) is a perfect fifth. The interval between the A (string two) and the D (string three) is a perfect fifth, and so on. This, my friends, makes all the difference in the world!

Because of this symmetrical tuning, we can move melodies and chord progressions "across" and up and down the mandolin fingerboard to different keys with relative ease. Guitars are tuned in fourths and a third which makes certain types of transposition very difficult. A guitarist always has to take into account that interval of a third between strings two and three.

Look at the tablature to the first song in *The Parking Lot Picker's Songbook*, "All the Good Times," on page 10. As played in the key of G, you'll see that all the notes fall on either the second or third strings. (Note: string one, the highest pitched string, is tuned to E; string two, the second highest pitched, is tuned to A; string three is tuned to D; string four, the lowest pitched, is tuned to G.) Because of the mandolin's symmetrical tuning, we can move this melody, lock, stock, and barrel, "over" one string to a new key. Instead of playing the first note on the second fret of the second string, play it on the second fret of the third string and follow the same tablature positions. Here's the first line of the new key to get you started.

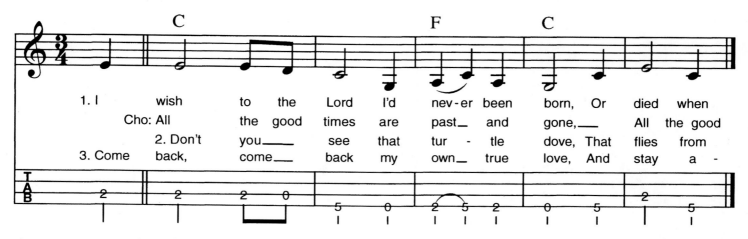

As you try to move the melody over one string, keep your fretting hand in the same position you use when you play "All the Good Times" in the original key of G.

By moving the melody in this way you've transposed it to the key of C, which is the first suggested female key. It is a little odd to think that we moved the melody down in pitch to move it to a higher key. You will have to pitch your voice correctly to sing along in the new key.

If you are the genius that most of us mandolin players are, you are already thinking, "If I can move the melody **down** from the original to string three, can I also move it **up** one string to start the melody on string one?" The answer is yes!

Look again at the original version of "All the Good Times" in the key of G. This time move the melody up one string so that your first note is on the first string second fret. Again, here's the tablature to the first line to get you started.

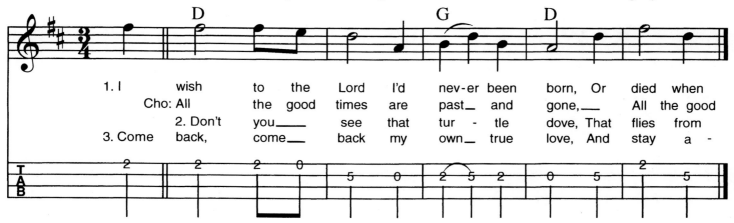

By moving the melody in this way you've transposed it to the key of D, which is the second suggested female key. Is this great, or what? Of course, if the melody spans three strings, you'll only be able to move it one way and to one other key. You can move the melody the other way, you just may have to move a few notes around that aren't automatically playable.

You can do the same type of transposing by moving whole chord progressions across the fingerboard. You'll need to use closed position chords, that is, chords that don't have any unfretted strings. Here are the closed position bluegrass chop chords to "Aunt Dinah's Quilting Party" in the key of A from page 20.

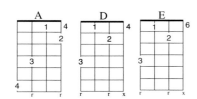

Let's move each of the chords "over" one string. Move the A chord so that your first finger frets the third string at the fourth fret. Your fourth finger will be lost in space with no string to fret. Also, your first string is unfretted. You'll need to mute it. (Remember: we have to use chords with no open string notes.) Wait a minute, doesn't this form look like the D chord from the original progression? That's because it *is* the same form and *is* a D chord. Now let's move the D chord from the original progression "over" one string so your first finger frets the fourth string at the fourth fret. This yields a two-string G chord with the first and second strings open. Not so good. Try changing the chord as shown with the first string muted.

     You can move this form up two frets to make the A.

Try to think of these chords as a complete I-IV-V progression, not as individual chords. Since the vast majority of the songs in *The Parking Lot Picker's Songbook* are I-IV-V progressions, you'll be able to use this transposition method extensively. You can also substitute the full four string G and A chop chords for the new G and A above.

This transposition moved the chord progression of "Aunt Dinah's Quilting Party" from the key of A to the key of D, which is the first suggested female key. I think of this as transposing from the "outside to the inside," "outside" being a full four-string chop chord like the A, "inside" being a three-string chop chord like the D. Obviously, one could just as easily transpose from the inside to the outside starting with D and transposing to A. In addition, one can move these sets of closed position chords up and down the fingerboard. For example, if you move the original key of A chords up two frets, you'll transpose the song to the key of B. Move them down two frets from the original key of A position and you'll transpose the song to the key of G. The "Transposer Wheel" on page 302 will also be helpful in transposing.

Of course there are several other fascinating ways to move melodies, chords and progressions around on the fingerboard. These exercises just scratch the surface. The best part is that you just can't do it this easily on either the guitar or the banjo. Mandolin rules! For a full examination of the subject using chords and solos, check out my *Getting into Bluegrass Mandolin* book/CD set from Mel Bay Publications. No home should be without a copy!

Special thanks to Craig Miller of Mandolin World News and Dawg Productions for granting permission to publish many of the historic photos of the great mandolin players.

Here's hoping you enjoy this collection of great songs! Visit me online at www.musixnow.com. Lots of music, tablature and MP3s to download and learn. My e-mail address is dix@musixnow.com

— Dix Bruce

Dix Bruce is a musician and writer from the San Francisco Bay Area. He has authored over forty books, recordings, and videos for Mel Bay Publications. Dix performs and does studio work on guitar, mandolin, and banjo and has recorded two LPs with mandolin legend Frank Wakefield, eight big band CDs with the Royal Society Jazz Orchestra, his own collection of American folk songs entitled "My Folk Heart" on which he plays guitar, mandolin, autoharp and sings, and a CD of string swing and jazz entitled "Tuxedo Blues." He contributed two original compositions to the soundtrack of Harrod Blank's acclaimed documentary film "Wild Wheels." He has released four CDs of traditional American songs and originals with guitarist Jim Nunally, most recently a collection of "brother duet" style recordings entitled "Brothers at Heart." Dix arranged, composed, and played mandolin on the soundtracks to four different editions of the best selling computer game "The Sims."

Books and instructional DVDs: *(For song lists and full details, as well as info on new books, CDs and DVDs, contact Musix, e-mail: info@musixnow.com)*

The Parking Lot Picker's Songbook for Guitar, Mandolin & Banjo (with Bill Evans).
You Can Teach Yourself Country Guitar.
You Can Teach Yourself Mandolin.
Getting into Bluegrass Mandolin.
Bluegrass Guitar Solos.
Gypsy Swing & Hot Club Rhythm for Mandolin and *Gypsy Swing & Hot Club Rhythm for Guitar*. Jam all night long with a hot Gypsy Swing band and learn twelve great standards recorded by Django Reinhardt and Stephane Grappelli.
BackUp Trax: Old Time Fiddle Tunes Vol. I. Jam all night long with the band on old time and fiddle tunes.
BackUp Trax: Swing & Jazz Vol. I. Jam all night long with a great band. You play all the leads and the band never gets tired!
BackUp Trax: Traditional Jazz & Dixieland. Jam all night long with the band on the basic Dixieland repertoire.
BackUp Trax: Early Jazz & Hot Tunes. Jam all night long with the band on more traditional jazz standards.
Basic Swing Guitar (DVD). Learn swing chord rhythm on the classics of the genre.
Basic Country Flatpicking Guitar (DVD). Explores easy Carter-style solos.

Recordings:
Brothers at Heart by Dix Bruce & Jim Nunally. Brother duet-style songs, & hot guitar picking (FGM CD 111).
From Fathers to Sons by Dix Bruce & Jim Nunally. Folk, bluegrass, & hot guitar picking (Musix CD/C 104).
In My Beautiful Dream by Dix Bruce & Jim Nunally. Great new songs & old classics by the duo. (Musix CD 106).
The Way Things Are by Dix Bruce & Jim Nunally. More hot picking & great new songs by the duo. (Musix CD 105).
My Folk Heart by Dix Bruce, solo & small group, traditional American folk music (Musix CD/C101). With Jim Nunally, Tom Rozum, and John Reischman.

Tuxedo Blues by Dix Bruce, string swing & jazz (Musix CD/C102). With Bob Alekno on mandolin, David Balakrishnan on violin, Mike Wollenberg on bass.

photo by Gene Tortora

Dix Bruce

All the Good Times

M: G; F: C or D
CD 1-Track 1

Traditional

B. Monroe, Monroe Bros., Flatt & Scruggs, R. Allen & F. Wakefield, Ken. Colonels, J. Martin

Amazing Grace

M: G; F: C or D
CD 1-Track 2

John Newton, ca. 1779

D. Watson, R. Stanley, Osborne Bros., Lewis Family, J. Garcia & D. Grisman   11

Angel Band

M: *G;* **F:** *C or D*

CD 1-Track 3

Hascall & Bradbury, ca. 1860

1. My lat - est sun is sink - ing fast, My race is near - ly run, My
2. Oh, bear my long - ing heart to Him, Who bled and died for me. Whose
3. I know I'm nearing the ho - ly ranks, Of friends and kin - dred dear. I've
4. I've al - most gained my heaven - ly home, My spir - it loud - ly sings, Thy

strong - est trials___ now are past, My tri - umph has be - gun.___
blood now cleans - es from all sin, And gives me vic - tor - y.___
brushed the dew on Jor - dan's banks, The cross - ing must be near.___
ho - ly ones, be - hold, they come, I hear the noise of wings.___

Cho: Oh come an - gel band, Come and a - round me stand, Oh bear me a - way on your snow-white wings, To

my im - mor - tal home,___ Oh bear me a - way on your snow-white wings, To my im - mor - tal home.__

Angelina Baker

M: C; F: F or G
CD 1-Track 4

Stephen Foster, 1850

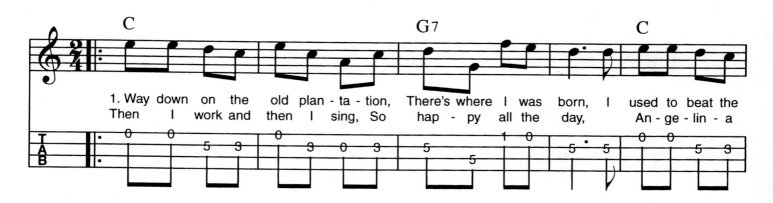

1. Way down on the old plan-ta-tion, There's where I was born, I used to beat the
Then I work and then I sing, So hap-py all the day, An-ge-lin-a

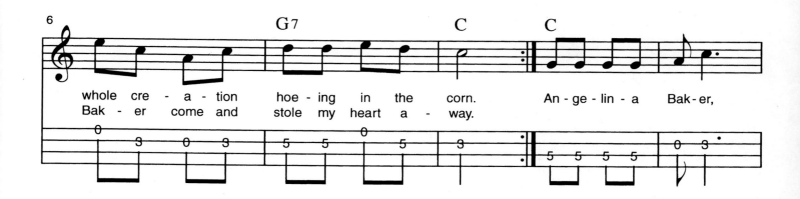

whole cre-a-tion hoe-ing in the corn. An-ge-lin-a Bak-er,
Bak-er come and stole my heart a-way.

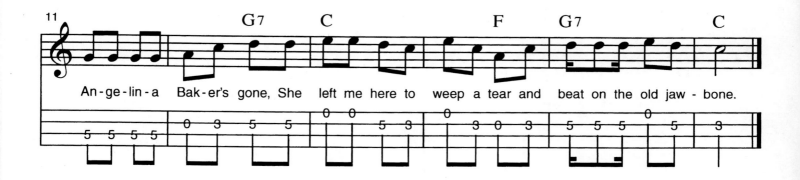

An-ge-lin-a Bak-er's gone, She left me here to weep a tear and beat on the old jaw-bone.

2. I've seen my Angelina in the Springtime and the Fall,
    C   G7
I've seen her in the cornfield and I've seen her at the ball,
    C   G7
And every time I met her she was smiling like the sun,
    C   G7   C
But now I'm left to weep a tear cause Angelina's gone.

3. Angelina is so tall, she never sees the ground,
She has to take a wellumscope to look down on the town.
Angelina likes the boys, as far as she can see 'em,
She used to run old master 'round, to ask him for to free 'em.

4. Early in the morning of a lovely summer day,
I asked for Angelina, and they say "she's gone away."
I don't know where to find her, 'cause I don't know where she's gone,
She left me here to weep a tear, and beat on the old jawbone.

Angels Rock Me To Sleep

M: G; F: C or D
CD 1-Track 5

Traditional

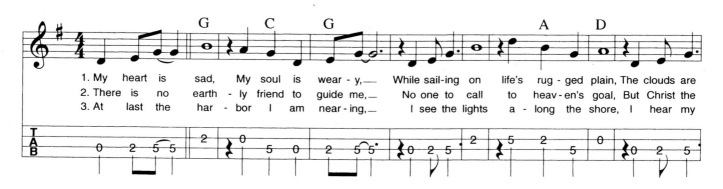

1. My heart is sad, My soul is wear - y,— While sail-ing on life's rug - ged plain, The clouds are
2. There is no earth - ly friend to guide me,— No one to call to heav - en's goal, But Christ the
3. At last the har - bor I am near-ing,— I see the lights a - long the shore, I hear my

dark, The day is drear - y,——— It seems all earth - ly help is vain. Cho: An - gels rock me to
sav - ior stands be - side me,— To cheer and com - fort my poor soul.
friends and loved ones cheer-ing,— I'll soon be safe for ev - er more.

sleep in the cra - dle of love, bear me o-ver the deep, to hea-ven a - bove, When sha-dows shall

fall,— and the sav-ior shall call, An-gels rock me to sleep,— In the cra-dle of love.—

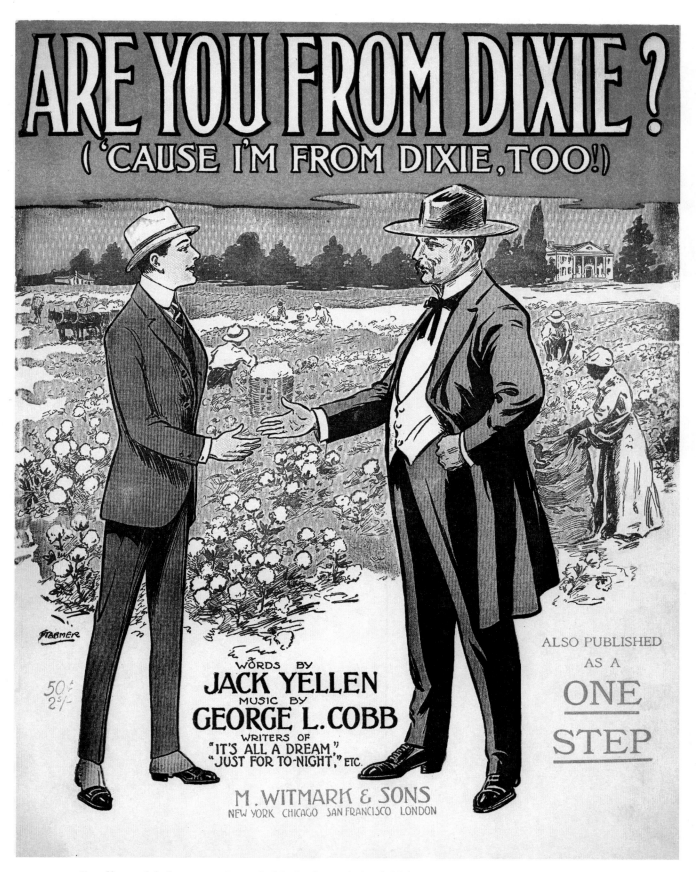

I collect old sheet music and this is the original 1915 cover "Are You From Dixie?"

Are You From Dixie?

M: C; F: F or G
CD 1-Track 6

Cobb & Yellin, 1915

1. Hel - lo there stran - ger, how do you do? There's some - thing I'd like
2. It was a way back in old eigh - ty nine, When first I crossed that

to say to you, You seem sur - prised, I re - co - gnize,
Mas - on Dixon line, Gee! but I've yearned, longed to re - turn,

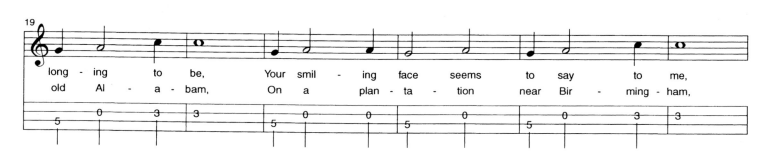

I'm no de - tect - ive but I just sur - mised. You're from a place I'm
To all the good folks I left be - hind. My home is way down in

long - ing to be, Your smil - ing face seems to say to me,
old Al - a - bam, On a plan - ta - tion near Bir - ming - ham,

You're from my own land, my sun - ny home - land, Tell me, can it be?
And there's one thing cer - tain, I'm sure - ly flir - tin', With those south bound trains.

Are You Washed in the Blood of the Lamb?

M: G; F: C or D
CD 1-Track 7

Elisha A. Hoffman, 1878

3. When the bridegroom cometh will your robes be white?
               D
Are you washed in the blood of the Lamb?
    G   **C**
Will your soul be ready for the mansions bright,
   G   **D**   **G**
And be washed in the blood of the Lamb?

4. Lay aside the garments that are stained with sin,
And be washed in the blood of the Lamb;
There's a fountain flowing for the soul unclean,
O be washed in the blood of the Lamb!

Arkansas Traveller

M: G; F: C or D
CD 1-Track 8

Traditional

1. Oh, once up-on a time in Ark-an-sas, An old man sat in his lit-tle cab-in door, And he

fidd-led at a tune that he liked to hear, A joll-y old tune that he played by ear. It was

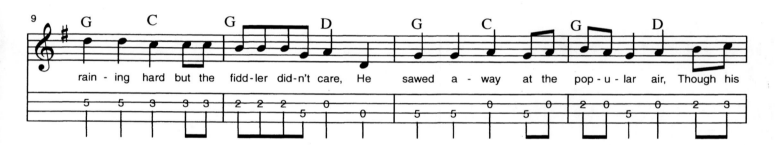

rain-ing hard but the fidd-ler did-n't care, He sawed a-way at the pop-u-lar air, Though his

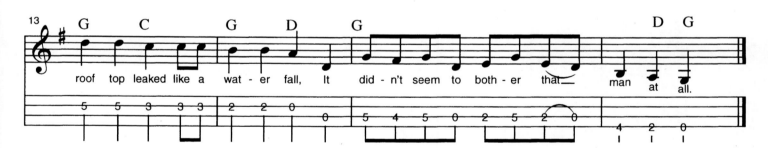

roof top leaked like a wat-er fall, It did-n't seem to both-er that man at all.

2.
G
A traveller was riding by that day,
D
And stopped to hear him a-practicing away.
G
The cabin was afloat and his feet were wet,
                    D   G
But still the old man didn't seem to fret.
       G   C   G   D
So the stranger said: "Now the way it seems to me,
   G   C   G   D
You'd better mend your roof," said he.
       G   C   G   D
But the old man said, as he played away:
   G   D   G
"I couldn't mend it now, it's a rainy day."

3. The traveller replied: "That's all quite true,
But this, I think, is the thing for you to do;
Get busy on a day that is fair and bright,
Then pitch the old roof till it's good and tight."
But the old man kept on a-playing at his reel,
And tapped the ground with his leathery heel:
"Get along," said he, "for you give me a pain;
My cabin never leaks when it doesn't rain."

Aunt Dinah's Quilting Party

M: A; F: D or E
CD 1-Track 9

Kyle & Fletcher, 1856

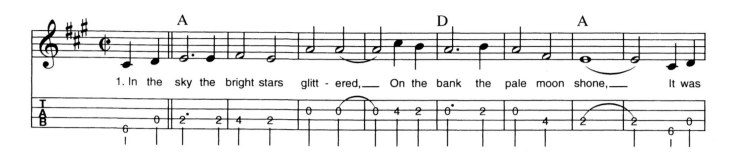

1. In the sky the bright stars glitt - ered,___ On the bank the pale moon shone,___ It was

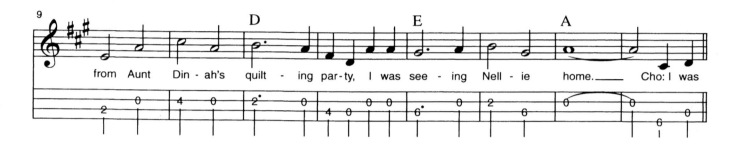

from Aunt Din - ah's quilt - ing par - ty, I was see - ing Nell - ie home.___ Cho: I was

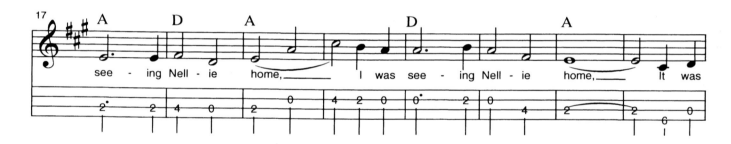

see - ing Nell - ie home,_____ I was see - ing Nell - ie home,___ It was

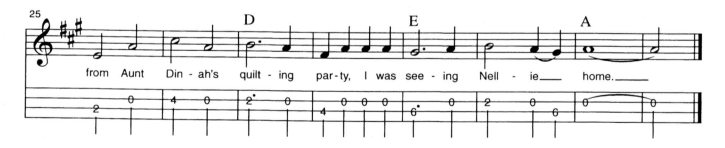

from Aunt Din - ah's quilt - ing par - ty, I was see - ing Nell - ie___ home.___

        A
2. On my arm a soft hand rested,
     D   A
Rested light as ocean foam,
                  D
And 'twas from Aunt Dinah's quilting party,
   E   A
I was seeing Nellie home. *(Chorus)*

3. On my lips a whisper trembled,
Trembled 'til it dared to come,
And 'twas from Aunt Dinah's *(etc., chorus)*

4. On my life new hopes were dawning,
And those hopes have lived and grown,
And 'twas from Aunt Dinah's *(etc., chorus)*

Away in a Manger

M: G; F: C or D
CD 1-Track 10

Luther & Muller

Banks of the Ohio

M: D; F: G or A
CD 1-Track 11

Traditional

1. I asked my love_____ to take a walk, Just to walk a lit-tle ways,
2. I held a knife_____ a-gainst her breast, As deep in-to my arms she pressed,

As we walked,_____ and as we talked, All a-bout_____ our wed-ding day. Cho: On-ly
She cried, "Oh Willie,_____ don't mur-der me, I'm un-pre-pared_____ for e-ter-ni-ty."

say_____ that you'll be mine, In our home_____ we'll hap-py be. Down be-side_____

_____ where the wat-ers flow,_____ On the banks_____ of the O-hi-o._____

          D   A7
3. I took her by her lily white hand,
                         D
Led her down that bank of sand,
                         G
There I pushed her in to drown,
                 D   A7   D
And watched her as she floated down.

4. I started home 'tween twelve and one,
Crying "God, what have I done?
I've killed the girl I love you see,
Because she would not marry me."

5. Next morning was about half past four,
The sheriff knocked upon my door,
Says "Young man, come go with me,
Down beside the deep blue sea."

A Beautiful Life

M: G; F: C or D
CD 1-Track 12

Wm. Golden, 1918

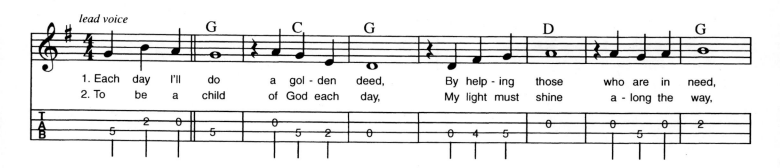

1. Each day I'll do a gol - den deed, By help - ing those who are in need,
2. To be a child of God each day, My light must shine a - long the way,

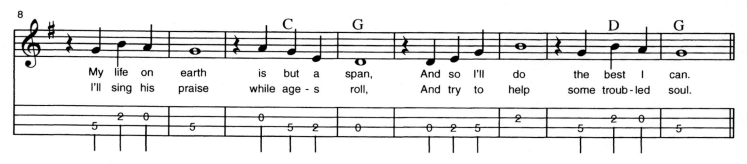

My life on earth is but a span, And so I'll do the best I can.
I'll sing his praise while age - s roll, And try to help some troub - led soul.

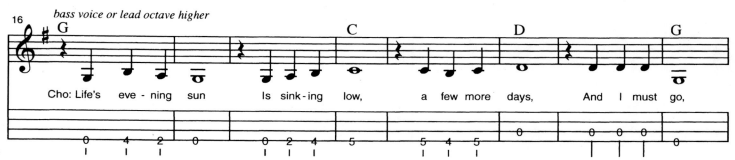

bass voice or lead octave higher

Cho: Life's eve - ning sun Is sink - ing low, a few more days, And I must go,

lead voice

To meet the deeds that I have done, Where there will be no sett - ing sun.___

       G   C   G
3. The only life that will endure,
         D   G
Is one that's kind and good and pure,
              C   G
And so for God I'll take my stand,
            D   G
Each day I'll lend a helping hand.

4. While going down life's weary road,
I'll try to lift some traveler's load,
I'll try to turn the night to day,
Make flowers bloom along the way.

Beautiful Star of Bethlehem

M: D; F: G or A
CD 1-Track 13

Boyce & Pace

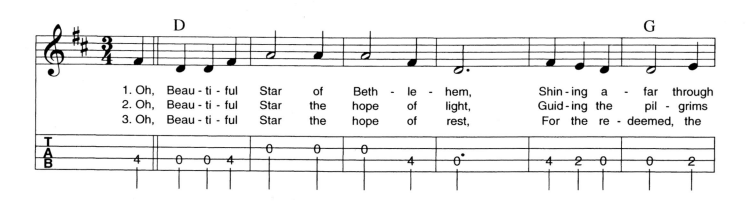

1. Oh, Beau-ti-ful Star of Beth-le-hem, Shin-ing a-far through
2. Oh, Beau-ti-ful Star the hope of light, Guid-ing the pil-grims
3. Oh, Beau-ti-ful Star the hope of rest, For the re-deemed, the

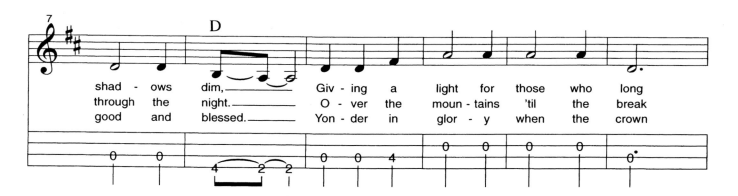

shad-ows dim, Giv-ing a light for those who long
through the night. O-ver the moun-tains 'til the break
good and blessed. Yon-der in glor-y when the crown

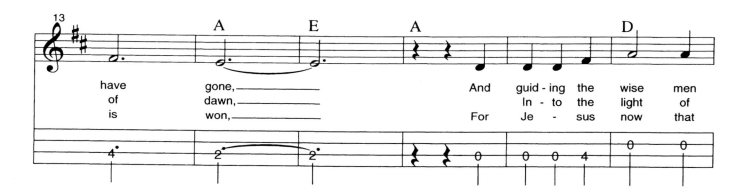

have gone, And guid-ing the wise men
of dawn, In-to the light of
is won, For Je-sus now that

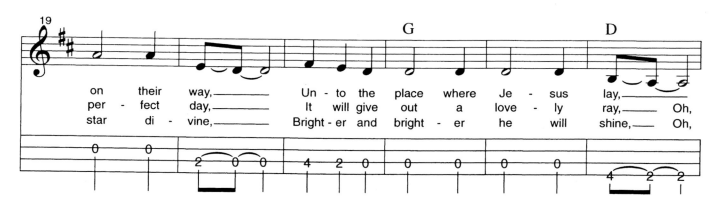

on their way, Un-to the place where Je-sus lay, Oh,
per-fect day, It will give out a love-ly ray, Oh,
star di-vine, Bright-er and bright-er he will shine, Oh,

24   *Stanley Bros., R. Stanley, Larry Sparks, Patty Loveless*

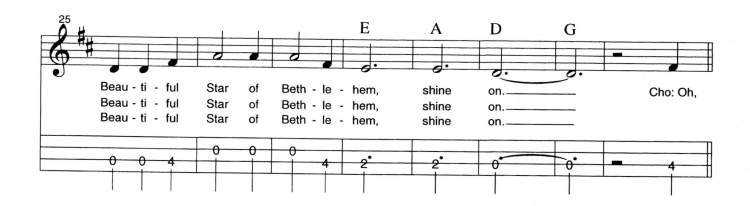

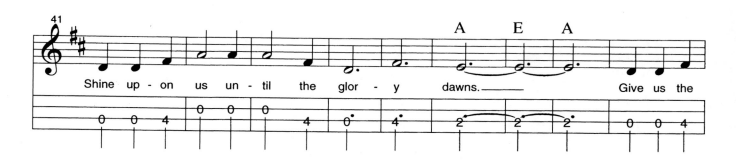

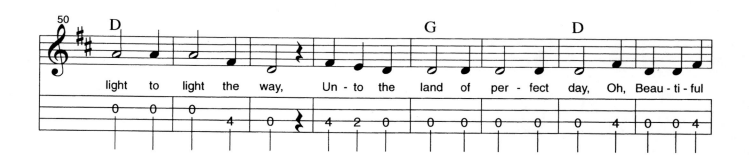

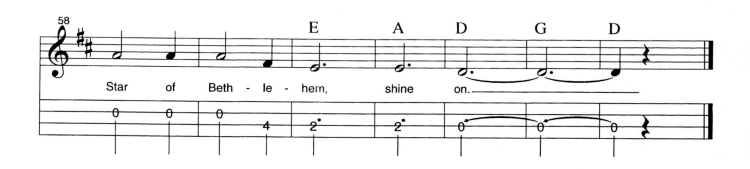

Bile Them Cabbage Down

M: G; F: C or D
CD 1-Track 14, medley pt. 1

Traditional

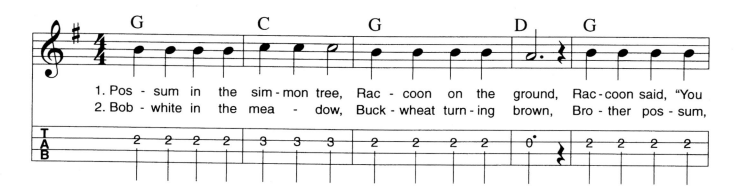

1. Pos - sum in the sim - mon tree, Rac - coon on the ground, Rac - coon said, "You
2. Bob - white in the mea - dow, Buck - wheat turn - ing brown, Bro - ther pos - sum,

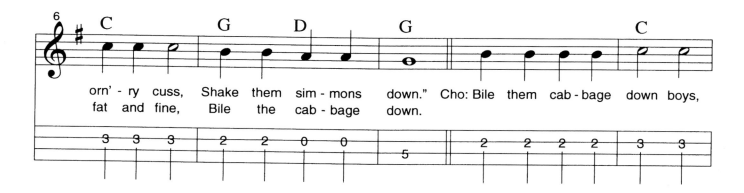

orn' - ry cuss, Shake them sim - mons down." Cho: Bile them cab - bage down boys,
fat and fine, Bile the cab - bage down.

Make the hoe cake brown, The on - ly song that I can sing, Is bile them cab-bage down.

G C 3. Pork roast in the oven G D Taters turning brown, G C Buttermilk and cornbread too, G D G Bile them cabbage down. 4. Corn blades rustling in the breeze, Pumpkins on the ground, Squirrels chirping in the trees, Bile them cabbage down.	5. I bought my gal a bicycle, She learned to ride it well, She ran into a telephone pole, And broke it all to pieces. 6. Grandpa had a muley cow, She was muley when she was born, It took the jaybird forty years, To fly from horn to horn. 7. Grandpa had a setting hen, He set her as you know, Set her on three buzzard eggs, Hatched out one old crow.

Black Eyed Susie

M: G; F: C or D
CD 1-Track 14, medley pt. 2

Traditional

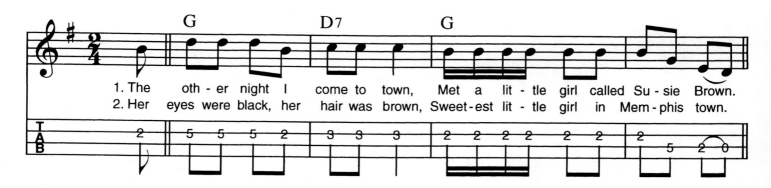

1. The oth-er night I come to town, Met a lit-tle girl called Su-sie Brown.
2. Her eyes were black, her hair was brown, Sweet-est lit-tle girl in Mem-phis town.

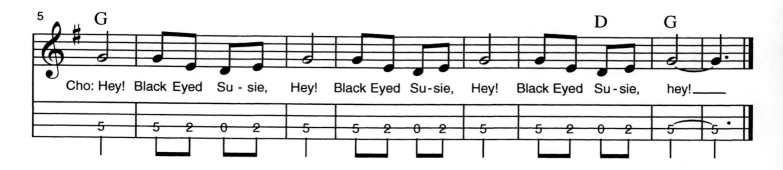

Cho: Hey! Black Eyed Su-sie, Hey! Black Eyed Su-sie, Hey! Black Eyed Su-sie, hey!____

```
G              D
3. All I need to make me happy
G
Two little boys to call me pappy,
```

```
G
Cho: Hey! Black Eyed Susie,
Hey! Black Eyed Susie,
              D7    G
Hey! Black Eyed Susie, hey!
```

4. One named Paul and the other one Davey,
One loves ham and the other one gravy. (Chorus)

5. Some got drunk and some got woozy,
I went home with Black Eyed Susie. (Chorus)

6. I fell in love with her that night,
Sent for the preacher and the preacher was tight. (Chorus)

7. We said "I do" by the lantern light,
Promised that preacher we'd never fight. (Chorus)

Blue Ridge Mountain Blues

M: G ; F: C or D
CD 1-Track 15

Cliff Hess

1. When I was young and in my prime, I left my home in Car-o-line,— Now
2. I see a win-dow with a light, I see two heads of snow-y white,—

all I do is sit and pine, For all those folks I left be-hind. Cho. 1: I've got those
I seem to hear them both recite, "Where is my wan-dering boy to-night?"

Blue Ridge Moun-tain blues, Want to hear those hound dogs bay, I want to

hunt the pos-sum when the corn tops blos-som, In that Blue Ridge far a - way.

G		D	
3. I'll always do right by my Ma,

I'll always do right by my Pa,

G

D

I'll hang around that cabin door,

G

No work, no worry anymore.

Cho. 2: I've got those Blue Ridge Mountain blues,

G

I want to stand right here and say,

G

C

My grip is packed to travel and I'm scratching gravel,

D7   G

To the Blue Ridge far away.

B. Monroe, Jim & Jesse, Flatt & Scruggs, D. Watson, Bill Clifton

The Bluebirds are Singing for Me

M: C; F: F or G
CD 1-Track 16

Mac Wiseman

Bound to Ride

M: G; F: C or D
CD 1-Track 17

Traditional

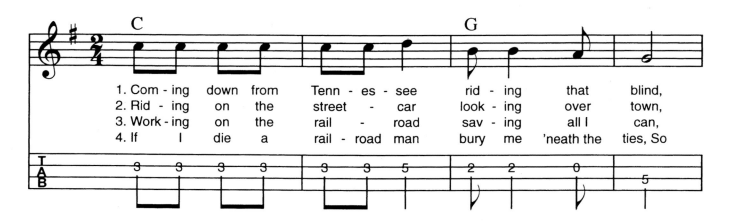

1. Com - ing   down   from   Tenn - es - see   rid - ing   that   blind,
2. Rid - ing   on   the   street - car   look - ing   over   town,
3. Work - ing   on   the   rail - road   sav - ing   all I   can,
4. If   I   die   a   rail - road man   bury   me   'neath the   ties, So

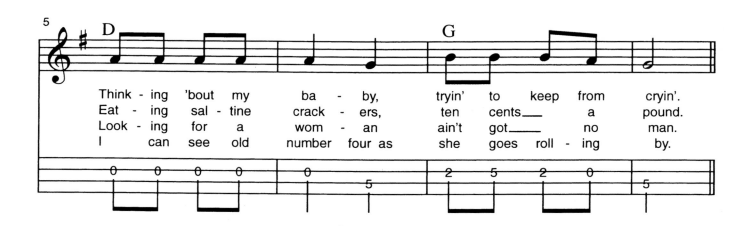

Think - ing   'bout   my   ba - by,   tryin'   to   keep   from   cryin'.
Eat - ing   sal - tine   crack - ers,   ten   cents___   a   pound.
Look - ing   for   a   wom - an   ain't   got___   no   man.
I   can   see   old   number   four as   she   goes   roll - ing   by.

Cho: Hon - ey babe, I'm bound to ride,   Don't you want to go?___

Bright Morning Stars

M: C; F: F or G
CD 1-Track 18

Traditional

1. Bright morn - ing stars are— ris - ing, Bright morn - ing stars are ris - ing, Bright—
2. Oh, where are our dear— fath - ers? Oh, where are our dear fath - ers? They're—
3. Oh, where are our dear— moth-ers? Oh, where are our dear moth - ers? They've—

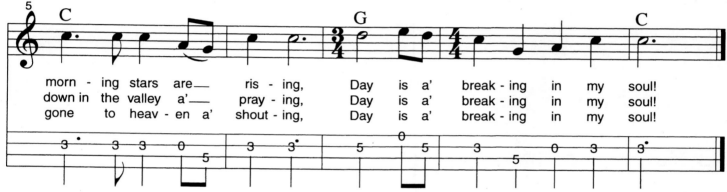

morn - ing stars are— ris - ing, Day is a' break - ing in my soul!
down in the valley a'— pray - ing, Day is a' break - ing in my soul!
gone to heav - en a' shout - ing, Day is a' break - ing in my soul!

Bring Back to Me My Wandering Boy

M: G; F: C or D
CD 1-Track 19

Traditional

1. Out in the cold world and far a-way_ from home, Some moth-er's boy is wand-ering all a-
2. Out in the hall - way, there stands a va - cant chair, And an old pair of shoes that he used to
3. Well I rem - em - ber those part-ing words he said, "We'll meet up yonder, where tears are nev-er

lone, No one to guide him or keep his foot - steps right, Some moth - er's boy is
wear, Emp - ty is the cra - dle he used to_ love so well, Oh, how I miss him
shed, In that land of sun - shine a - way from toil_ and care, When life is over, I'll

home - less to - night. Cho: Oh, bring back to me my wan - der - ing boy,_
no tongue can tell.
meet you up there."

There is no oth-er_ that's left to give me joy, Tell him his moth - er with

fad - ed cheeks and hair, Is at the old home a - wait-ing him there._____

B. Monroe, Flatt & Scruggs, Blue Sky Boys, Carter Fam., J. Val

Buffalo Gals

M: C; F: F or G
CD 1-Track 20

Traditional

C

2. I danced with a gal with a hole in her stockin',
   G7   C
Her heel kept a-rockin', her knees kept a-knockin',
I danced with a gal with a hole in her stockin',
   G7   C
We danced by the light of the moon.

Chorus after each verse.

3. I asked her if she'd like to talk, (like to talk 2X)
Her feet took up the whole sidewalk,
Oh, she was fair to see.

4. I asked her if she'd have a dance, (have a dance 2X)
I thought that I might have a chance,
To shake a foot with her.

5. I asked her if she'd be my wife, (be my wife 2X)
Then I'd be happy all my life,
If she'd marry me.

The Bully of the Town

M: G; F: C or D
CD 1-Track 21

Unknown, 1895

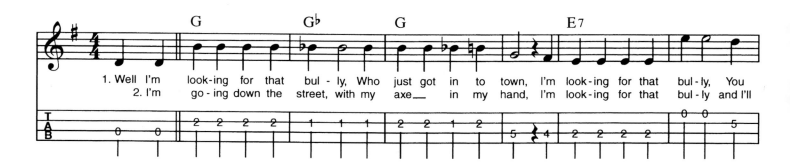

1. Well I'm look-ing for that bul - ly, Who just got in to town, I'm look-ing for that bul - ly, You
2. I'm go - ing down the street, with my axe___ in my hand, I'm look-ing for that bul - ly and I'll

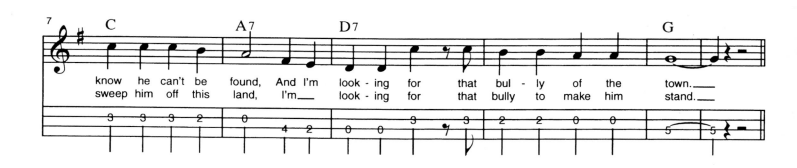

know he can't be found, And I'm look - ing for that bul - ly of the town.___
sweep him off this land, I'm___ look - ing for that bully to make him stand.___

Cho: As I walk this le - vee 'round,_____ eve - ry night I can be found,_____

As I walk this le - vee 'round,_____ I'm look-ing for that bul - ly of the town._____

```
       G            Gb      G
```
3. I'll take my long razor, I'm going to carve him deep,
```
    E7                    C              A7
```
And when I see that bully, I'll lay him down to sleep,
```
     D7                        G
```
I'm looking for that bully to make him weep.

4. I went a winging, down at Parson Jones',
Took along my trusty blade to carve that fellow's bones,
Just a'looking for that bully to hear his groans.

5. I walked in the front door, the men were prancing high,
For that levee fella, I skinned my foxy eye,
Just a'looking for that bully and he wasn't nigh.

6. I asked Miss Pansy Blossom, if she would wing a reel,
She says, "Laws, Mr. Johnson, how high you make me feel,"
Then you ought to see me shake my sugar heel.

7. I rose up like a black cloud and took a look around,
There was that new bully, standing on the ground,
I've been looking for you fella and I've got you found.

8. When I got through bully, a doctor and a nurse,
Were no good to that man, so they put him in a hearse,
A cyclone couldn't have torn him up much worse.

9. You don't hear about that fella, that treated folks so free,
Go down upon the levee and his face you'll never see,
There's only one boss bully and that is me.

10. When you see me coming, hoist your windows high,
When you see me going, hang your heads and cry,
I'm looking for that bully and he must die.

11. My madness is a rising, and I'm not going to get left,
I'm getting so bad that I'm scared of myself,
I was looking for that bully now he's on the shelf.

Bury Me Beneath the Willow

M: D; F: G or A
CD 1-Track 22

Traditional

1. My heart is sad and I am lonely, For the only one I love, When shall I see her oh no never, 'Til we meet in heaven above. Cho: So

2. To-mor-row was to be our wedding, God, oh God where can she be? She's gone a' courting with an-oth-er, And no lon-ger cares for me.

3. She told me that she did not love me, I could not be-lieve 'twas true, Un-til an an-gel soft-ly whis-pered, "She no lon-ger cares for you."

4. Place on my grave a snow white li-ly, To prove my love for her was true, To show the world I died of griev-ing, For her love I could not win.

bur-y me be-neath the wil-low, Un-der the weep-ing wil-low tree,

When she hears that I am sleep-ing, Then per-haps she'll weep for me.

Carter Fam., Rice and Skaggs, C. White, W. Guthrie, Ken. Colonels

Bill Monroe, the Father of Bluegrass in 1980.

C-H-I-C-K-E-N

M: C; F: F or G
CD 1-Track 23

Perrin & Slater, 1902

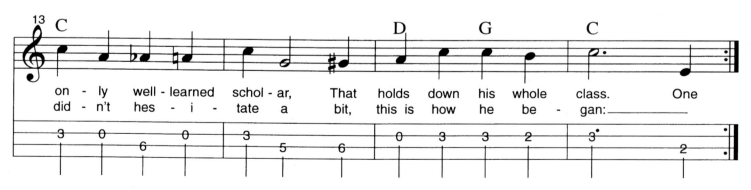

Greenbriar Boys, Sam McGee, Kathy Kallick

Cho: "C," that's the way to be-gin, "H," that's the next let-ter in,

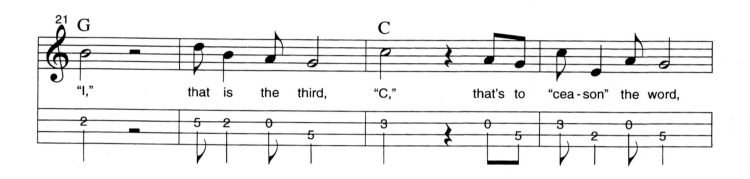

"I," that is the third, "C," that's to "cea-son" the word,

"K," that's a' fill-ing——— in, "E," I'm near——— the end,

"C-H-I-C-K-E-N," that's the way to spell "chick-en."———

Can't You Hear Me Callin'?

M: *D* ; **F:** *G or A*
CD 1-Track 24

Bill Monroe

Careless Love

M: F ; F: Bb or C
CD 1-Track 25

Traditional

F   C7   F
2. Sorrow, sorrow to my heart,
                  C7
Sorrow, sorrow to my heart,
F   F7   Bb   Bbm
Sorrow, sorrow to my heart,
F   C7   F
Since we two have been apart.

3. What, oh what will Momma say? (3X)
When she learns I've gone astray?

4. Once I wore my apron low, (3X)
Scarcely keep you from my door.

5. Now my apron strings don't pin, (3X)
You pass my door and you don't come in.

Children Go Where I Send Thee

M: D; F: G or A
CD 1-Track 26

Traditional

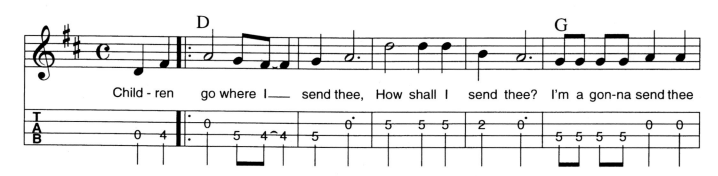

Child - ren go where I— send thee, How shall I send thee? I'm a gon-na send thee

1st X, no repeat, go on: 2nd X, repeat, go on;
3rd time, repeat twice, go on; etc.

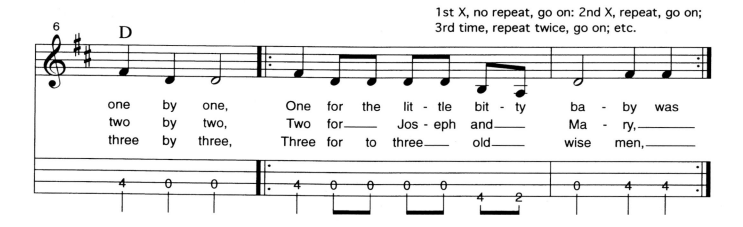

one by one, One for the lit - tle bit - ty ba - by was
two by two, Two for—— Jos - eph and—— Ma - ry,——
three by three, Three for to three—— old—— wise men,——

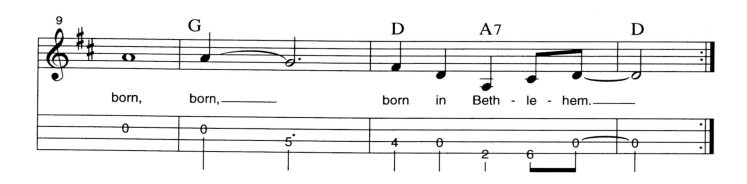

born, born,——— born in Beth - le - hem.———

Four for the four who stood at the door,
Five for the Hebrew children,
Six for the six who didn't get fixed,
Seven for the seven who couldn't get to heaven,
Eight for the eight who didn't get straight,
Nine was the nine that stood in the line,
Ten for the ten commandments.

The Church in the Wildwood

M: A; F: D or E
CD 1-Track 27

Wm. Pitts, ca. 1850s

1. There's a church in the val - ley by the wild - wood, No love - li - er place in the dale, No
2. How sweet on a clear Sab-bath morn - ing, To listen to the clear ring-ing bell, It's
3. There, close by the church in the val - ley, Lies one that I loved so well, She
4. There, close by the side of that loved one, 'Neath the trees where the wild flow-ers bloom, When the

spot is so dear to my child - hood, As the lit - tle brown church in the vale. Cho: Oh,
tones so sweet - ly are cal - ling, Oh, come to the church in the vale.
sleeps, sweet - ly sleeps, 'neath the wil - low, Dis - turb not her rest in the vale.
fare - well hymn shall be chant-ed, I shall rest by her side in the tomb.

come to the church by the wild - wood, Oh, come to the church in the dale, No

spot is so dear to my child - hood, As the lit - tle brown church in the vale.

Carter Fam. 43

Cindy

M: G; F: C or D
CD 1-Track 28

Traditional

1. I wish I was an ap - ple A' hang - ing on a tree, And ev - ery time that
2. And If I was a sugar tree, A' stand - ing in the town,—— Ev - ery time my

Cin - dy passed, She'd take a big bite out of me. Cho: Get a - long home, Cin - dy,
Cin - dy passed, I'd shake—some sug - ar—— down.

Cin - dy, Get a - long home,— Get a - long home, Cin - dy, Cin - dy, I'll mar - ry you some day.

G
3. The first time I saw Cindy,
D
She was standing in the door,
G
Her shoes and stockings in her hand,
D   G
Her feet all over the floor.

4. She took me to her parlor,
She cooled me with her fan,
She said I was the prettiest thing,
In the shape of mortal man.

5. She kissed me and she hugged me,
She called me "Sugar Plum,"
She throwed her arms around me,
I thought my time had come.

6. Oh, Cindy is a pretty girl,
Cindy is a peach,
She threw her arms around my neck,
And hung on like a leech.

7. If I had a thread and needle,
Fine as I could sew,
I'd sew that gal to my coat tails,
And down the road I'd go.

Columbus Stockade Blues

M: *G ; **F:** C or D*
CD 1-Track 29

Traditional

B. Monroe, Ken. Colonels, W. Guthrie, B. Clifton, D. Watson, N. Blake

Cotton-Eyed Joe

M: G; F: C or D
CD 1-Track 30

Traditional

1. Don't you re-mem-ber, don't you know, Dad-dy worked a man they called
Cho: Where'd you come from, where'd you go? Where'd_____ you come_ from

Cot-ton Eyed Joe, Dad-dy worked a man called Cot-ton Eyed Joe._____
Cot-ton Eyed Joe? Where'd_ you come from Cot-ton Eyed Joe?_____

G   C
2. Had not been for Cotton-Eyed Joe,
G   C
I'd a'been married a long time ago,
G
I'd a'been married a long time ago.

3. Down in the cotton patch, way down low,
Everybody singing the Cotton-Eyed Joe. (2X)

4. I know a gal lives down below,
I used to go to see her but I don't no more. (2X)

5. I fell down and stubbed my toe,
Call for the doctor, Cotton Eyed Joe. (2X)

46   *C. White, D. Watson, Fiddlin' John Carson, M. Seeger, Ken. Colonels, NLCR, E. Taylor, Skillet Lickers, K. Hall, D. Reno & R. Smiley, Kathy Kallick*

Cowboy Jack

M: C; F: F or G
CD 1-Track 31

Traditional

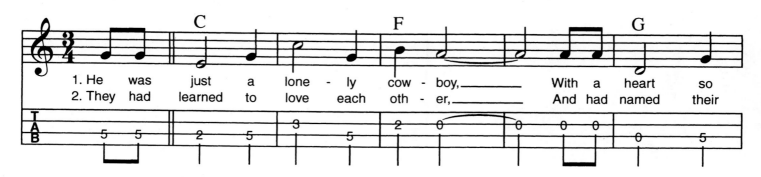

1. He was just a lone - ly cow - boy,_____ With a heart so
2. They had learned to love each oth - er,_____ And had named so their

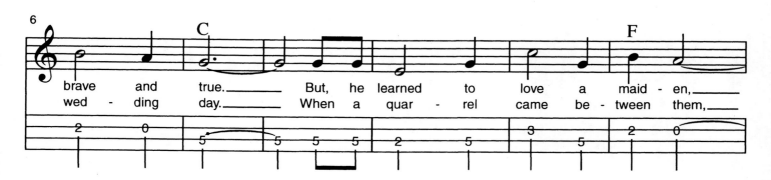

brave and true._____ But, he learned to love a maid - en,_____
wed - ding day._____ When a quar - rel came be - tween them,_____

— With eyes of heaven's own blue._____
— And Jack, he rode a - way._____

     C   F
3. He joined a band of cowboys,
    G   C
And tried to forget her name.
                  F
But, out on the lonely prairie,
    G   C
She waits for him the same.

4. Your sweetheart waits for you, Jack,
Your sweetheart waits for you.
Out on the lonely prairie,
Where the skies are always blue.

5. One night as the work was finished,
Just at the close of day.
Someone said to, "sing a song, Jack,
T'will drive dull care away."

6. When he began his singing,
His mind it wandered back.
For he sang of a maiden,
Who waited for her Jack.

7. Jack left the camp next morning,
He was breathing his sweetheart's name.
He says, "I'll ask forgiveness,
For I know that I'm to blame."

8. But, when he reached the prairie,
He found a new made mound.
And his friends they sadly told him,
They had laid his loved one down.

9. They said as she was dying,
She breathed her sweetheart's name.
And asked them with her last breath,
To tell him when he came.

10. "Your sweetheart waits for you, Jack,
Your sweetheart waits for you.
Out on the lonely prairie,
Where the skies are always blue."

The Crawdad Song

M: G; F: C or D
CD 1-Track 32

Traditional

G

Cho: You get a line and I'll get a po - le hon - ey, You get a line and
1. Set on the bank 'til my feet got — co - ld hon - ey, Set on the bank 'til my

I'll get a pole ___ ba - be, You get a line and I'll get a pole, ___
feet got — cold ___ ba - be, Set on the bank 'til my feet got — cold, It's a

we'll go down to the craw - dad hole, ___ Hon - ey, ba - a - by mine.
sight to see the craw - dads — jump in that hole, ___

G   D7

2. Yonder come a man with a sack on his back honey, Yonder come a man with a sack on his back babe,
G   G7   C   G   D7 G
Yonder come a man with a sack on his back, He's got more crawdads than he can pack, Honey, baby mine.

3. He fell down and he broke that sack honey, He fell down and he broke that sack babe,
He fell down and he broke that sack, Was a sight to see the crawdads backing back, Honey, baby mine.

4. What did the hen duck say to the drake honey? What did the hen duck say to the drake babe?
What did the hen duck say to the drake, "There ain't no crawdads in that lake," Honey, baby mine.

Cripple Creek

M: A; F: D or E
CD 1-Track 33

Traditional

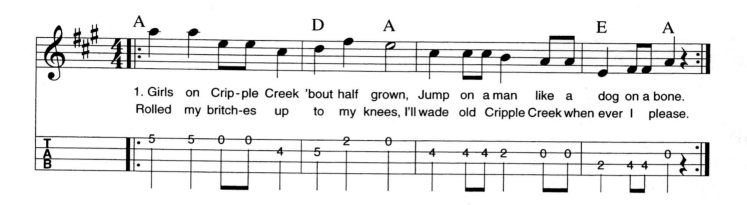

1. Girls on Crip-ple Creek 'bout half grown, Jump on a man like a dog on a bone.
Rolled my britch-es up to my knees, I'll wade old Cripple Creek when ever I please.

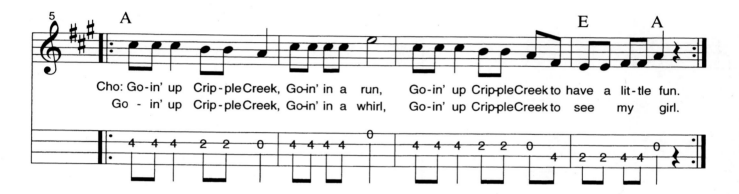

Cho: Go-in' up Crip-ple Creek, Go-in' in a run, Go-in' up Cripple Creek to have a lit-tle fun.
Go - in' up Crip-ple Creek, Go-in' in a whirl, Go-in' up Cripple Creek to see my girl.

A   D   A
2. Cripple Creek's wide and Cripple Creek's deep,
          E A
I'll wade old Cripple Creek before I sleep.
A   D   A
I got a girl and she loves me,
       E   A
She's as sweet as sweet can be.

3. I went down to Cripple Creek,
To see what them girls had to eat.
I got drunk and fell against the wall,
Old corn likker was the cause of it all.

4. I got a girl and she loves me,
She's as sweet as she can be.
She got eyes of baby blue,
Makes my gun shoot straight and true.

Monroe Bros., Flatt & Scruggs, R. Stanley, Jimmy Martin, C. White, D. Watson, Fiddlin' Doc Roberts, K. Hall, A. Munde,
Country Gentlemen, John McEuen

Crying Holy

M: G; F: C or D
CD 1-Track 34

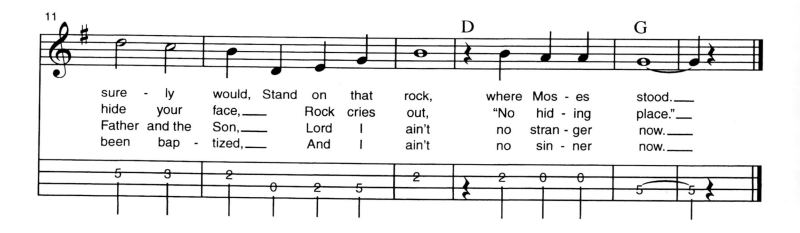

B. Monroe, Flatt & Scruggs, Carter Fam., J.D. Crowe, Country Gentlemen, J.E. Mainer

The Cuckoo

M: Dm; F: Gm or Am
CD 1-Track 35

Traditional

1. Oh the cuck - oo,_____ she's a pretty bird,_____ And she war - bles_____
2. Jack of Dia - monds,_____ Jack of Dia - monds,_____ I – know you_____

— as she flies._____ And she nev - er,_____ says
— of – old._____ You – robbed my_____ poor

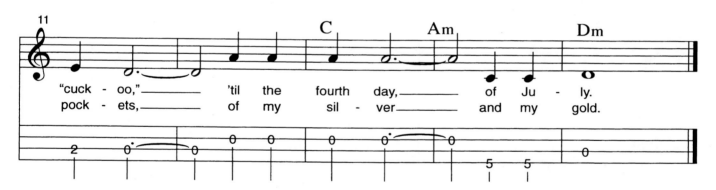

"cuck - oo,"_____ 'til the fourth day,_____ of Ju - ly.
pock - ets,_____ of my sil - ver_____ and my gold.

Dm
3. I've played cards in England,
    C   **Am Dm**
I've played cards in Spain,
I'll bet you ten dollars,
    C   **Am**   **Dm**
I'll beat you next game.

4. My horses ain't hungry,
They won't eat your hay,
I'll drive on a little further,
I'll feed 'em on the way.

5. Gonna build me log cabin,
On a mountain so high,
So I can see Willie,
When he goes on by.

6. Oh the cuckoo, she's a pretty bird,
I wish that she was mine.
She never drinks water,
She always drinks wine.

Daniel Prayed

M: G; F: C or D
CD 1-Track 36

Traditional

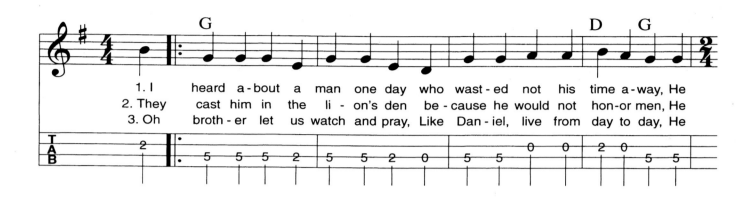

1. I   heard a-bout   a   man   one   day   who   wast-ed   not   his   time a-way, He
2. They   cast him in   the   li - on's den   be - cause he would not   hon-or men, He
3. Oh   broth - er   let   us watch   and pray, Like Dan - iel, live from   day to day, He

prayed to   God,____   ev - ery morn-ing   noon   and   night.____   He
prayed to   God,____   ev - ery morn-ing   noon   and   night.____   Their
prayed to   God,____   ev - ery morn-ing   noon   and   night.____   He

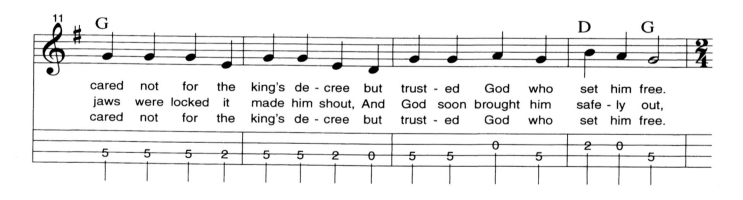

cared   not   for   the   king's de-cree   but   trust - ed   God   who   set   him free.
jaws   were locked   it   made him shout, And   God   soon brought him   safe - ly   out,
cared   not   for   the   king's de-cree   but   trust - ed   God   who   set   him free.

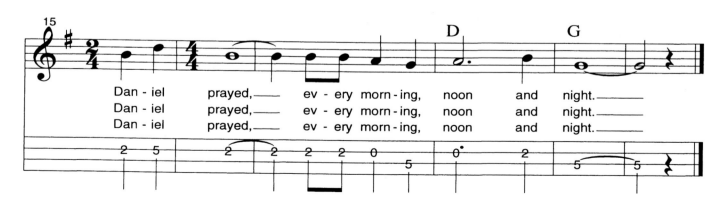

Dan - iel   prayed,____   ev - ery morn-ing,   noon   and   night.____
Dan - iel   prayed,____   ev - ery morn-ing,   noon   and   night.____
Dan - iel   prayed,____   ev - ery morn-ing,   noon   and   night.____

Cho: Dan - iel served the liv - ing God while here up - on this earth he trod, He

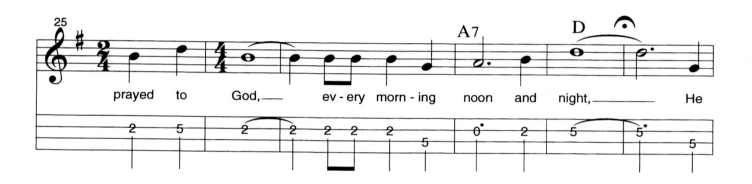

prayed to God,___ ev - ery morn - ing noon and night,_____ He

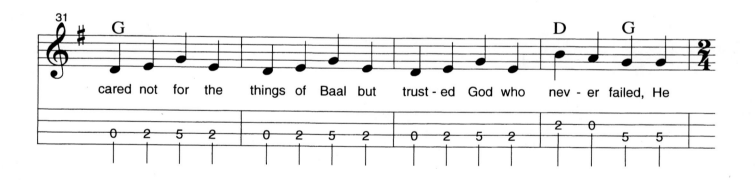

cared not for the things of Baal but trust - ed God who nev - er failed, He

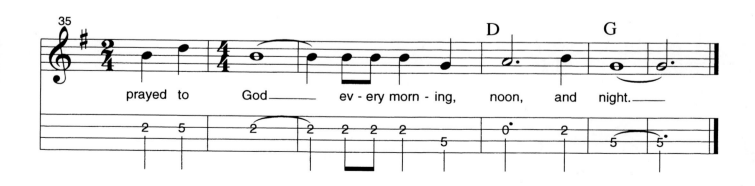

prayed to God___ ev - ery morn - ing, noon, and night.___

Danny Boy

M: C; F: F or G
CD 1-Track 37

Traditional

B. Monroe, Jim Hurst, Butch Waller

Darling Corey

M: C; F: F or G
CD 1-Track 38, medley pt. 1

Traditional

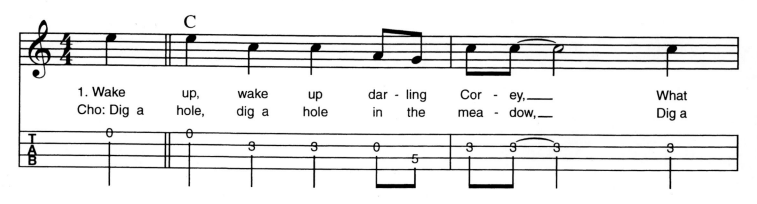

1. Wake up, wake up dar - ling Cor - ey,___ What
Cho: Dig a hole, dig a hole in the mea - dow,__ Dig a

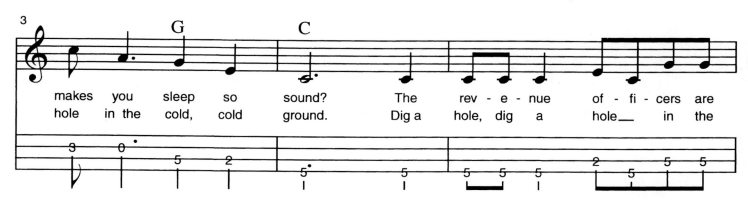

makes you sleep so sound? The rev - e - nue of - fi - cers are
hole in the cold, cold ground. Dig a hole, dig a hole__ in the

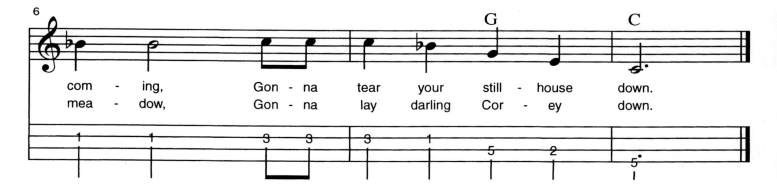

com - ing, Gon - na tear your still - house down.
mea - dow, Gon - na lay darling Cor - ey down.

C

3. Well, the first time I saw darling Corey,
           G   C
She was sittin' on the banks of the sea,
Had a forty-four around her body,
         G C
And a banjo on her knee.

4. Go away, go away darling Corey,
Quit hanging around my bed.
Bad liquor has ruined my body,
Pretty women gone to my head.

5. Can't you hear those bluebirds a'singing?
Don't you hear that mournful sound?
They're preaching darling Corey's funeral,
In some lonesome graveyard ground.

6. Wake up, wake up darling Corey,
Go and get my gun,
I ain't no man for trouble,
But I'll die before I'll run.

Darling Nellie Gray

M: C; F: F or G
CD 1-Track 38, medley pt. 2

B.R. Hanby, 1856

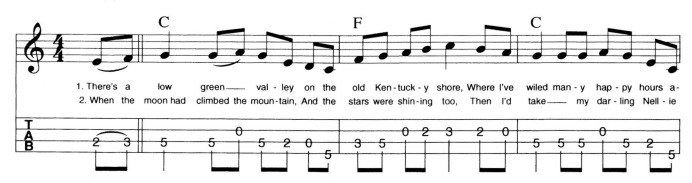

1. There's a low green valley on the old Ken-tuck-y shore, Where I've wiled man-y hap-py hours a-
2. When the moon had climbed the moun-tain, And the stars were shin-ing too, Then I'd take my dar-ling Nell-ie

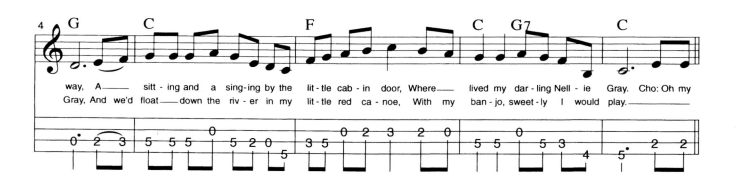

way, A sitt-ing and a sing-ing by the lit-tle cab-in door, Where lived my dar-ling Nell-ie Gray. Cho: Oh my
Gray, And we'd float down the riv-er in my lit-tle red ca-noe, With my ban-jo, sweet-ly I would play.

poor Nell-ie Gray, they have tak-en her a-way, And I'll nev-er see my dar-ling an-y-more, I'm

sitt-ing by the riv-er, and I'm weep-ing all the day, For she's gone from the old Ken-tuck-y shore.

Stanley Bros., Goose Island Ramblers, B. Clifton, M. Wiseman, D. Bruce & J. Nunally

```
         C                                          F
3. My canoe is under water and my banjo is unstrung,
             C                     G
Lord, I'm tired of living anymore,
        C                                    F
My eyes shall look downward, my songs shall be unsung,
             C          G7          C
While I stay on the old Kentucky shore.
```

4. One night I went to see her, "She's gone," the neighbors say,
The white man bound her with his chain,
They have taken her to Georgia, for to wear her life away,
As she toils in the cotton and the cane.

5. My eyes are growing blinded and I can not see my way,
Hark, there's someone knocking at the door.
I hear the angels calling, and I see my Nellie Gray,
Farewell, to the old Kentucky shore.

Last chous: Oh, my darling Nellie Gray, up in heaven, there they say,
That they'll never take you from me anymore.
I'm a'coming, coming, coming, as the angels clear my way,
Farewell, to the old Kentucky shore.

Darling Will You Ever Think of Me?

M: D; F: G or A
CD 1-Track 39

Dix Bruce

Copyright © by Dix Bruce • Dix Bruce Music, BMI

D   G
2. With the scent of summer fading,
D   A7
From the gentle autumn breeze,
D   G
As you pause in reflection,
Em A7   D
Darling will you think of me?
I will love you in September,
As in summer I will be,

Ever loving through December,
Darling will you think of me? (Chorus)

3. Worlds away my heart is beating,
Always lost in revery,
Pleading though the night won't answer,
Darling will you think of me?
Can I ever find escape love,
From your tender memory?
Need I ask and be heartbroken,
Darling will you think of me? (Chorus)

Deep Elem Blues

M: *C;* **F:** *F or G*
CD 1-Track 40

Traditional

Diamonds in the Rough

M: G; F: C or D
CD 1-Track 41

C.W. Bryson

```
       G                             C                    G
2. I used to dance the polka, the schottische and the waltz,
                              D
I also loved the theater, its glitter vain and false,
       G                             C               G
And Jesus, when He found me, He found me very tough,
                                          D       G
But praise the Lord, He saved me, a diamond in the rough.
```

3. One day, my precious comrades, you, too, were lost in sin,
When some one sought your rescue, and Jesus took you in,
When you are tried and tempted, by sinners' stern rebuff,
Don't turn away in anger, they're diamonds in the rough.

4. While reading through the Bible, some wondrous sights I see,
I read of Peter, James, and John, by the sea of Gallilee,
And when the Savior called them, their work was rude enough,
Yet they were precious diamonds, He gathered in the rough.

5. Now keep your lamps all burning, the lamps of holy love,
And unto every sinner point out the way above,
The dying love of Jesus, will help you love the tough,
He'll polish into beauty, the diamond from the rough.

Do Lord

M: A; F: D or E
CD 1-Track 42

Traditional

1. I've got a home in glo-ry-land that out-shines the sun, I've got a home in
Cho: Do Lord, oh do Lord, oh do re-member me, Do Lord, oh
2. I took Je-sus as my sav-ior, you take him too, I took Je-sus

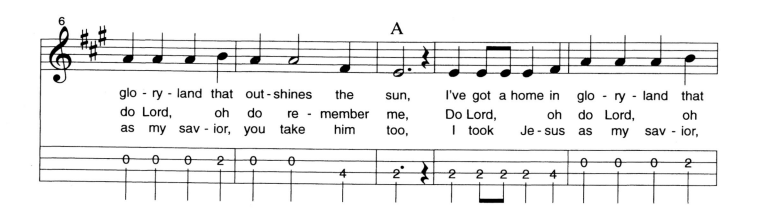

glo-ry-land that out-shines the sun, I've got a home in glo-ry-land that
do Lord, oh do re-member me, Do Lord, oh do Lord, oh
as my sav-ior, you take him too, I took Je-sus as my sav-ior,

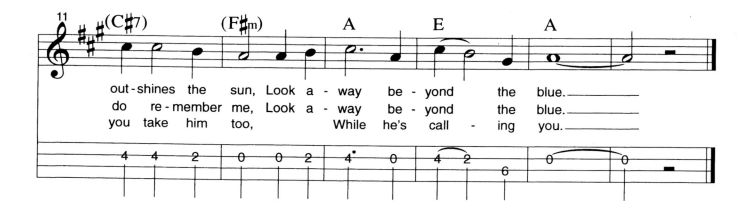

out-shines the sun, Look a-way be-yond the blue.
do re-member me, Look a-way be-yond the blue.
you take him too, While he's call-ing you.

Don't Let Your Deal Go Down

M: G; F: C or D
CD 1-Track 43

Traditional

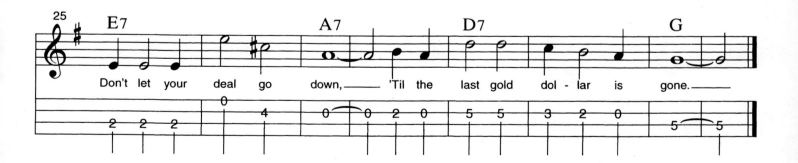

1. Well I've been all a - round this whole wide world, I've done most ev - ery thing,____ I've
2. When I left my____ love be - hind,____ She was stand - ing in the door,____ She
3. Now____ who's gon - na shoe your pretty little feet? And who's gonna glove your hand?____
4. Pa - pa will shoe my pretty little feet, And Mama will glove my hand.____
5. Where'd_ you get them high top shoes, The dress you wear so fine?

played cards with the king and the queen, The ace and the deuce and the trey.____
threw her arms a - round____ my neck said, "Daddy,____ please don't____ go."
Who's gonna kiss your ru - by____ lips?____ Who's gon - na be your____ man?____
You can kiss my red ru - by lips,____ When you get back a - gain.
Got them shoes from an en - gin - eer, Got the dress from a driver in the mine.____

Cho: Don't let your deal go down,____ Don't let your deal go down,____

Don't let your deal go down,____ 'Til the last gold dol - lar is gone.____

Flatt & Scruggs, NLCR, C. Poole, Ken. Colonels, D. Watson, B. Keith, Fiddlin' John Carson, M. Wiseman

Don't This Road Look Rough and Rocky?

M: D; F: G or A
CD 1-Track 44

Traditional

1. Dar - ling I have come to tell you,___ Though it al - most breaks my heart,___
2. Don't you hear the night birds cry - ing,___ On some dark and lone - ly sea,___
3. One more kiss be - fore I leave you,___ One more kiss be - fore we part.___

That be - fore the morn - ing dar - ling,___ We'll be man - y miles a - part.___
While of oth - ers you are think - ing,___ Won't you some - times think of me?___
You have caused me lots of trou - ble,___ Dar - ling, you have broke my heart.___

Cho: Don't this road look rough and rock - y?___ Don't that sea look wide and deep?___

Don't my ba - by look the sweet - est,___ When she's in my arms a - sleep?___

Don't You Hear Jerusalem Moan?

M: G; F: C or D
CD 1-Track 45

Traditional

Down Among the Budded Roses

M: C; F: F or G
CD 1-Track 46

Traditional

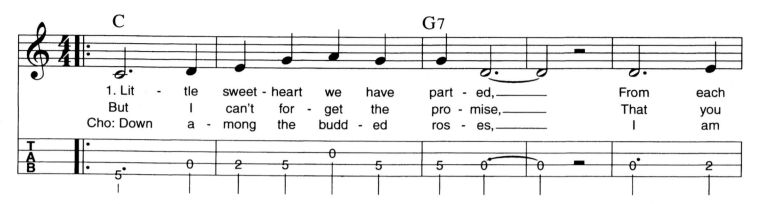

Lyrics under staff (verse 1 / verse 2 line / chorus):
1. Lit - tle sweet - heart we have part - ed,_____ From each
But I can't for - get the pro - mise,_____ That you
Cho: Down a - mong the budd - ed ros - es,_____ I am

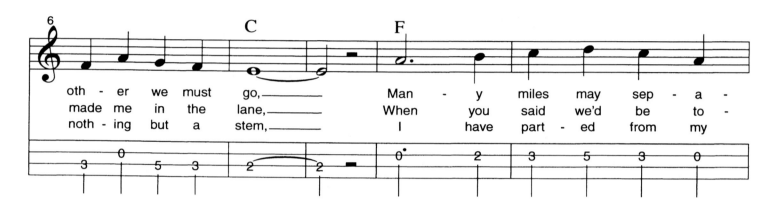

oth - er we must go,_____ Man - y miles may sep - a -
made me in the lane,_____ When you said we'd be to -
noth - ing but a stem,_____ I have part - ed from my

rate us,_____ In this world of care and woe._____
geth - er,_____ When the ros - es bloom a - gain.
dar - ling,_____ Nev - er more to meet a - gain.

C   G7   C
2. Now this parting gives me sorrow, And it almost breaks my heart,
F   C   G7   C
Tell me darling will you love me, When we meet, no more to part.
             G7   C
Or will this parting be forever, Will there be no coming day,
F   C   G7   C
When our hearts will be united, And all sorrows pass away?

3. Darling, meet me up in heaven, That's my true and earnest prayer,
If you love me here on earth dear, Then I'm sure you'll love me there.

Down in the Valley to Pray

M: G; F: C or D
CD 1-Track 47

Traditional

Cho: As I went down in the val - ley to pray, Stud - y - ing a - bout the good old way and

who will wear the star - ry crown? Oh, Lord, show me the way.

1. Oh, child - ren let's go down,——— Come on down, Don't you want to go down?——
2. Oh, moth - er let's go down,——— Come on down, Don't you want to go down?——

Oh, child - ren let's go down,——— Down in the val - ley to pray.
Oh, moth - er let's go down,——— Down in the val - ley to pray.

Additional verses:
Oh, brother, father, etc.

Down in the Willow Garden

M: E; F: A or B
CD 1-Track 48

Traditional

1. Down in the wil-low gar-den, where me and my love did meet, And
2. I drew my sa-ber through her, which was a blood-y knife, I
3. Now he sits by his cabin door, a' wip-ing his tear-brimmed eyes,

there we sat a-court-ing, my love fell off to sleep. I
threw her in to the riv-er, which was a dread-ful sight. My
Mourn-ing for his only son, out on the scaf-fold high. My

had a bot-tle of bur-glar's wine, which my true love did not know, And
fa-ther of-ten told me, that money would set me free, If
race is run be-neath the sun, the devil is wait-ing for me, For

there I poi-soned that dear lit-tle girl, down by the banks be-low.
I would mur-der that dear lit-tle miss, whose name was Rose Connel-ly.
I did mur-der that dear lit-tle girl, whose name was Rose Connel-ly.

Down the Road

M: G; F: C or D
CD 1-Track 49

Traditional

1. Now down the road a-bout a mile or two, Lives a lit-tle girl named Pear-ly Blue,
2. Now any - time you want to know, Where I'm heading it's down the road,

About so high and her hair is brown, Pret-ti-est thing, boys, in this town.
Got my girl on the line, You'll find her there most any old time.

      G   Em
3. Now every time I get the blues,
      G   D   G
I walk the soles right off my shoes,
                              Em
I don't know why I love her so,
         G   D   G
That gal of mine lives down the road.

4. Now everyday and Sunday too.
I go to see my Pearly Blue,
Before you hear that rooster crow,
You'll see me headed down the road.

5. Now old man ___ * he owned a farm,
From the hog lot to the barn,
From the barn to the rail,
He made his living by carrying the mail.

* *your name here*

Flatt & Scruggs, Greenbriar Boys, D. Watson, Country Gentlemen, BG Album Band   69

Drifting Too Far From the Shore

M: G; F: C or D
CD 1-Track 50

Chas. Moody

Monroe Bros., B. Monroe, Blue Sky Boys, Country Gentlemen, Boone Creek, Grisman-Garcia-Rice, Stanley Bros., Seldom Scene, Old & in the Way, IIIrd Tyme Out

East Virginia Blues

M: E; F: A or B
CD 1-Track 51

Traditional

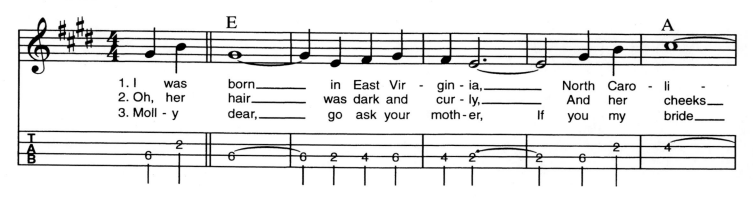

1. I was born_____ in East Vir - gin - ia,_____ North Caro - li -
2. Oh, her hair_____ was dark and cur - ly,_____ And her cheeks__
3. Moll - y dear,_____ go ask your moth - er, If you my bride____

— na I did go,_____ There I met_____ a fair young
— were ros - y red,_____ On her breast_____ she wore white
— might e - ver be,_____ If she says no,_____ come back and

maid - en,____ Though her age,_____ I did not know._____
lin - en,____ Where I longed_____ to lay my head._____
tell__ me,____ And I'll run_____ a - way with thee._____

    E
4. No I'll not go ask my mother,
     A   E
Where she lies on her bed of rest,
     A   E
For at her side she holds a dagger,
     B7   E
To kill the one that I love best.

5. I don't want your green back dollar,
I don't want your watch and chain,
All I want is your heart darling,
Say you'll take me back again.

6. The ocean's deep and I can't wade it,
And I have no wings to fly,
I'll just get some blue-eyed boatman,
For to row me over the tide.

7. I'll go back to East Virginia,
North Carolina ain't my home,
I'll go back to East Virginia,
Leave old North Carolina alone.

8. Oh, you know I'd like to see you,
At my door you're welcome in,
At my gate I'll always greet you,
For you're the girl I tried to win.

Carter Fam., Flatt and Scruggs, Stanley Bros., R. Stanley, J.D. Crowe, Country Gentlemen, Kathy Kallick, NLCR   71

Fair and Tender Ladies

M: D; F: G or A
CD 1-Track 52

Traditional

1. Come all ye fair___ and ten-der la - dies,___ Take warn-ing how___
2. They'll tell to you___ some lov-ing stor - ies,___ They'll tell you that___
3. I wish I was___ a lit-tle spar-row,___ And I had wings___
4. Oh, love is hand - some, love is charm-ing,___ Love is pret -

___ you court young men,___ They're like a star___ of a sum - mer's
___ they love you well,___ Then a - way they'll go___ and___ court some
___ and I could fly,___ Then a - way I'd go___ to my false true
ty while it's new,___ But love grows cold___ as___ love grows

morn - ing,___ They'll first ap - pear___ and then they're gone.___
oth - er,___ And leave you here___ in grief to dwell.___
lov - er,___ And when he'd ask___ I would de - ny.___
old - er,___ And fades a - way___ like morn - ing dew.___

Country Gentlemen, Ken. Colonels, J.Val, Osborne Bros., P. Rowan

Fathers Have a Home Sweet Home

M: G; F: C or D
CD 1-Track 53

Traditional

Additional verses:
Mothers, brothers, sisters, etc.

Feast Here Tonight

M: D; F: G or A
CD 1-Track 54

Traditional

1. There's a rab-bit in the log and I ain't got my dog, How will I get him? I
2. I'll build__ me a fire and I'll roast that old hare, Roll him in the flames to make him
3. I'm go-ing down the track with my coat ripped up my back, Soles on my shoes are nearly

know,__ I'll get me a briar and I'll twist it in his hair, That way I'll
brown, Have a feast here to - night while the moon is shin-ing bright, Just find me a
gone,__ Just a lit - tle ways a - head there's a farm - er's__ shed, That's where I'll

get him I know.__ I know,__ I know,__ That way I'll get him I know,
place__ to lie down.__ To lie down,__ to lie down,__ Find me a place__ to lie down,
rest my weary bones.__ Weary bones,__ weary bones,__ That's where I'll rest my weary bones,

I'll get me a briar and I'll twist it in his hair, That way I'll get him I know.__
Have a feast here to - night while the moon is shining bright, Find me a place to lie down.__
Just a lit - tle ways a - head there's a farm - er's__ shed, That's where I'll rest my weary bones.__

Monroe Bros., B. Monroe, R. Stanley, Stanley Bros., D. Grisman, Lilly Bros., Scruggs/Watson/Skaggs

The Foggy Mountain Top

M: G; F: C or D
CD 1-Track 55

Traditional

Verse 1 often used as chorus

Carter Fam., Monroe Bros., B. Monroe, Flatt & Scruggs, NLCR, E. Taylor, D. Grisman, The Bluegrass Band, W. Guthrie

Footprints in the Snow

M: C; F: F or G
CD 1-Track 56

Harry Wright, ca. 1880

1. Some folks like the sum-mer time, When they can walk a - bout, Stroll-ing through the meadow green, It's
2. I dropped in to see her, There was a big round moon, Her moth-er said she just went out, She would
3. Now she's up in heav - en, She's with an an - gel band, I know I'm going to see her,

pleas - ant there's no doubt. But give me the win-ter-time, when the snow is on the ground, For I
be re - turn - ing soon. I found her lit - tle foot - prints, and I traced them through the snow, I
in that prom-ised land. Eve - ry time the snow falls, It brings back mem - o - ries, Oh, I

found her when the snow was on the ground. Cho: I traced her lit-tle foot-prints in the
found her when the snow was on the ground.
found her when the snow was on the ground.

snow, I found her lit-tle foot-prints in the snow, Lord I bless that hap-py

day, When Nel - lie lost her way, I found her when the snow was on the ground.

B. Monroe, Flatt & Scruggs, Stanley Bros., R. Stanley, C. White, Ken. Colonels, D. Watson, B. Kincaid, Muleskinner

This is the original 1899 cover for "The Girl I Loved in Sunny Tennessee."

The Girl I Loved in Sunny Tennessee

M: G; F: C or D
CD 1-Track 57, medley pt. 1

*Braisted & Carter,
ca. 1899*

1. On one morn - ing bright and clear, To my old home I drew near, Just a
2. It was but a few short years since I'd kissed a - way her tears, As I
3. As the train drew up at last, Old fa - mil - iar scenes I passed, And I
4. As I whis - pered, "Moth - er dear, Where is Mar - y, she's not here!" All the

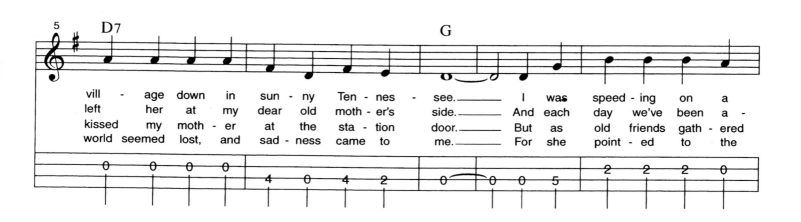

vill - age down in sun - ny Ten - nes - see.____ I was speed - ing on a
left her at my dear old moth - er's side.____ And each day we've been a -
kissed my moth - er at the sta - tion door.____ But as old friends gath - ered
world seemed lost, and sad - ness came to me.____ For she point - ed to the

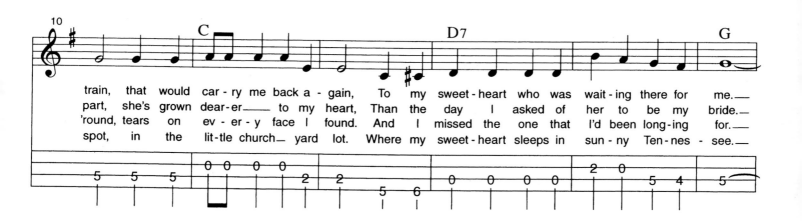

train, that would car - ry me back a - gain, To my sweet - heart who was wait - ing there for me.__
part, she's grown dear - er____ to my heart, Than the day I asked of her to be my bride.__
'round, tears on ev - er - y face I found. And I missed the one that I'd been long - ing for.__
spot, in the lit - tle church__ yard lot. Where my sweet - heart sleeps in sun - ny Ten - nes - see.__

Cho: We could hear___ the old folks sing-ing,___ As she bid___ fare-well to

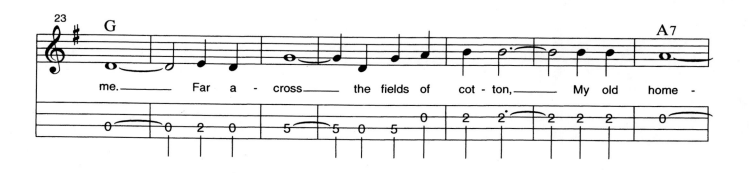

me.___ Far a - cross___ the fields of cot - ton,___ My old home -

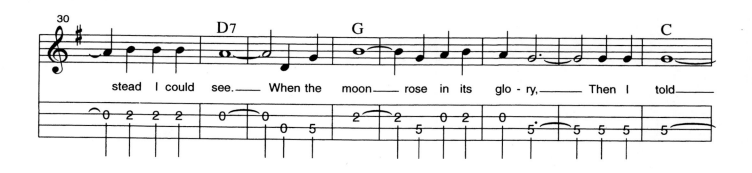

stead I could see.___ When the moon___ rose in its glo - ry,___ Then I told___

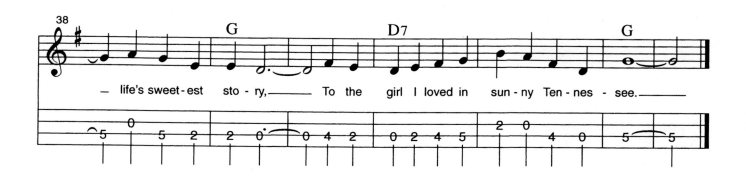

— life's sweet-est sto - ry,___ To the girl I loved in sun - ny Ten - nes - see.___

Give Me Oil in My Lamp

M: G; F: C or D
CD 1-Track 57, medley pt. 2

Traditional

Give Me the Roses While I Live

M: G; F: C or D
CD 1-Track 58

Cornelius & Rowe

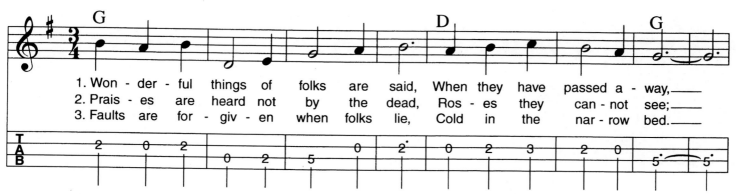

1. Won - der - ful things of folks are said, When they have passed a - way,____
2. Prais - es are heard not by the dead, Ros - es they can - not see;____
3. Faults are for - giv - en when folks lie, Cold in the nar - row bed.____

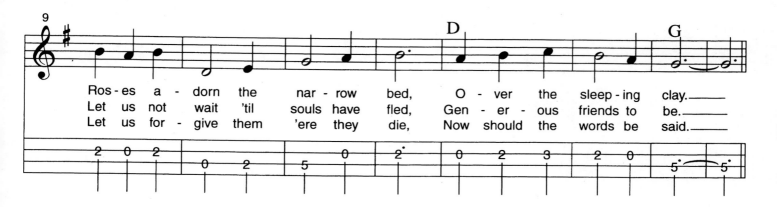

Ros - es a - dorn the nar - row bed, O - ver the sleep - ing clay.____
Let us not wait 'til souls have fled, Gen - er - ous friends to be.____
Let us for - give them 'ere they die, Now should the words be said.____

Cho: Give me the ros - es while I live, Try - ing to cheer me on.____

Use - less the flow - ers that you give, Af - ter the soul is gone.____

Carter Fam., Stanley Bros., R. Stanley, Jimmy Martin   81

Going Down This Road Feeling Bad

M: G; F: C or D
CD 1-Track 59, medley pt. 1

Traditional

     G   G7
2. They feed me on corn bread and beans,
     C   G G7
They feed me on corn bread and beans,
     C   G
They feed me on corn bread and beans, Lord, Lord,
     D   G
And I ain't gonna be treated this a way.

3. I'm going where the chilly winds don't blow, (etc.)
4. I'm going where the water tastes like wine, (etc.)
5. I'm going where the weather suits my clothes, (etc.)

Jam sessions can sometimes be very large! This old time jam — with seven banjos no less — took place at the 2006 California Bluegrass Association's Music Camp in Grass Valley.

Large or small, jam sesions are all lots of fun!

Grandfather's Clock

M: G; F: C or D

Henry Clay Work, 1876

CD 1-Track 59, medley pt. 2

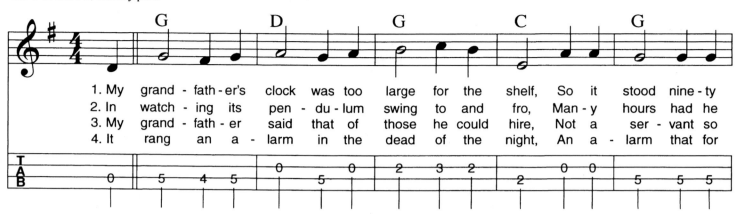

1. My grand-fath-er's clock was too large for the shelf, So it stood nine-ty
2. In watch-ing its pen-du-lum swing to and fro, Man-y hours had he
3. My grand-fath-er said that of those he could hire, Not a ser-vant so
4. It rang an a-larm in the dead of the night, An a-larm that for

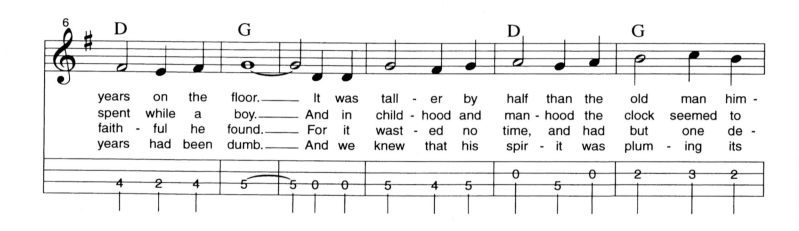

years on the floor.____ It was tall-er by half than the old man him-
spent while a boy.____ And in child-hood and man-hood the clock seemed to
faith-ful he found.____ For it wast-ed no time, and had but one de-
years had been dumb.____ And we knew that his spir-it was plum-ing its

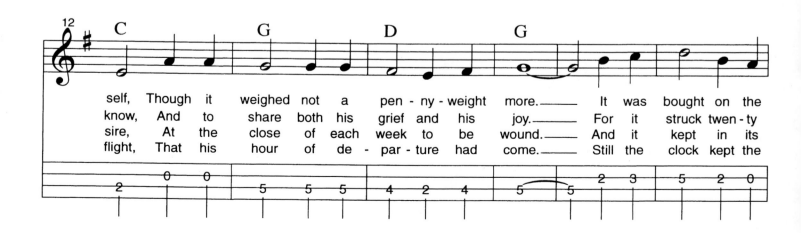

self, Though it weighed not a pen-ny-weight more.____ It was bought on the
know, And to share both his grief and his joy.____ For it struck twen-ty
sire, At the close of each week to be wound.____ And it kept in its
flight, That his hour of de-par-ture had come.____ Still the clock kept the

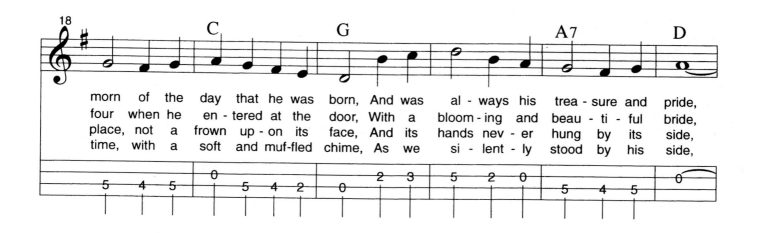

morn of the day that he was born, And was al - ways his trea - sure and pride,
four when he en - tered at the door, With a bloom - ing and beau - ti - ful bride,
place, not a frown up - on its face, And its hands nev - er hung by its side,
time, with a soft and muf-fled chime, As we si - lent - ly stood by his side,

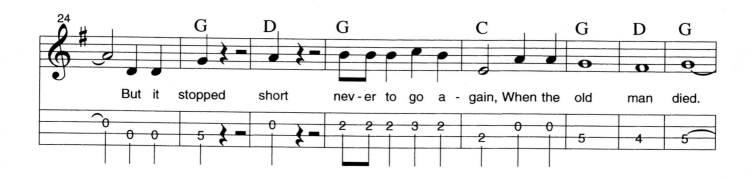

But it stopped short nev - er to go a - gain, When the old man died.

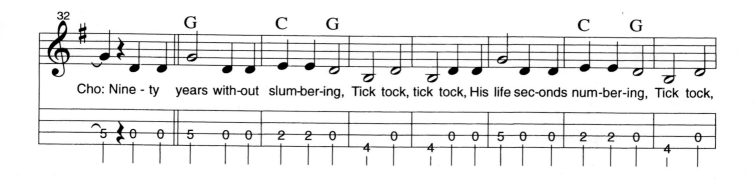

Cho: Nine - ty years with-out slum-ber-ing, Tick tock, tick tock, His life sec-onds num-ber-ing, Tick tock,

tick tock, It stopped short nev - er to go a - gain, When the old man died.

Great Speckled Bird

M: G; F: C or D
CD 1-Track 60

Traditional

1. What a beau - ti - ful thought I am think - ing,_____ Con - cern - ing the great speck - led bird._____ Re - mem - ber her name is re - cord - ed,_____ In the pag - es of God's Ho - ly Word._____

2. De - sir - ing to low - er her stan - dard,_____ They watch ev - ery move that she makes,_____ They long to find fault with her teach - ing,_____ But real - ly they find no mis - take._____

G   C
3. I am glad to have learned of her meekness,
D   G
I'm proud that my name is in her book,
  G   C
For I want to be one never fearing,
  D   G
The face of my Saviour's to look.

4. All the other birds flocking 'round her
And she is despised by the squad,
But the great speckled bird in the Bible,
Is one with the great church of God.

5. In the presence of all her despisers,
With a song never uttered before,
She will rise and be gone in a moment,
'Til the great tribulation is o'er.

6. When He cometh descending from heaven,
On the clouds as He writes in His word,
I'll be joyfully carried to meet Him,
On the wings of the great speckled bird.

7. She is spreading her wings for a journey.
She's going to leave by and by,
When the trumpet shall sound in the morning,
She'll rise and go up in the sky.

Green Pastures

M: A; F: D or E
CD 1-Track 61

Traditional

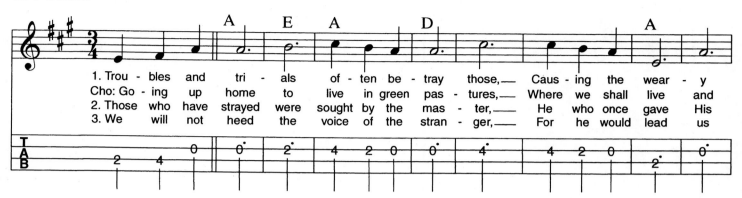

1. Trou - bles and tri - als of - ten be - tray those,— Caus - ing the wear - y
Cho: Go - ing up home to live in green pas - tures,— Where we shall live and
2. Those who have strayed were sought by the mas - ter,— He who once gave His
3. We will not heed the voice of the stran - ger,— For he would lead us

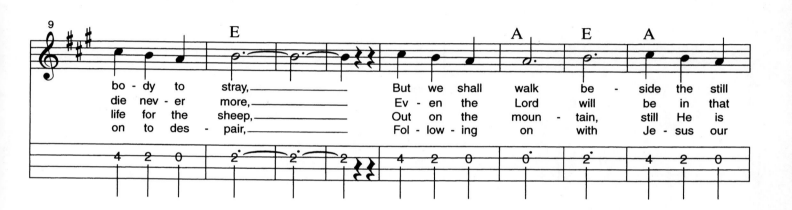

bo - dy to stray,— But we shall walk be - side the still
die nev - er more,— Ev - en the Lord will be in that
life for the sheep,— Out on the moun - tain, still He is
on to des - pair,— Fol - low - ing on with Je - sus our

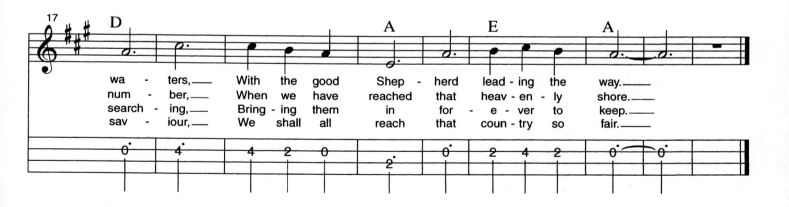

wa - ters,— With the good Shep - herd lead - ing the way.—
num - ber,— When we have reached that heav - en - ly shore.—
search - ing,— Bring - ing them in for - e - ver to keep.—
sav - iour,— We shall all reach that coun - try so fair.—

Groundhog

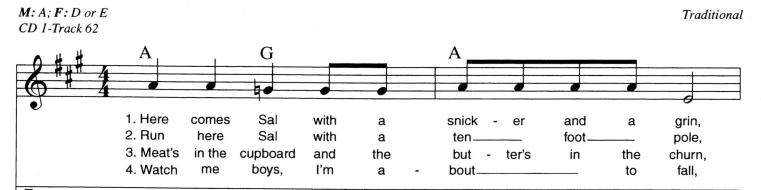

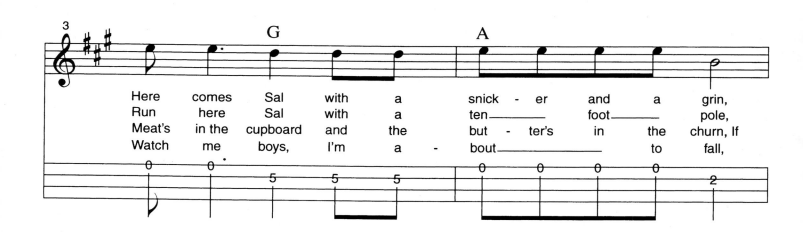

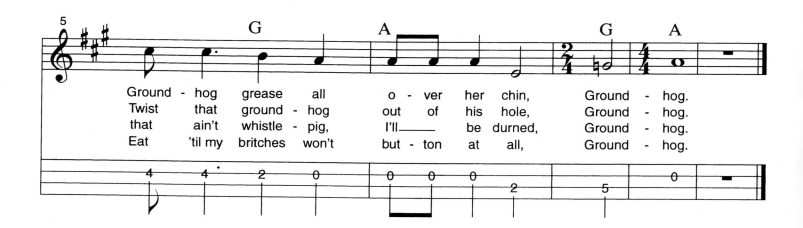

Stanley Bros., D. Watson, NLCR, Dillards

Hallelujah! I'm Ready

M: C; F: F or G
CD 1-Track 63

Traditional

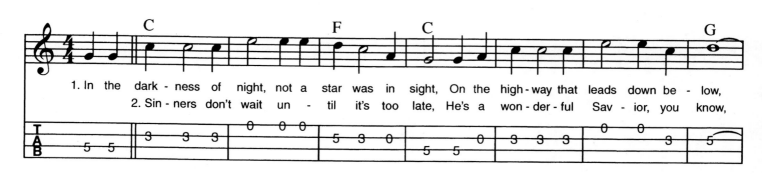

1. In the dark - ness of night, not a star was in sight, On the high - way that leads down be - low,
2. Sin - ners don't wait un - til it's too late, He's a won - der - ful Sav - ior, you know,

But Je - sus came in to save us all from sin, Hal - le - lu - jah, I'm read - y to go. Cho: Hal - le -
Well I fell on my knees, and he an - swered my pleas, Hal - le - lu - jah, I'm read - y to go.

lu - jah,____ ____ I'm read - y,____ I can hear the voic - es sing - ing soft and low,____
(I'm read - y), (Hal - le - lu - jah),

____ Hal - le - lu - jah,____ I'm read - y, Hal - le - lu - jah, I'm read - y to go.____
(I'm read-y), Hal - le - lu - jah),

Hand Me Down My Walking Cane

M: G; F: C or D

CD 1-Track 64, medley pt. 1

Traditional

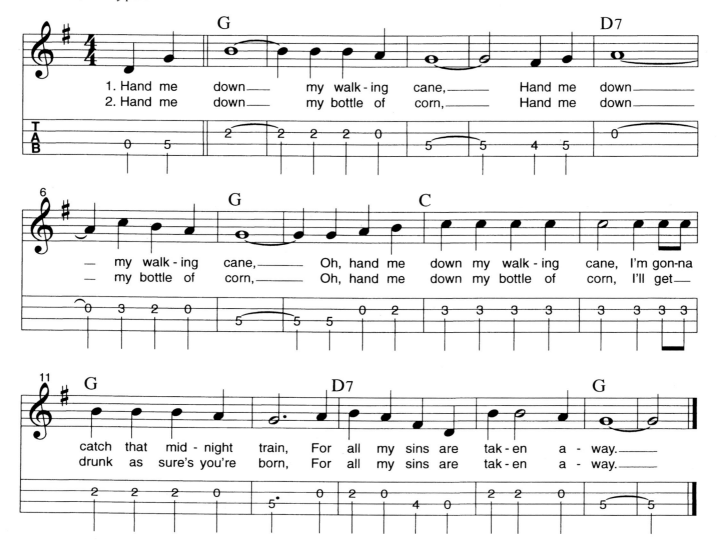

G

3. Oh, I got drunk and I landed in jail,
       D7   G
Oh, I got drunk and I landed in jail,
            C
Oh, I got drunk and I landed in jail,
          G
With no one to go my bail,
   D7   G
For all my sins are taken away.

4. The meat is tough, and the beans are bad, (3X)
Oh, my God, I can't eat that,
For all my sins are taken away.

5. The devil chased me 'round a stump, (3X)
I thought he'd catch me at every jump,
For all my sins are taken away.

Goose Island Ramblers, Osborne Bros., Skillet Lickers, N. Blake

Handsome Molly

M: G; F: C or D
CD 1-Track 64, medley pt. 2

Traditional

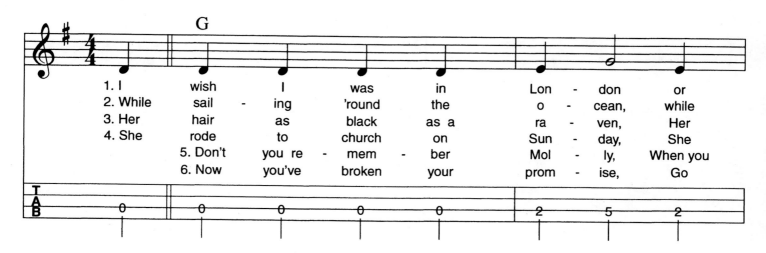

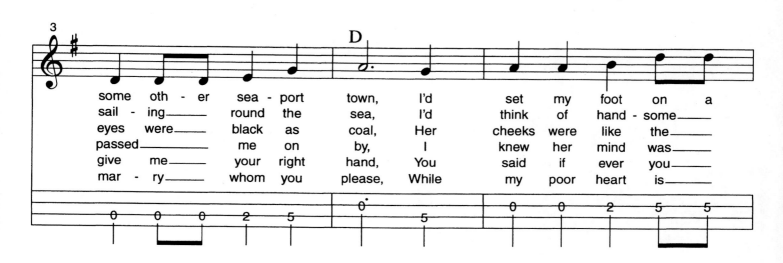

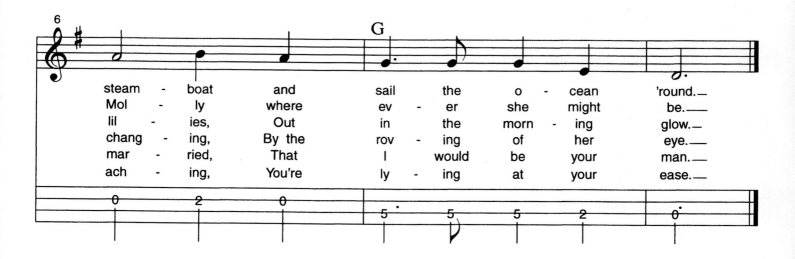

Flatt & Scruggs, Stanley Bros., R. Stanley, D. Watson, N. Blake, Grayson & Whitter, Country Gentlemen

Hard Times, Come Again No More

M: D; F: G or A

CD 1-Track 65, medley pt. 1

Stephen Foster

1. Let us pause in life's pleas-ures and count its man-y tears, While we all sup sor-row with the
2. While we seek mirth and beau-ty, And mus-ic light and gay, There are frail forms faint-ing at the
3. There's a pale droop-ing maid-en, Who toils her life a-way, With a worn heart whose bet-ter days are
4. 'Tis a sigh that is waft-ed, A-cross the troub-led wave, 'Tis a wail that is heard up-on the

poor, There's a song that will lin-ger for-ev-er in our ears, Oh! hard times, come a-gain no
door; Though their voic-es are si-lent, Their plead-ing looks will say, Oh! hard times come a-gain no
o'er: Though her voice would be mer-ry, 'tis sigh-ing all the day, Oh! hard times come a-gain no
shore, 'Tis a dirge that is mur-mured, A-round the low-ly grave, Oh! hard times come a-gain no

more. Cho: 'Tis the song, the sigh of the wear-y, hard times, hard times, come a-gain no more, Man-y
more.
more.
more.

days you have ling-ered a-round my cab-in door, Oh! hard times, come a-gain no more.

Have Thine Own Way, Lord

M: D; F: G or A
CD 1-Track 65, medley pt. 2

Pollard & Stebbins,1907

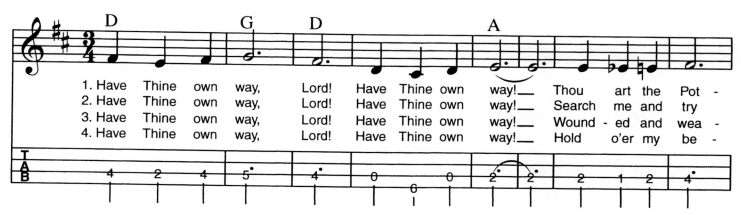

1. Have Thine own way, Lord! Have Thine own way!__ Thou art the Pot -
2. Have Thine own way, Lord! Have Thine own way!__ Search me and try
3. Have Thine own way, Lord! Have Thine own way!__ Wound - ed and wea -
4. Have Thine own way, Lord! Have Thine own way!__ Hold o'er my be -

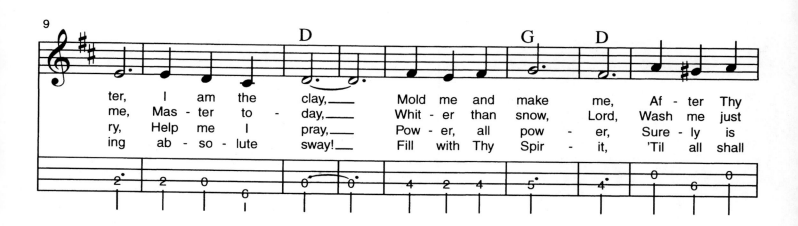

ter, I am the clay,__ Mold me and make me, Af - ter Thy
me, Mas - ter to - day,__ Whit - er than snow, Lord, Wash me just
ry, Help me I pray,__ Pow - er, all pow - er, Sure - ly is
ing ab - so - lute sway!__ Fill with Thy Spir - it, 'Til all shall

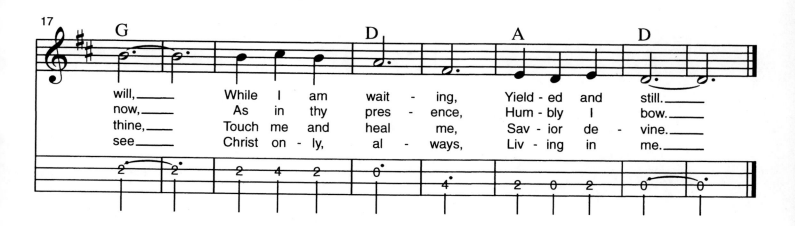

will,___ While I am wait - ing, Yield - ed and still.___
now,___ As in thy pres - ence, Hum - bly I bow.___
thine,___ Touch me and heal me, Sav - ior de - vine.___
see___ Christ on - ly, al - ways, Liv - ing in me.___

He Was a Friend of Mine

M: G; F: C or D
CD 1-Track 66

Traditional

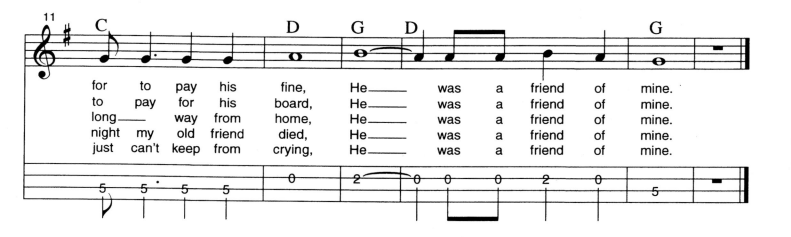

Country Gentlemen, Grateful Dead

Frank Wakefield, one of bluegrass music's greatest innovators, in 1983

He Will Set Your Fields on Fire

M: *A;* **F:** *D or E*
CD 1-Track 67

Ballew & Brackett

Monroe Bros., B. Monroe, Flatt & Scruggs, C. White, Country Gentlemen, Reno & Smiley

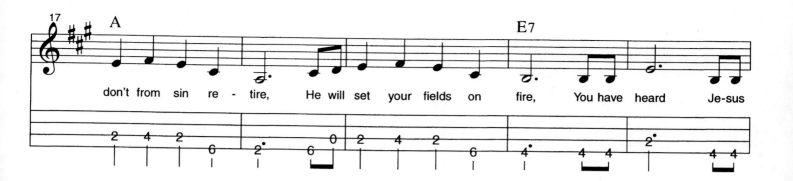

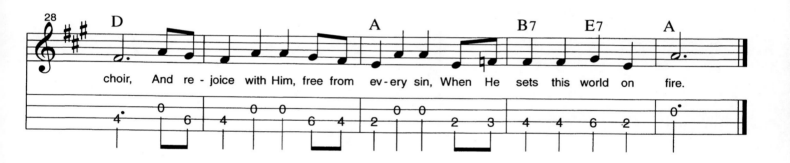

High on a Mountain

M: D; F: G or A
CD 1-Track 68

Ola Belle Reed

1. As I looked at the val-leys down be-low, They were green just as far as I could see, As my mem-o-ry re-turned,____ oh, how my heart did yearn, For you and the days that used to be.

2. Oh, I wonder if you ev-er think of me, Or if time has blotted out your mem-o-ry, As I lis-ten to the breeze, whis-per gen-tly through the trees, I'll always cher-ish what you meant to me.

Cho: High on a moun-tain the wind blow-ing free, Think-ing a-bout the days that used to be, High on a moun-tain, oh, stand-ing all a-lone, Won-der-ing where the years of my life have flown.

Highway of Sorrow

M: C; F: F or G
CD 1-Track 69

Bill Monroe

B. Monroe, D. Grisman, Del McCoury, D. Watson, Johnson Mtn. Boys

Hills of Roane County

M: G; F: C or D
CD 1-Track 70

Traditional

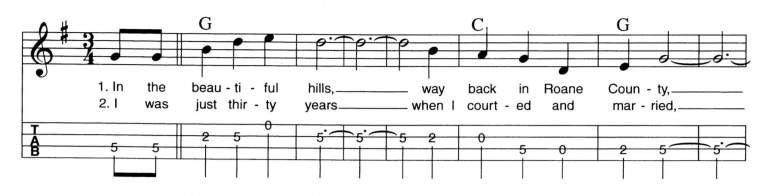

1. In the beau - ti - ful hills,_____ way back in Roane Coun - ty,_____
2. I was just thir - ty years_____ when I court - ed and mar - ried,_____

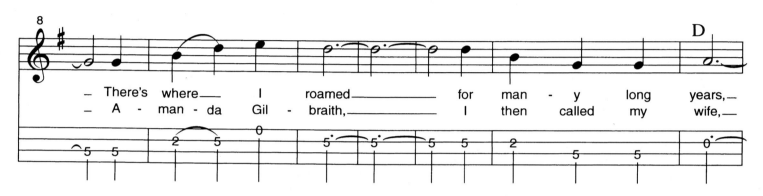

_ There's where_ I roamed_____ for man - y long years,_
_ A - man - da Gil - braith,_____ I then called my wife,_

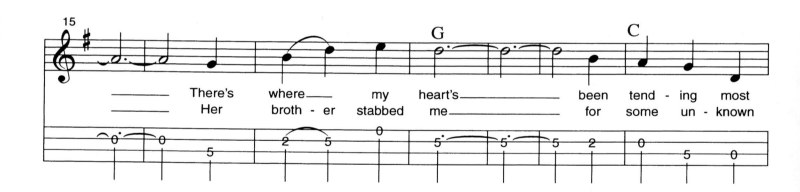

_____ There's where_ my heart's_____ been tend - ing most
_____ Her broth - er stabbed me_____ for some un - known

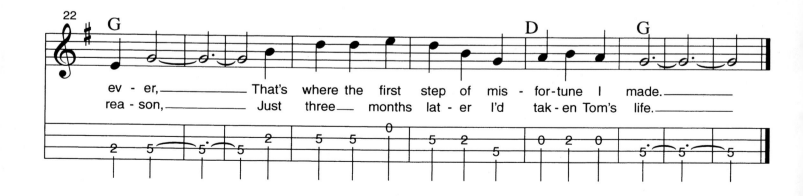

ev - er,_____ That's where the first step of mis - for-tune I made._____
rea - son,_____ Just three_ months lat - er I'd tak - en Tom's life._____

B. Monroe, Stanley Bros., Blue Sky Boys, Mac Wiseman, T. Rice,

```
          G          C          G
3. For twenty five years this whole world I rambled,
                              D
I went to old England to France and to Spain,
              G          C          G
But I thought of my home way back in Roane County,
                    D          G
I boarded a steamer and came back again.
```

4. I was captured and tried in the village of Kingston,
Not a man in the county would speak one kind word,
When the jury came in with the verdict next morning,
"A lifetime in prison" was the words that I heard.

5. When the train pulled out, poor Mother stood weeping,
And sister she sat, alone with a sigh,
And the last words I heard was, "Willie God bless you,"
Was, "Willie God bless you, God bless you, good bye."

6. Sweet Martha was grave but Corey was better,
There's better and worse, although you can see,
Boys when you write home from the prison in Nashville,
Place one of my songs in your letter for me.

7. In the scorching hot sand of the foundry I'm working,
Toiling and working my poor life away.
They'll measure my grave on the banks of old Cumberland,
Just as soon as I've finished the rest of my days.

8. No matter what happens to me in Roane County,
No matter how long my sentence may be,
I'll love my home way back in Roane County,
It's a' way back down in East Tennessee.

His Eye is on the Sparrow

M: C; F: F or G
CD 1-Track 71

Martin & Gabriel, 1906

D. Lawson

Hold Fast to the Right

M: G; F: C or D
CD 1-Track 72

Traditional

Hold to God's Unchanging Hand

M: F ; F: Bb or C
CD 1-Track 73

Wilson & Eiland

Stanley Bros., Jimmy Martin, D. Grisman

Home Sweet Home

M: D; F: G or A
CD 1-Track 74

Payne & Bishop

Honey in the Rock

M: G; F: C or D
CD 1-Track 75

Traditional

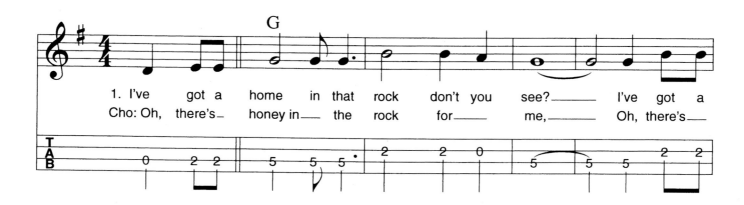

Lyrics under staff 1:
1. I've got a home in that rock don't you see?_____ I've got a
Cho: Oh, there's— honey in— the rock for—— me,—— Oh, there's—

Lyrics under staff 2:
home in that rock don't you see?—— I've got a home in that rock, just be-
honey in— the rock for—— me,—— Oh, there's— honey in— the rock, just be-

Lyrics under staff 3:
yond the moun-tain top, I've got a home in that rock don't you see?——
yond the moun-tain top, Oh, there's— honey in— the rock for—— me.——

G
2. God gave Noah the rainbow sign don't you see?
                                      D
God gave Noah the rainbow sign don't you see?
   G
God gave Noah the rainbow sign,
                            Em
No more water but the fire next time,
        G   D   G
God gave Noah the rainbow sign don't you see?

3. Oh, I'm climbing up the King's highway, (2X)
Got old Satan on my track,
Never think of looking back,
Oh, I'm climbing up the King's highway.

Three of my favorite mandolin players, left to right,
David Grisman, Buck White, and Ricky Skaggs, ca 1980.

Ruth McClain, of The McClain Family Band, elegant-
ly demonstrates the delicate balance of mandolinhood
and motherhood. Early 1980s.

Hop High Ladies

M: D; F: G or A
CD 1-Track 76

Traditional

1. Did you ev-er go to meet-ing Un-cle Joe, Un-cle Joe? Did you
2. Will your horse___ car-ry dou-ble, Un-cle Joe, Un-cle Joe? Will your

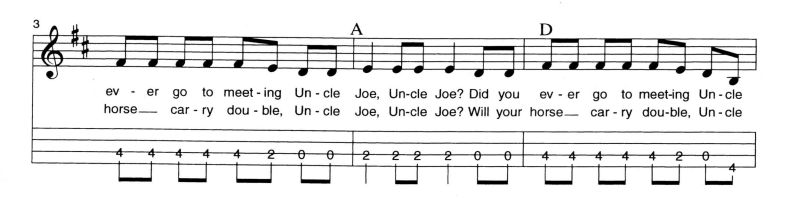

ev-er go to meet-ing Un-cle Joe, Un-cle Joe? Did you ev-er go to meet-ing Un-cle
horse___ car-ry dou-ble, Un-cle Joe, Un-cle Joe? Will your horse___ car-ry dou-ble, Un-cle

Joe, Un-cle Joe? I don't mind the wea-ther so the wind don't blow.___
Joe, Un-cle Joe? I don't mind the wea-ther so the wind don't blow.___

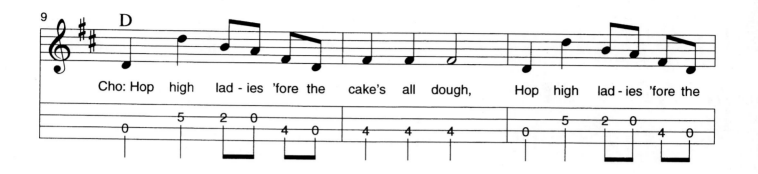

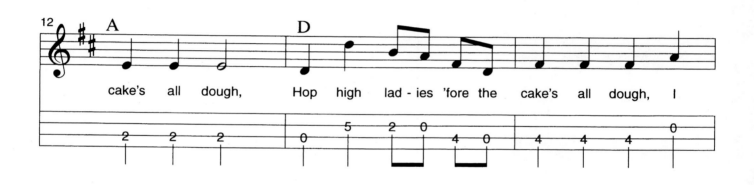

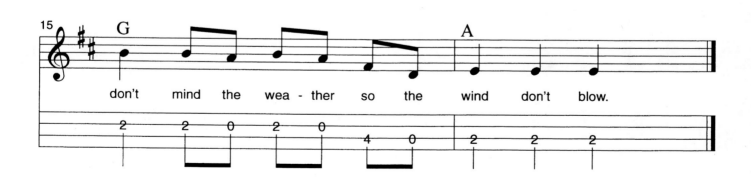

Hot Corn, Cold Corn

M: C; F: F or G
CD 1-Track 77

Traditional

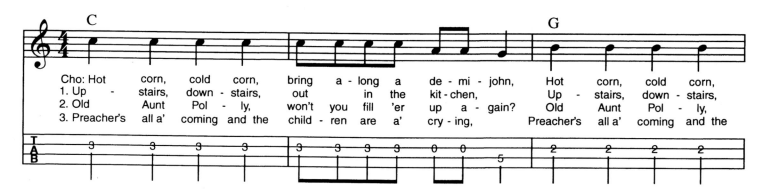

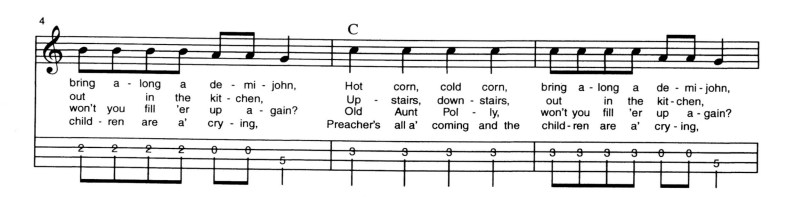

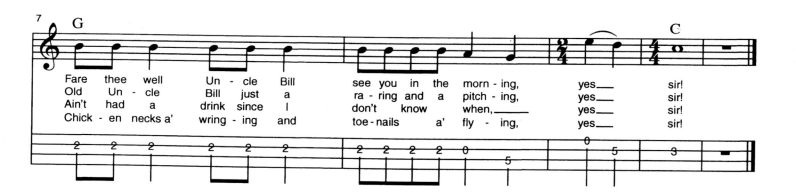

Flatt & Scruggs, Holy Modal Rounders, Here Today, Grisman, Garcia, Rice, NLCR, Dry Branch Fire Squad, D. Bruce

How Can You Treat Me So?

M: E; F: A or B
CD 1-Track 78

Dix Bruce

E
4. I been broke and I been busted, I been robbed by people I trusted,
    B7   E
But how can you treat me so?
        E
I might win and I might lose, I might be in love, I might have the blues,
        B7   E
But how can you treat me so?

Cho 2: All I ever wanted was you,
I've done my part, baby I been true,
When the whole wide world turned me away,
You opened your arms and you would let me stay.

5. In sickness and in health,
Life can be heaven or it can be hell,
But how can you treat me so?

D. Bruce & J. Nunally   **111**

I Ain't Gonna Work Tomorrow

M: C; F: F or G
CD 1-Track 79

Traditional

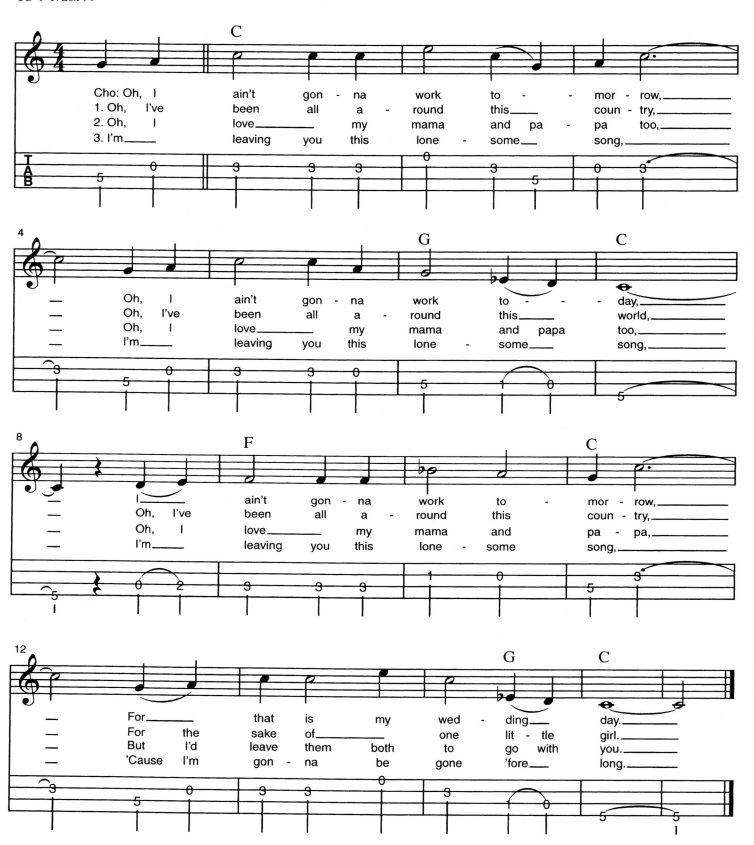

Carter Fam., Flatt & Scruggs, Country Gentlemen, Louvin Bros.

I Know You Rider

M: A mixolydian; F: D or E mixolydian
CD 1-Track 80

Traditional

1. I know you rid - er, gon - na miss me when — I'm gone, —
2. Laid down last night, — Lord, I could not take — my rest, —

— I know you rid - er, Gon - na miss me when — I'm gone, — Gon - na
— Laid down last night, — Lord, I could not — take my rest, — My —

miss your ba - by, from roll - ing in — your arms. —
mind was wan - d'ring like the wild geese in — the West. —

  A   G D A
3. I'm going down to the river, set in my rockin' chair, (2X)
   G   D   G D A
And if the blues don't find me, gonna rock away from here.

4. I know my baby sure is bound to love me some, (2X)
Throws her arms around me like a circle 'round the sun.

5. The sun's gonna shine in my back door some day, (2X)
The wind's gonna rise and blow my blues away.

6. I wish I was a headlight on a northbound train, (2X)
I'd shine my light through the cold Colorado rain.

7. Just as sure as the bird flies in the sky above, (2X)
Life ain't worth living if you ain't with the one you love.

I Never Will Marry

M: G; F: C or D
CD 1-Track 81, medley pt. 1

Traditional

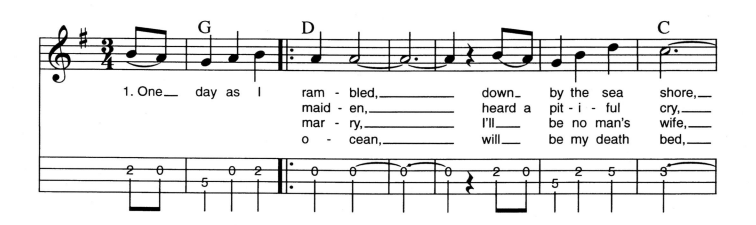

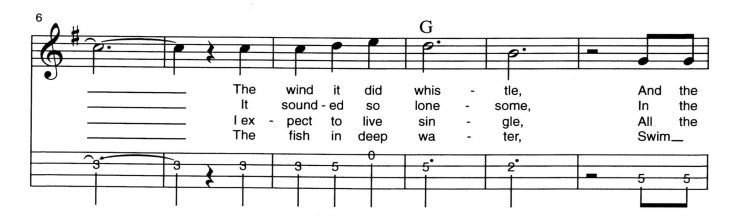

G   D   C

4. My love's gone and left me, he's the one I adore,

               G   D   G

He's gone where I never shall see him no more.

5. She plunged her dear body, in the waters so deep,
She closed her pretty blue eyes, in the water to sleep.

I Shall Not Be Moved

M: G; F: C or D
CD 1-Track 81, medley pt. 2

Traditional

1. Glo - ry hal - le - lu - jah, I shall not be moved, Anch - ored in Je -
Cho: I___ shall___ not be I shall not be moved, I___ shall___

ho - vah, I shall not be moved, Just like a tree that's
not be I shall not be moved, Just like a tree that's

plant - ed by the wa - ters, I shall not be moved.___
plant - ed by the wa - ters, I shall not be moved.___

G   D
2. In his love abiding, I shall not be moved,
                 G
And in Him confiding, I shall not be moved.
      C   G
Just like a tree that's planted by the waters,
     D   G
I shall not be moved.

3. Though all Hell assail me, I shall not be moved,
Jesus will not fail me, I shall not be moved. (etc.)

4. Though the tempest rages, I shall not be moved,
On the Rock of Ages, I shall not be moved. (etc.)

I Wonder How the Old Folks Are at Home

M: G; F: C or D
CD 1-Track 82

*Lambert & Van
der Sloot, 1909*

B. Monroe, R. Stanley, Ken. Colonels, Mac Wiseman, D. Watson, Osborne Bros., Jim & Jesse, Lilly Bros. & D. Stover

Ricky Skaggs, left, and Kentucky Thunder. Band members from left to right are Ricky Skaggs, Darrin Vincent, Jim Mills, Paul Brewster and Cody Kilby.

I'll Be All Smiles Tonight

M: A; F: D or E
CD 1-Track 83

T.B. Ransom, 1879

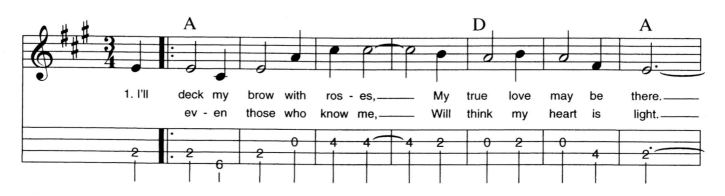

1. I'll deck my brow with ros - es,_____ My true love may be there._____
ev - en those who know me,_____ Will think my heart is light._____

— The_ gems that oth-ers_ gave me,_____ Will shine with - in my hair._____ And
Though my heart may break_ to - mor-row,_____ I'll

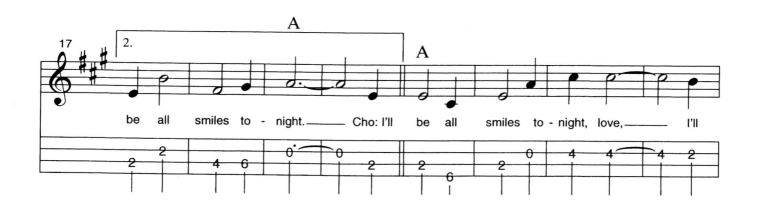

be all smiles to - night._____ Cho: I'll be all smiles to - night, love,_____ I'll

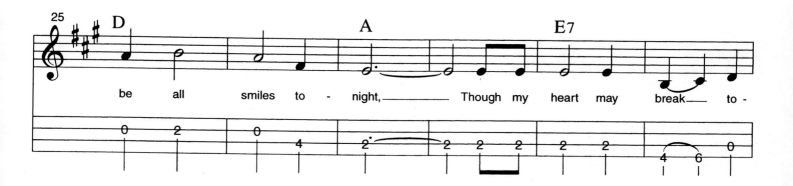

be all smiles to - night,_____ Though my heart may break___ to -

mor - row,_____ I'll be all smiles to - night._____

A
2. And when the door he entered,
   D   A
With a bride upon his arm.
   E
I stood and gazed upon him,
                        A
As though he were some charm.

So, now he smiles on his love,
   D   A
As once he smiled on me.
   E
He meant not to deceive me,
                        A
There'll be no change in me.

(Chorus after each verse)

3. And when the dance commences,
Oh, how I will rejoice,
I'll sing a song he taught me
Without one faltering voice;
When flatterers come around me
They will think my heart is light,
Though my heart will break tomorrow
I'll be all smiles tonight.

4. And when the dance is over,
And all have gone to rest,
I'll think of him, dear mother,
The one that I love best.
He once did love, believe me,
But he's grown cold and strange,
He sought not to deceive me,
False friends have brought this change.

I'll Fly Away

M: G; F: C or D
CD 1-Track 84

A.E. Brumley, 1932

1. Some glad morn-ing when this life is o'er, I'll fly a-way,
2. When the shad-ows of this life have gone, I'll fly a-way,
3. Just a few more wear-y days and then, I'll fly a-way,

To a home on God's ce-les-tial shore, I'll fly a-way.
Like a bird from these pri-son walls I'll fly, I'll fly a-way.
To a land where joys will nev-er end, I'll fly a-way.

Cho: I'll fly a-way, Oh glo-ry, I'll fly a-way,

When I die hal-le-lu-jah by and by, I'll fly a-way.

I'm Working on a Building

M: D; F: G or A
CD 1-Track 85

Traditional

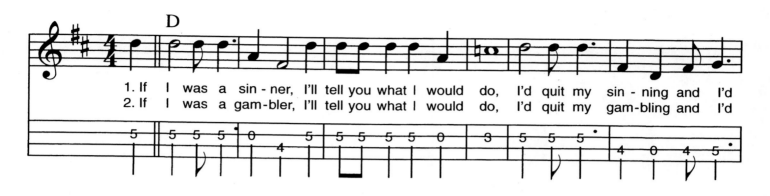

1. If I was a sin-ner, I'll tell you what I would do, I'd quit my sin-ning and I'd
2. If I was a gam-bler, I'll tell you what I would do, I'd quit my gam-bling and I'd

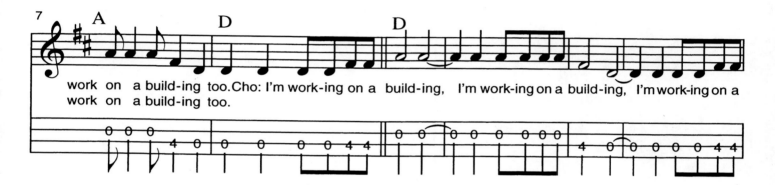

work on a build-ing too. Cho: I'm work-ing on a build-ing, I'm work-ing on a build-ing, I'm work-ing on a
work on a build-ing too.

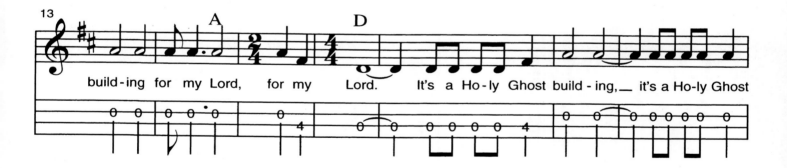

build-ing for my Lord, for my Lord. It's a Ho-ly Ghost build-ing,— it's a Ho-ly Ghost

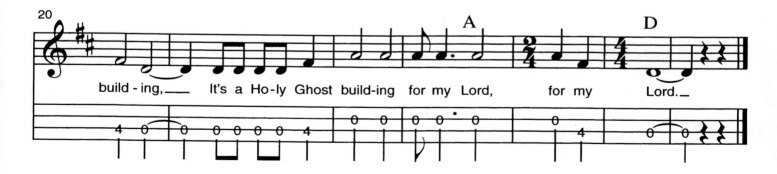

build-ing,— It's a Ho-ly Ghost build-ing for my Lord, for my Lord.—

3. If I was a drunkard, I'll tell you what I would do, (etc.)
4. If I was a cheater, I'll tell you what I would do, (etc.)
5. If I was a liar, I'll tell you what I would do, (etc.)
6. If I was a preacher, I'll tell you what I would do,
I'd keep on preaching and I'd work on a building too.

Carter Fam., B. Monroe, Stanley Bros., R. Stanley, Ken. Colonels, Hot Rize, Johnson Mtn. Boys, Seldom Scene 121

In the Garden

M: G; F: C or D
CD 1-Track 86

C.A. Miles, 1912

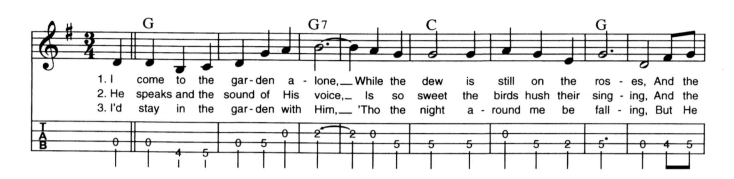

1. I come to the gar-den a - lone,__ While the dew is still on the ros - es, And the
2. He speaks and the sound of His voice,__ Is so sweet the birds hush their sing - ing, And the
3. I'd stay in the gar-den with Him,__ 'Tho the night a - round me be fall - ing, But He

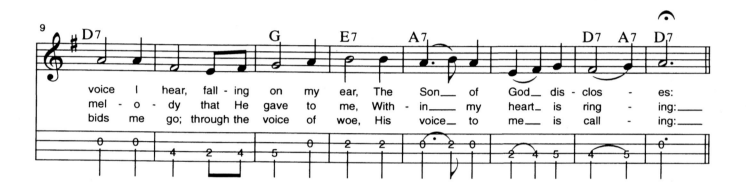

voice I hear, fall - ing on my ear, The Son__ of God__ dis - clos - es:
mel - o - dy that He gave to me, With - in__ my heart__ is ring - ing:__
bids me go; through the voice of woe, His voice__ to me__ is call - ing:__

Cho: And He walks with me, And He talks with me, And He tells me I am His own.__

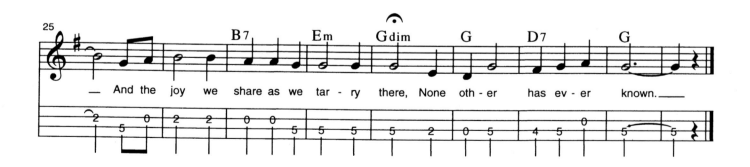

__ And the joy we share as we tar - ry there, None oth - er has ev - er known.__

In the Pines

M: D; F: G or A
CD 1-Track 87

Traditional

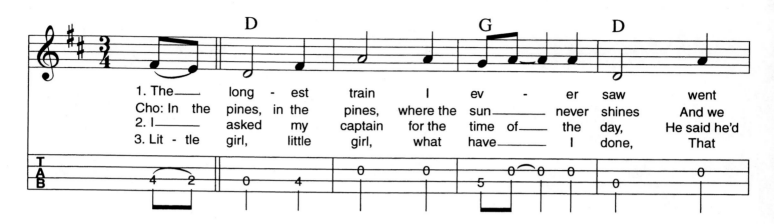

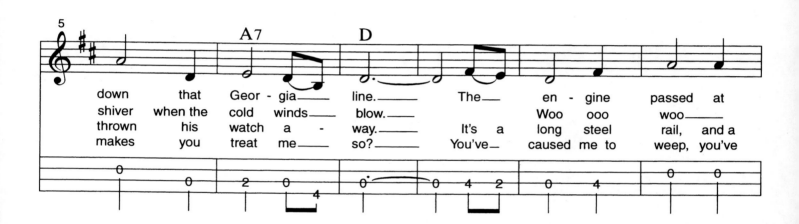

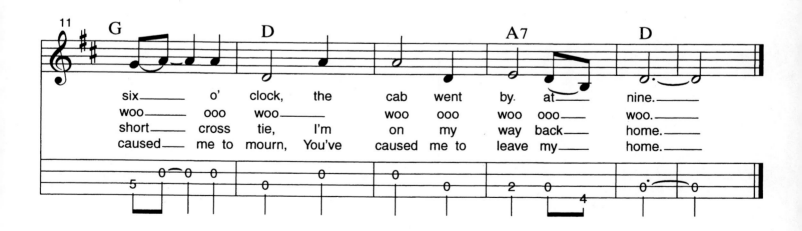

B. Monroe, Jimmy Martin, R. Stanley, C. White, Ken. Colonels, Boone Creek, Grateful Dead, Louvin Bros., Mac Wiseman,
Osborne Bros., Seldom Scene 123

It's Mighty Dark to Travel

M: G; F: C or D
CD 1-Track 88, medley pt. 1

Bill Monroe

Photo by Dix Bruce

I worked for David Grisman, shown here in 1983, as editor of Mandolin World News. David was the magazine's publisher and main benefactor. He's a great believer in education and learning in addition to being the greatest, most creative musician I ever met. I couldn't begin to catalog all the music he's led me to, all the master musicians he's introduced me to, or all the books, tapes, records, and concert tickets he so generously shared. Thanks for the education man!

Jesse James

M: G; F: C or D
CD 1-Track 88, medley pt. 2

Garshade, ca. 1882

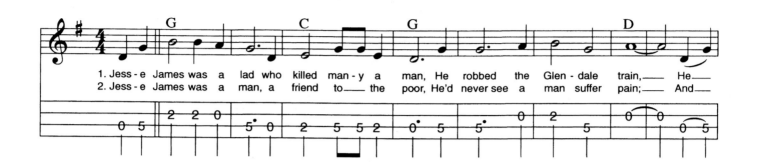

1. Jess-e James was a lad who killed man-y a man, He robbed the Glen-dale train,— He—
2. Jess-e James was a man, a friend to— the poor, He'd never see a man suffer pain;— And

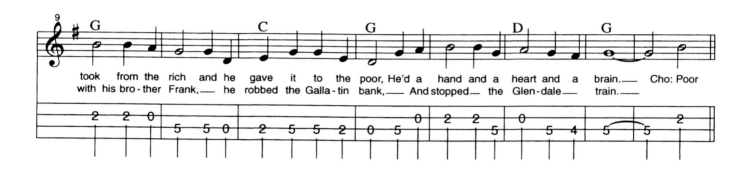

took from the rich and he gave it to the poor, He'd a hand and a heart and a brain.— Cho: Poor
with his bro-ther Frank,— he robbed the Galla-tin bank,— And stopped— the Glen-dale— train.—

Jess-e had a wife to mourn for his life, Three child-ren they were brave,— But the

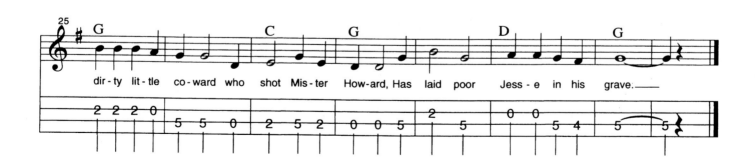

dir-ty lit-tle co-ward who shot Mis-ter How-ard, Has laid poor Jess-e in his grave:—

126   R. Stanley, Osborne Bros., Fiddlin' John Carson, Country Gentlemen, W. Guthrie

```
           G                        C              G
3. It was on a Wednesday night and the moon was shining bright,
                        D
They robbed the Glendale train,
           G                    C          G
And the people they did say, for many miles away,
              D           G
It was robbed by Frank and Jesse James.
```

(Repeat chorus after each verse)

4. It was with his brother Frank that he robbed the Gallatin bank,
And carried the money from the town;
It was in this very place that they had a little chase,
And they shot Captain Sheets to the ground.

5. They went to the crossing, not very far from there,
And there they did the same;
With the agent on his knees, he delivered up the keys,
To the outlaws, Frank and Jesse James.

6. It was Robert Ford, that dirty little coward,
I wonder how he does feel,
He ate Jesse's bread and he slept in Jesse's bed,
Then he laid poor Jesse in his grave.

7. It was on a Saturday night and Jesse was at home
Talking with his family brave,
Robert Ford came along like a thief in the night,
And laid poor Jesse in his grave.

8. The people held their breath when they heard of Jesse's death,
And wondered how he ever came to die.
It was one of the gang, called little Robert Ford,
He shot poor Jesse on the sly.

9. Jesse went to his rest with his hand on his breast,
The devil will be upon his knee,
He was born one day in the county of Clay,
And came from a solitary race.

Jimmie Brown, the Newsboy

M: D; F: G or A
CD 1-Track 89

W.S. Hays, 1875

1. I_____ sell the morn - ing pa - per sir my name is Jim - my Brown,_____
2. You can hear me yell - ing "Morn - ing Star"_____ running a - long the street,_____
3. Nev-er mind_____ sir how I look, don't look at me and frown,_____
4. I'm_____ aw - ful cold_____ and hun - gry sir, my clothes are might - y thin,_____
5. My_____ fath - er died_____ a drunk - ard sir, I've heard my moth - er say,_____
6. My_____ moth - er al - ways tells me sir I've nothing in the world to lose,_____

_____ Ev - ery bod - y knows that I'm_____ the news - boy of the town._____
_____ Got no hat_____ up - on my head,_ no shoes up - on my feet._____
_ I sell the morn - ing pap - er sir,_ my name is Jim - mie Brown._____
_ I wander a - bout_____ from place to place_ my dail - y bread to win._____
_____ I am help - ing moth - er sir,_ as I jour - ney on my way._____
_ I'll get a place_____ in heav - en sir_ to sell the Gos - pel News._____

Carter Fam., Flatt & Scruggs, B. Monroe, C. White, Mac Wiseman

Sam Bush, the virtuosic originator of "new grass" music, in 1981.

John Hardy

M: G; F: C or D
CD 1-Track 90

Traditional

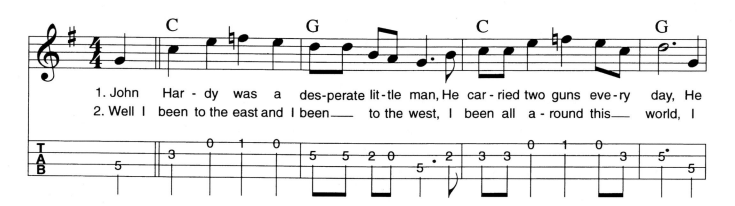

1. John Har - dy was a des-perate lit-tle man, He car - ried two guns eve-ry day, He
2. Well I been to the east and I been to the west, I been all a - round this world, I

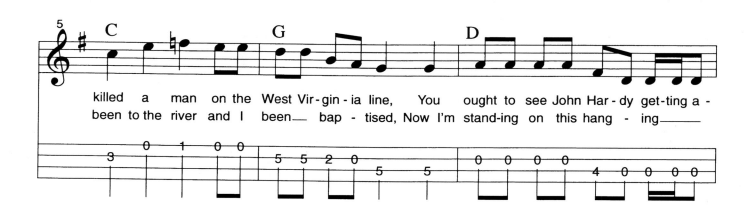

killed a man on the West Vir-gin - ia line, You ought to see John Har - dy get-ting a -
been to the river and I been bap - tised, Now I'm stand-ing on this hang - ing

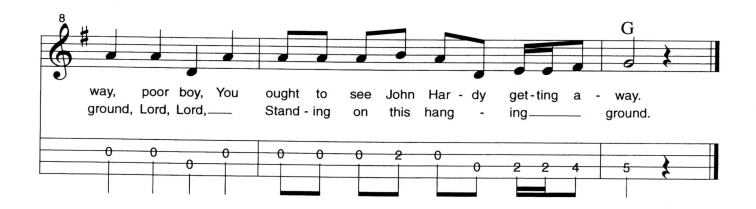

way, poor boy, You ought to see John Hardy get-ting a - way.
ground, Lord, Lord, Stand - ing on this hang - ing ground.

Carter Fam., Flatt & Scruggs, B. Monroe. Ken. Colonels, Poor Richard's Almanac

```
        C                    G
3. Hangman, hangman, hold your rope,
C           G
Just a little while,
   C                    G
I thought I heard my father's voice,
      D
He travelled ten thousand long miles, Lord, Lord,
                              G
Travelled ten thousand long miles.
```

4. Did you bring me any silver or gold,
Or money to pay my fee?
Or did you come to see me hung,
Upon this hanging tree, Lord, Lord,
Upon this hanging tree?

5. No, I didn't bring no silver nor gold,
Nor money to pay your fee,
But I did come to see you hung,
Upon that hanging tree, Lord, Lord,
Upon that hanging tree.

6. Hangman, hangman, hold your rope,
Just a little while,
I thought I heard my sweetheart's voice,
She travelled ten thousand long miles, Lord, Lord,
Travelled ten thousand long miles.

7. Oh yes, I brought that silver and gold,
And money to pay your fee,
I have come for to take you home,
And keep you there with me, Lord, Lord,
And keep you there with me.

8. Well, John Hardy run for that old state line,
It was there he thought he'd go free,
But a man walked up and took him by the arm,
Saying "Johnny walk along with me, Lord, Lord,
Johnny walk along with me."

9. Well the first one to visit John Hardy in his cell,
Was a little girl dressed in blue,
She came down to that old jail cell,
Singing "Johnny, I've been true to you, Lord knows,
Johnny I've been true to you."

10. Then the next one to visit John Hardy in his cell,
A little girl dressed in red,
She came down to that old jail cell,
Singing "Johnny, I'd rather see you dead, Lord, Lord,
God knows, Johnny I'd rather see you dead."

11. John Hardy stood in his old jail cell,
The tears running down from his eyes,
He said "I've been the death of many poor boy,
But my six-shooter never told a lie, Lord, Lord,
No my six-shooter never told a lie."

John Henry

M: C; F: F or G
CD 1-Track 91

Traditional

1. When John Hen-ry was a lit-tle ba-by,——— Just a' sit-ting on his pap-py's
2. John——— Hen-ry had a litt-le wo-man,——— And her name——— was Pol-ly

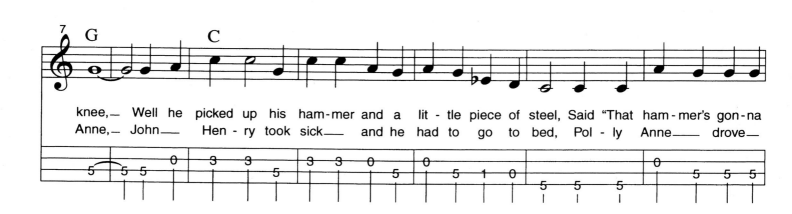

knee,— Well he picked up his ham-mer and a lit-tle piece of steel, Said "That ham-mer's gon-na
Anne,— John——— Hen-ry took sick——— and he had to go to bed, Pol-ly Anne——— drove———

be the death of me, Lord, Lord, Ham-mer's gon-na be the death of me."———
steel——— like a man, Lord, Lord, Polly Anne——— drove——— steel——— like a man.———

B. Monroe, Flatt & Scruggs, Stanley Bros., R. Stanley, Jimmy Martin, Ken. Colonels, D. Watson, W. Guthrie, Skillet Lickers,
Fiddlin' John Carson, Dry Branch Fire Squad

C
3. Captain said to John Henry,
                              G
"Gonna bring me a steam drill 'round,
          C
Gonna take that steam drill out on the job,
Gonna drive that steel on down, Lawd, Lawd,
                    G   C
Gonna drive that steel on down."

4. John Henry told his captain,
Said, "A man ain't nothin' but a man,
And before I'd let that steam drill beat me down,
I'll die with this hammer in my hand, Lawd, Lawd,
I'll die with the hammer in my hand."

5. Now the captain told John Henry,
"I believe this mountain's caving in,"
John Henry said to his captain, "Oh my,
It's my hammer just a'sucking wind, Lawd, Lawd,
It's my hammer just a' sucking wind."

6. John Henry told his captain,
"Looky yonder what I see,
Your drill's done broke and your hole's done choke,
And you can't drive steel like me, Lawd, Lawd,
And you can't drive steel like me."

7. John Henry was hammering on the mountain,
And his hammer was striking fire,
He drove so hard 'til he broke his poor heart,
And he laid down his hammer and he died, Lawd, Lawd,
Laid down his hammer and he died.

8. They took John Henry to the graveyard,
And they buried him in the sand,
And every locomotive come roaring by,
Says, "Yonder lies a steel driving man, Lawd, Lawd,
Yonder lies a steel driving man."

Jordan

M: G; F: C or D
CD 1-Track 92

Traditional

1. Oh sin-ner as you tread life's jour-ney, Take Je-sus as your dai-ly guide, Though you may feel pure and
2. That aw - ful— day of judge-ment, Is com-ing in the by and by, We'll— see our Lord des-

saint - ly, With - out him walk-ing by your side,— But when you come to make the cross-ing, At the
cend-ing, In glor - y— from on high,— Oh, let us keep in touch with Jes - us, And—

end-ing of your pil-grim way, If you e-ver will meet our Sav-iour, You'll sure-ly meet him on that day—
in his grace the love—of God, We may be— ev - er called rea - dy, When he calls us o - ver Jor-dan's tide.—

Cho 1: Now look at that cold Jor-dan, Look at those deep— wat-ers, Look at that wide

riv-er, Oh, hear the migh-ty bil-lows roll. You bet-ter take Je-sus with you, He's a true com-

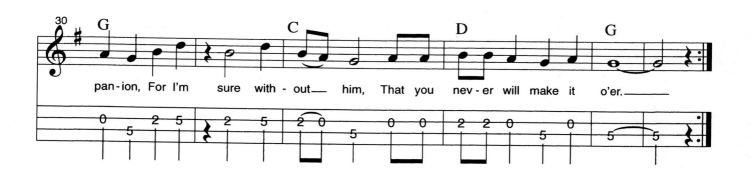

pan-ion, For I'm sure with-out him, That you nev-er will make it o'er.

Tag: Oh what, oh what you gon-na do? Oh what, oh what you gon-na say? Oh

how, oh how you gon-na feel? When you come to the end of the way?

Just a Closer Walk with Thee

M: A; F: D or E
CD 1-Track 93

Traditional

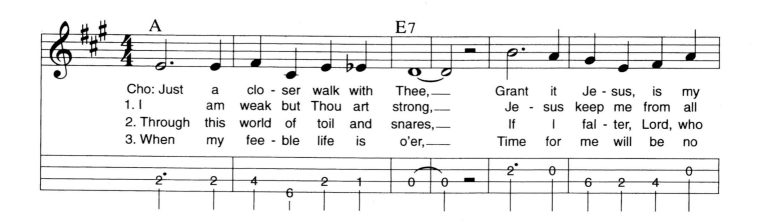

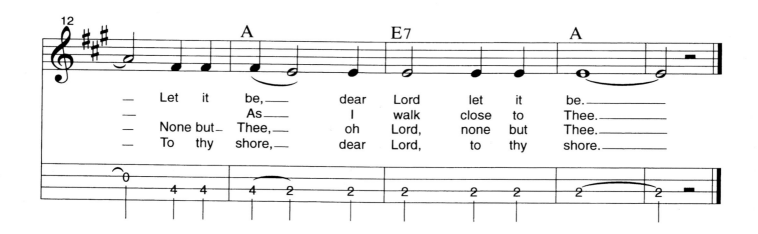

Just as I Am

M: C; F: F or G
CD 1-Track 94

Elliott & Bradbury

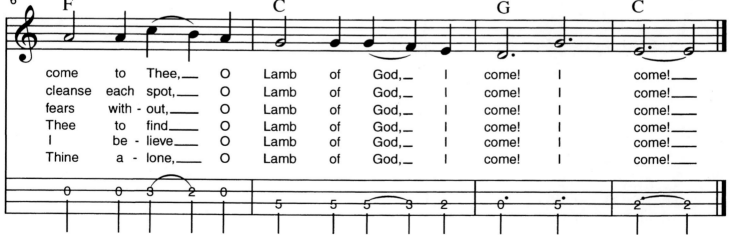

Just Over in the Gloryland

M: A; F: D or E
CD 1-Track 95, medley pt. 1

Acuff & Dean, 1906

1. I've a home prepared, where the saints abide, Just over in the Gloryland! And I
2. I am on my way to those mansions fair, Just over in the Gloryland! There to
3. What a joyful thought that my Lord, I'll see, Just over in the Gloryland! And with
4. With the blood washed throng, I will shout and sing, Just over in the Gloryland! Glad ho-

long to be by my Savior's side, Just over in the Gloryland! Cho: Just
sing God's praise and His glory share, Just over in the Gloryland!
kindred saved, there forever be, Just over in the Gloryland!
sannas to Christ, the Lord and King, Just over in the Gloryland!

over in the Gloryland, I'll join the happy angel band, Just over in the Gloryland! Just

over in the Gloryland, There with the mighty host I'll stand, Just over in the Gloryland!

B. Monroe, Stanley Bros., R. Stanley, Jim & Jesse, Ken. Colonels, J.E. Mainer

Katy Cline

M: A; F: D or E
CD 1-Track 95, medley pt. 2

Traditional

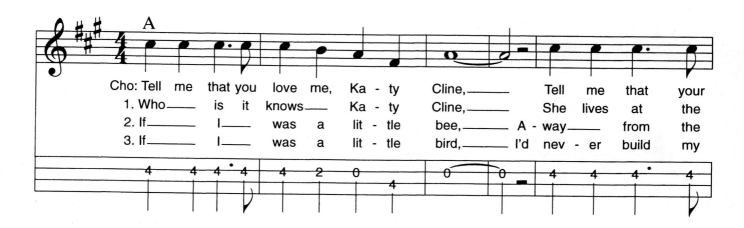

Cho: Tell me that you love me, Ka - ty Cline,_____ Tell me that your
1. Who_____ is it knows_____ Ka - ty Cline,_____ She lives at the
2. If_____ I_____ was a lit - tle bee,_____ A - way_____ from the
3. If_____ I_____ was a lit - tle bird,_____ I'd nev - er build my

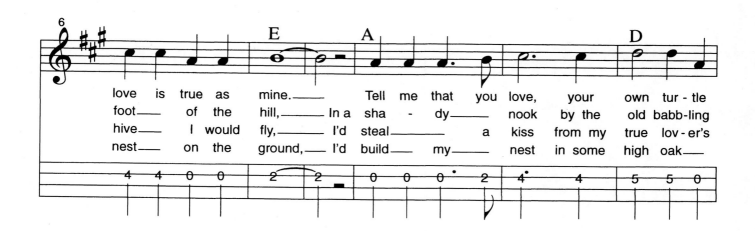

love is true as mine._____ Tell me that you love, your own tur - tle
foot_____ of the hill,_____ In a sha - dy_____ nook by the old babb-ling
hive_____ I would fly,_____ I'd steal_____ a kiss from my true lov-er's
nest_____ on the ground,_____ I'd build_____ my_____ nest in some high oak_____

dove, Tell me that you love me Ka - ty Cline._____
brook, That runs_____ by her dear old fath - er's mill._____
lips, Then back_____ to the hive_____ I would fly._____
tree, Where the bad_____ boys_____ could - n't tear it down._____

Katy Daley

M: C ; F: F or G
CD 1-Track 96

Traditional

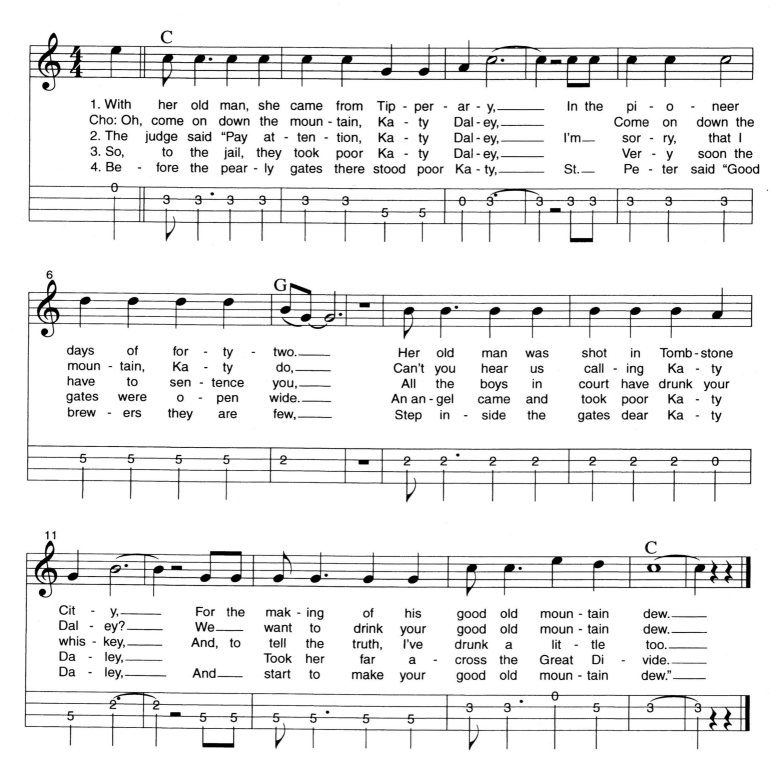

Katy Dear

M: D ; F: G or A
CD 1-Track 97

Traditional

1. Oh, Ka - ty dear,_____ go ask your moth - er,_____ If you can
2. Oh Will - ie dear,_____ I can - not ask__ her,_____ She's in her

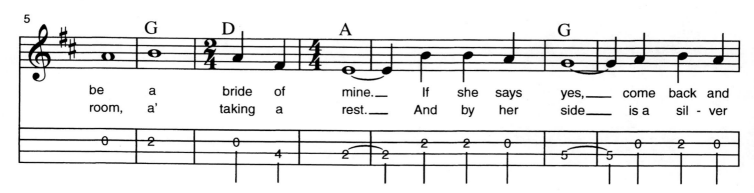

be a bride of mine.__ If she says yes,__ come back and
room, a' taking a rest.__ And by her side__ is a sil - ver

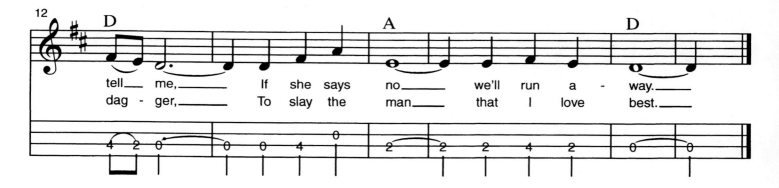

tell__ me,_____ If she says no_____ we'll run a - way._____
dag - ger,_____ To slay the man__ that I love best._____

        G   D
3. Oh, Katy dear, go ask your father,
        G   D   A
If you can be a bride of mine.
      G   D
If he says yes, come back and tell me,
       A   D
If he says no, we'll run a-way.

4. Oh, Willie dear, I cannot ask him,
He's in his room a' taking a rest,
And by his side, that silver dagger,
To slay the one, that I love best.

5. Then he picked up that silver dagger,
And stove it through his weary heart.
Saying, "Goodbye Katy, goodbye darling,
At last the time has come to part."

6. Then she picked up that bloody dagger,
And stove it through her lilly white breast,
Saying, "Goodbye Willie, goodbye mother,
I'll die with the one that I love best."

Keep on the Sunnyside

M: G; F: C or D

CD 1-Track 98, medley pt. 1

Blenkhorn & Entwisle

1. There's a dark and a trou-bled side of life, There's a bright and a sun-ny-side,
2. Though the storm in its fu-ry broke to-day, Crush-ing hopes that we cher-ished so
3. Let us greet with a song of hope each day, Though the mo-ments be cloud-y or

too, Though we meet with the dark-ness and strife,— The sun-ny-side we al-so may view.
dear, Storm and clouds will in time pass a-way,— The sun a-gain will shine bright and clear.
fair, Let us trust in our Sav-iour al-ways,— Who keep-eth eve-ry-one in His care.

Cho: Keep on the sun-ny-side, Al-ways on the sun-ny-side, Keep on the sun-ny-side of life, It will

help us ev-ery day, It will bright-en all the way, If we keep on the sun-ny-side of life.

Jim (right) and Jesse (left) McReynolds sing a trio with Jesse's son Keith McReynolds in early 1979. Jim and Jesse were part of the second generation of bluegrass musicans that followed Monroe in the early 1950s. The duo was known for its smooth "brother duet" vocals and for Jesse's phenomenal cross picking on the mandolin.

Knoxville Girl

M: G; F: C or D
CD 1-Track 98, medley pt. 2

Traditional

1. I met a lit-tle girl in Knox-ville, A town you all know well, And
2. She fell down on her bended knees, For mer-cy she did cry, "Oh,

ev-ery Sun-day eve-ning, Out in her home I'd dwell, We
Wil-lie dear, don't kill me here, I'm un-pre-pared to die," She

went to take an eve-ning walk, A-bout a mile from town, I
nev-er spoke an-oth-er word, I on-ly beat her more, Un-

picked a stick up off the ground, And knocked that fair girl down.
til the ground a-round me, With-in her blood did flow.

Louvin Bros., Stanley Bros., Blue Sky Boys, Mac Wiseman, Jimmy Martin, Osborne Bros.

```
        G
3. I took her by her golden curls,
      C                 G
I drug her 'round and 'round,
I threw her into the river,
          A                   D
That flows through Knoxville town,
      G
Go down, go down, you Knoxville girl,
        C               G
With dark and rolling eyes,
Go down, go down, you Knoxville girl,
          D           G
You'll never be my bride.
```

4. Starting back to Knoxville,
Got there about midnight,
My mother she was worried,
And woke up in a fright,
Saying, "Son, oh son, what have you done,
To bloody your clothes so?"
I told my anxious mother,
Been bleeding at my nose.

5. I called for me a candle,
To light myself to bed,
I called for me a handkerchief,
To bind my aching head,
Rolled and tumbled the whole night through,
As troubles were for me,
Like flames of Hell around my bed,
And in my eyes could see.

6. They carried me down to Knoxville,
They put me in a cell,
My friends all tried to get me out,
But none could go my bail,
I'm here to waste my life away,
Down in this dirty old jail,
Because I murdered that Knoxville girl,
The girl I loved so well.

Late Last Night

M: C; F: F or G
CD 2-Track 1

Traditional

1. It was late last night when Wil-lie came home, I heard him a' rap-ping on the door. He was
Cho: Way down town just a' fool-ing a - round, They took me to the jail, It's

slip - ping and a' slid - ing with his new shoes on, Pa - pa said, "Wil - lie don't you rap no more."
oh me, and it's oh my, No one to go my bail.

F   C
2. Wish I was over at my sweet Sally's house,
G   C
Sitting in that big armed chair,
F   C
One arm around this old guitar,
G   C
Other one around my dear.

3. This one old shirt is about all I got,
And a dollar is all I crave,
I brought nothing with me into this old world,
Ain't gonna take nothing to my grave.

4. I like the hills of West Virginia,
I like the hills of Tennessee,
North, south, east or west,
It's home, sweet home to me.

Leave it There

M: D; F: G or A
CD 2-Track 2

C.A. Tindley, 1916

D
G

3. When your enemies assail and your heart begins to fail,
D   A
Don't forget that God in heaven answers prayer;
D   G
He will make a way for you and will lead you safely through,
D   A   D
Take your burden to the Lord and leave it there.

4. When your youthful days are gone and old age is stealing on,
And your body bends beneath the weight of care;
He will never leave you then, He'll go with you to the end,
Take your burden to the Lord and leave it there.

5. If your mother leaves you here, grief and sorrow you must bear,
And you feel the only friend you have is gone,
But whenever you feel alone, He will take you in his arms,
Take your burden to the Lord and leave it there.

147

Let Me Rest at the End of My Journey

M: G; F: C or D
CD 2-Track 3

Traditional

B. Monroe, R. Stanley

The Letter Edged in Black

M: D; F: G or A
CD 2-Track 4

Hattie Nevada, 1897

1. I was stand-ing by my win-dow yes-ter-day morn-ing, With-out—— a thought of
2. He—— rang the bell and whist-led as—— he wait-ed, He—— said—— "Good

wor-ry or of care.—— When I saw the post-man com-ing up the
morn-ing, to you Jack,"—— But he lit-tle knew the sor-row that he

path-way,—— With such a hap-py face and jol-ly air.——
brought me,—— When he hand-ed me that let-ter edged in black.——

D   **A**

3. With trembling hands, I took that letter from him,

D

I broke the seal and this is what it said:

G

"Come home my boy, your dear old father wants you,

A   **D**

Come home my boy, your dear old mother's dead."

4. "Those angry words I wished I'd never spoken,
You know I didn't mean them don't you Jack?
I bow my head in sadness and in sorrow,
While I'm writing you this letter edged in black."

5. "The last words that your mother ever uttered,
Were 'Tell my boy, I want him to come back,'
May the angels bear me witness I am asking,
Your forgiveness in this letter edged in black."

(Repeat verse 2)

B. Kincaid, Goose Island Ramblers, Fiddlin' John Carson, Mac Wiseman   149

Life's Railway to Heaven

M: D; F: G or A
CD 2-Track 5

Traditional

Lyrics (verses 1–4):

1. Life is like_____ a moun-tain rail-road,_____ With an en-gin-eer that's brave._____ You must make____ the run suc-cess-ful_____ from the cra-dle to the grave._____ Watch the hills,_____ the curves the tun-nels,_____ Nev-er fal-ter, nev-er fail._____

2. You will roll_____ up grades of trial,_____ You will cross the bridge of strife._____ See that Christ____ is your Con-duct-or_____ on this light-ning train of life._____ Al-ways mind-ful of ob-struc-tion,_____ do your du-ty, nev-er fail._____

3. You will of-ten find ob-struc-tions,_____ look for storms of wind and rain._____ On a fill,____ or curve, or tres-tle,____ they will al-most ditch your train._____ Put your trust____ a-lone in Jes-us,_____ nev-er fal-ter, nev-er fail._____

4. As you roll_____ a-cross the tres-tle,_____ span-ning Jor-dan's swell-ing tide._____ You be-hold____ the Un-ion De-pot____ in-to which____ your train will glide._____ There you'll meet____ the Super-in-ten-dent,____ God the Fath-er, God the Son.___

150   *B. Kincaid, B. Monroe, Greenbriar Boys, Blue Sky Boys, Jim & Jesse, Nitty Gritty Dirt Band*

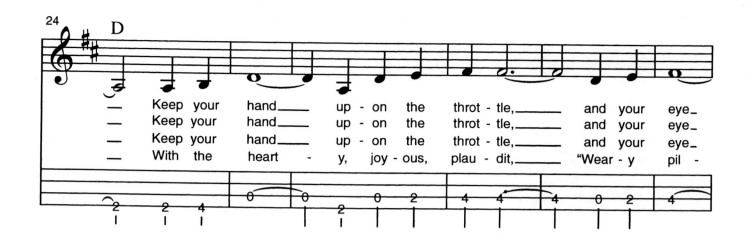

Keep your hand____ up - on the throt - tle,_____ and your eye_
Keep your hand____ up - on the throt - tle,_____ and your eye_
Keep your hand____ up - on the throt - tle,_____ and your eye_
With the heart - y, joy - ous, plau - dit,_____ "Wear - y pil -

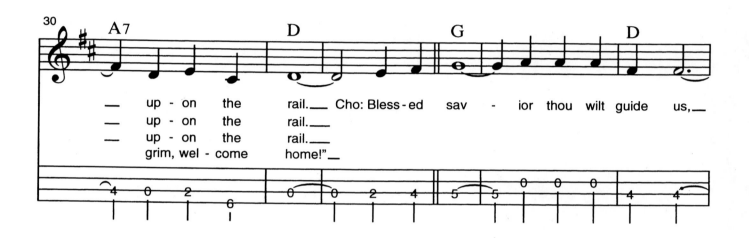

— up - on the rail.___ Cho: Bless - ed sav - ior thou wilt guide us,__
— up - on the rail.___
— up - on the rail.___
grim, wel - come home!"__

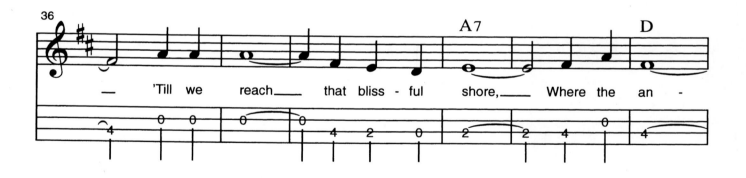

— 'Till we reach____ that bliss - ful shore,____ Where the an -

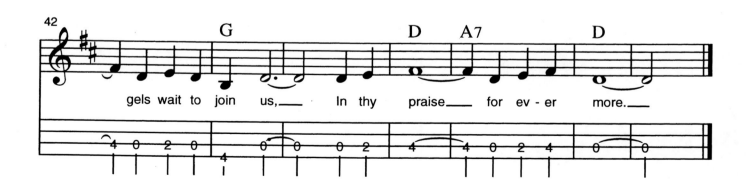

gels wait to join us,___ In thy praise___ for ev - er more.___

Li'l Liza Jane

M: *C*; **F:** *F or G*

Traditional

CD 2-Track 6

1. I got a gal and you got none, Li'l Li - za Jane, I got a gal that
2. Li - za Jane done come to me, Li'l Li - za Jane, Both as hap - py
3. Come my love and live with me, Li'l Li - za Jane, I will take good
4. House and lot in Bal - ti - more, Li'l Li - za Jane, Lots of child - ren

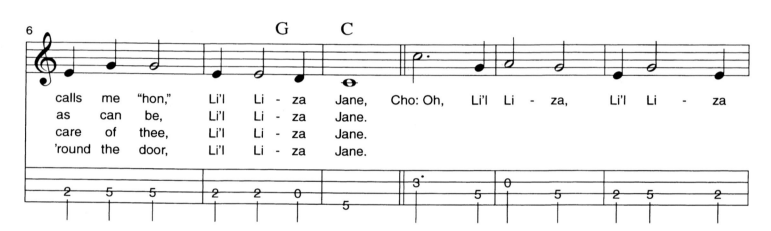

calls me "hon," Li'l Li - za Jane, Cho: Oh, Li'l Li - za, Li'l Li - za
as can be, Li'l Li - za Jane.
care of thee, Li'l Li - za Jane.
'round the door, Li'l Li - za Jane.

Jane, Oh Li'l Li - za, Li'l Li - za Jane.

Little Annie

M: C; F: F or G
CD 2-Track 7

Traditional

1. Once more I must leave you lit-tle An - nie,— We must part at the end of the lane, But you
2. When the sun shines— down— on the moun-tains,— And the wild sheep are wandering all a - lone, And the
3. Now the spring-time has come— on the moun-tains,— And I'm on my way back to the lane, For you

prom - ised me— lit - tle An - nie,— You'd be wait - ing when the spring-time comes a - gain. Cho: When the
birds and the bees— are— sing-ing,— Then it makes me think that spring-time won't be long.
prom - ised me— lit - tle An - nie,— You'd be wait - ing when the spring-time comes a - gain.

spring - time comes on the moun - tain,— And the wild flow - ers scat - ter o'er the plains, I will

watch for the leaves to re - turn to the trees, And I'll be wait - ing when the spring-time comes a - gain.

V. Williams, Lilly Bros. & Don Stover, L. Lewis & K. Kallick 153

Little Bessie

M: G; F: C or D
CD 2-Track 8

Crandall & Porter, 1875

1. Hug me clos - er, clos - er__ Moth - er,____ Put your arms__
2. Some - thing hurts me here dear__ Moth - er,____ Like a stone__
3. Just be - fore the lamps were light - ed,____ Just be - fore__
4. All at once a win - dow__ o - pened,____ On a field__

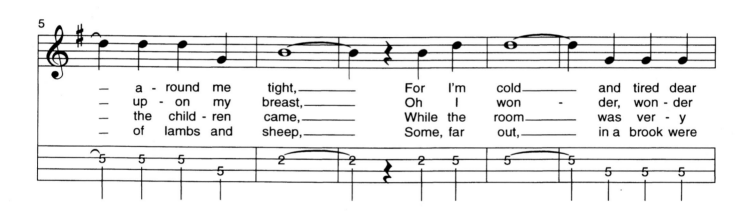

— a - round me tight,____ For I'm cold____ and tired dear
— up - on my breast,____ Oh I won - der, won - der
— the child - ren came,____ While the room____ was ver - y
— of lambs and sheep,____ Some, far out,____ in a brook were

Moth - er,____ And I feel so strange to - night.____
Moth - er,____ Why it is I can - not rest.____
qui - et,____ I heard some - one call my name.____
drink - ing,____ Some were ly - ing fast a - sleep.____

       G

5. In a moment I was looking,
On a world so bright and fair,
Which was filled with little children,
                         D   G
And they seemed so happy there.

6. They were singing, oh, so sweetly,
Sweetest songs I'd ever heard.
They were singing sweeter, Mother,
Than a darling little bird.

7. Come up here little Bessie,
Come up here and live with me,
Where little children never suffer,
Suffer through eternity.

8. Then I thought of all you told me,
Of that bright and happy land,
I was going when you called me,
When you came and kissed my hand.

9. I felt so sorry when you called me,
And from this world I soon must go,
Go to sleep and never suffer,
Then dear Mother don't be crying so.

10. And the mother pressed her closer,
To her own dear burning breast,
To the heart so near broken,
Lay the heart so near its rest.

11. At the solemn hour of midnight,
In the darkness calm and deep,
Lying on her mother's bosom,
Little Bessie fell asleep.

12. Far up yonder past the portals,
That are shining very fair,
Little Bessie now is tended,
By her Savior's loving care.

Little Birdie

M: G; F: C or D
CD 2-Track 9

Traditional

1. Lit - tle bir - die,_____ lit - tle bir - die, Come and sing_____
2. Lit - tle bir - die,_____ lit - tle bir - die, What_____ makes_____

— to me your song._____ Got a short time_____ to
— you fly so high?_____ When you know my_____ true

stay_____ here, And a long time to be_____ gone._____
lov - er, Is_____ sleep - ing in the_____ sky._____

      G   D
3. I'm a long way from old Dixie,
                G
And my old Kentucky home,
                      D
Now my parents are both dead and gone,
                G
Have no place to call my home.

4. Now I'd rather be a sailor,
'Way out upon the sea,
Then to be at home a married man,
With a baby on my knee.

5. For the married man, he sees trouble,
And the single boy sees none,
I expect to live single,
'Til my days on earth are done.

6. Now I'd rather be in some dark hollow,
Where the sun don't ever shine,
Then to see you love another,
When you promised to be mine.

Flatt & Scruggs, Stanley Bros., R. Stanley, R. Allen & F. Wakefield, Greenbriar Boys, NLCR, Cox Family, M. Seeger, King

Jesse McReynolds demonstrates his stunning mandolin crosspicking technique in 1979.

Jim (left) and Jesse McReynolds (right) relax after a show in Northern California in 1979.

Little Maggie

M: G; F: C or D
CD 2-Track 10, medley pt. 1

Traditional

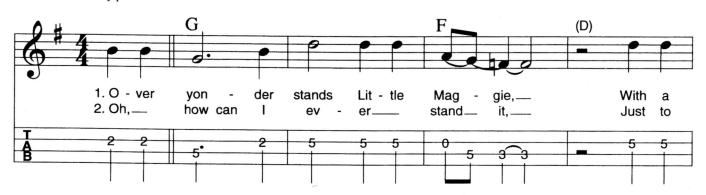

1. O - ver   yon - der   stands   Lit - tle   Mag - gie,___   With a
2. Oh,___   how can   I   ev - er___   stand___   it,___   Just to

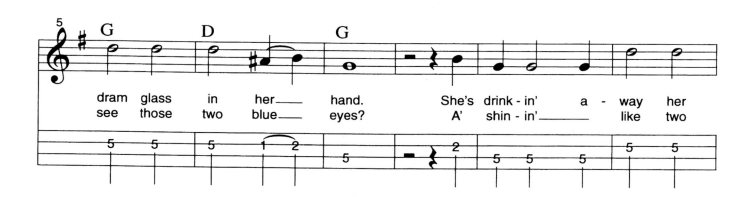

dram glass   in   her___   hand.   She's drink - in'   a - way   her
see those   two   blue___   eyes?   A' shin - in'_____   like   two

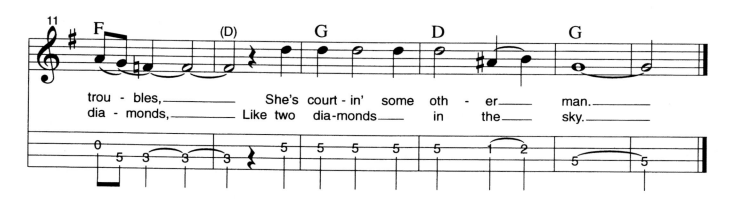

trou - bles,_____   She's court - in'   some   oth - er___   man.___
dia - monds,_____   Like two   dia-monds___   in   the___   sky.___

(D) = optional chord

Stanley Bros., R. Stanley, B. Monroe, Flatt & Scruggs, J. Martin, R. Allen & F. Wakefield, Grayson & Whitter, R. Skaggs

```
       G                     F        (D)
```
3. Last time I saw little Maggie,
```
             G          D          G
```
She was sitting on the banks of the sea.
```
                       F          (D)
```
With a forty-four around her,
```
           G        D        G
```
And a banjo on her knee.

4. Lay down your last gold dollar,
Lay down your gold watch and chain.
Little Maggie's gonna dance for daddy,
Listen to that old banjo ring.

5. Pretty flowers were made for blooming,
Pretty stars were made to shine.
Pretty girls were made for loving,
Little Maggie was made for mine.

6. March me down to the station,
With my suitcase in my hand.
I'm going away for to leave you,
I'm going to some far distant land.

7. I'd rather be in some dark hollow,
Where the sun don't never shine.
Then to know you're another man's darling,
And no longer a darling of mine.

8. Sometimes I have a nickel,
And sometimes I have a dime.
Sometimes I have ten dollars,
Just to pay little Maggie's fine.

9. Go away, go away little Maggie,
Go and do the best that you can.
I'll get me another woman,
You can get you another man.

Little Old Log Cabin in the Lane

M: G; F: C or D

W.S. Hays, 1871

CD 2-Track 10, medley pt. 2

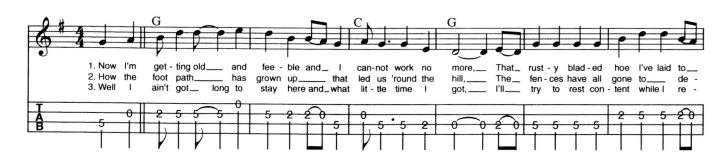

1. Now I'm get-ting old____ and fee-ble and__ I can-not work no more,____ That__ rust-y blad-ed hoe I've laid to__
2. How the foot path____ has grown up____ that led us 'round the hill,____ The__ fen-ces have all gone to____ de -
3. Well I ain't got__ long to stay here and__ what lit-tle time I got,____ I'll__ try to rest con-tent while I re -

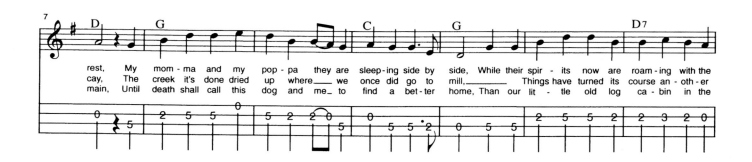

rest, My mom-ma and my pop-pa they are sleep-ing side by side, While their spir - its now are roam-ing with the
cay, The creek it's done dried up where____ we once did go to mill,____ Things have turned its course an-oth-er
main, Until death shall call this dog and me__ to find a bet-ter home, Than our lit - tle old log ca-bin in the

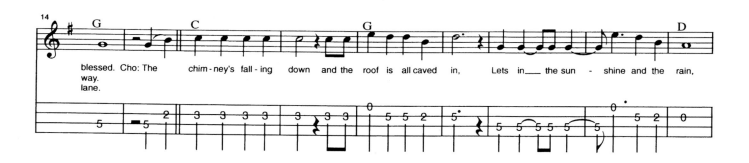

blessed. Cho: The chim-ney's fall-ing down and the roof is all caved in, Lets in____ the sun - shine and the rain,
way.
lane.

But they're an-gels watch-ing o - 'er me when I lay down to sleep, In my lit-tle old log ca-bin in the lane.____

Little Rosewood Casket

M: C; F: F or G
CD 2-Track 11

Goullaud & White, 1870

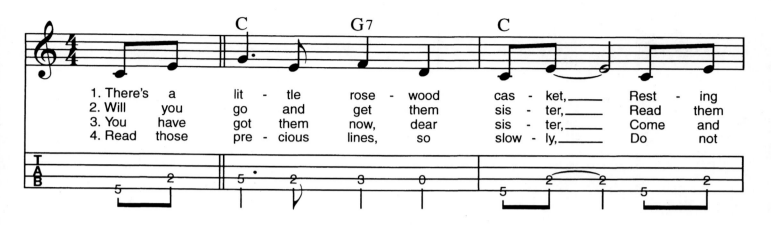

1. There's a lit - tle rose - wood cas - ket,_____ Rest - ing
2. Will you go and get them sis - ter,_____ Read them
3. You have got them now, dear sis - ter,_____ Come and
4. Read those pre - cious lines, so slow - ly,_____ Do not

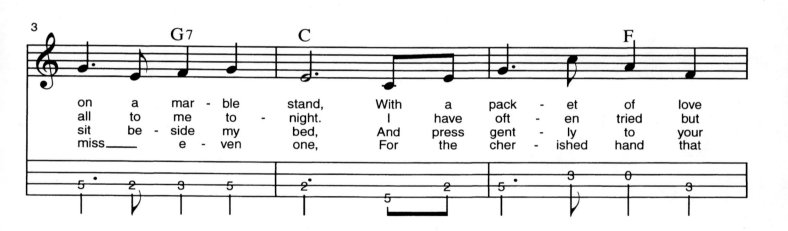

on a mar - ble stand, With a pack - et of love
all to me to - night. I have oft - en tried but
sit be - side my bed, And press gent - ly to your
miss_____ e - ven one, For the cher - ished hand that

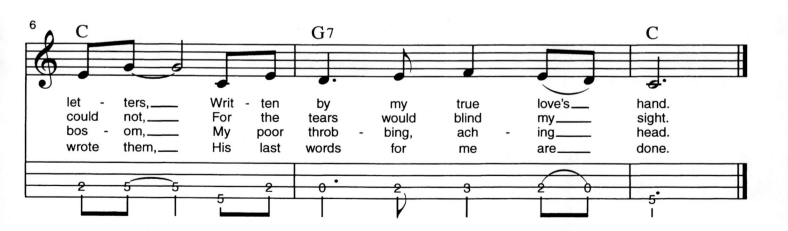

let - ters,_____ Writ - ten by my true love's__ hand.
could not,_____ For the tears would blind my_____ sight.
bos - om,_____ My poor tears throb - bing, ach - ing_____ head.
wrote them,__ His last words for me are_____ done.

Little Sadie

M: Em; F: Am or Bm
CD 2-Track 12

Traditional

Em
3. Standing on the corner reading a bill,
   D   **B7**
Up stepped the sheriff from Thomasville,
   D
Says, "Young man is your name Brown?
   B7   **Em**
Remember the night you blowed Sadie down?"

4. Oh, yes sir, my name is Lee,
I murdered little Sadie in the first degree,
First degree and the second degree,
If you got any papers will you read 'em to me?

5. Took me downtown, they dressed me in black,
They put me on the train and they took me back,
Had no one for to go my bail,
Crammed me back in the county jail.

6. Judge and the jury, took their stand,
Judge had his papers in his right hand,
Forty one days, forty one nights,
Forty one years to wear the ball and the stripes.

Little Willie

M: G; F: C or D
CD 2-Track 13

Traditional

1. When I was in my six-teenth year, Lit-tle
2. We were so far a-way from home, When little
3. My moth-er was so kind to me, And I
4. "It's nat-ure, nature, my dear little girl, It's

Will-ie court-ed me. He said if I'd
Will-ie said to me. "Go home, go home,
know she loves me too. You brought me far
nat-ure for to be. My mind is to

— run a-way with him, His dar-ling wife I could be.
— my dear little girl, My wife you can nev-er be."
— a-way from home, How can you leave me here?
— ram-ble 'round, And I bid this wide world a-dieu."

Lonesome Valley

M: G; F: C or D
CD 2-Track 14, medley pt. 1

Traditional

1. You've got to walk___ that lone-some val-ley,___ You've got to
2. My mother's got to walk___ that lone-some val-ley,___ She's got to

walk,___ it by your-self,___ Ain't no-bod-y here___ can walk it
walk,___ it by her-self,___ Ain't no-bod-y here___ can walk it

for you,___ You've got to walk,___ it by your-self.___
for her,___ She's got to walk,___ it by her-self.___

My brother's got to walk, etc.
My sister's got to walk, etc.
My father's got to walk, etc.
All sinners got to walk, etc.

Long Journey Home

M: G; F: C or D
CD 2-Track 14, medley pt. 2

Traditional

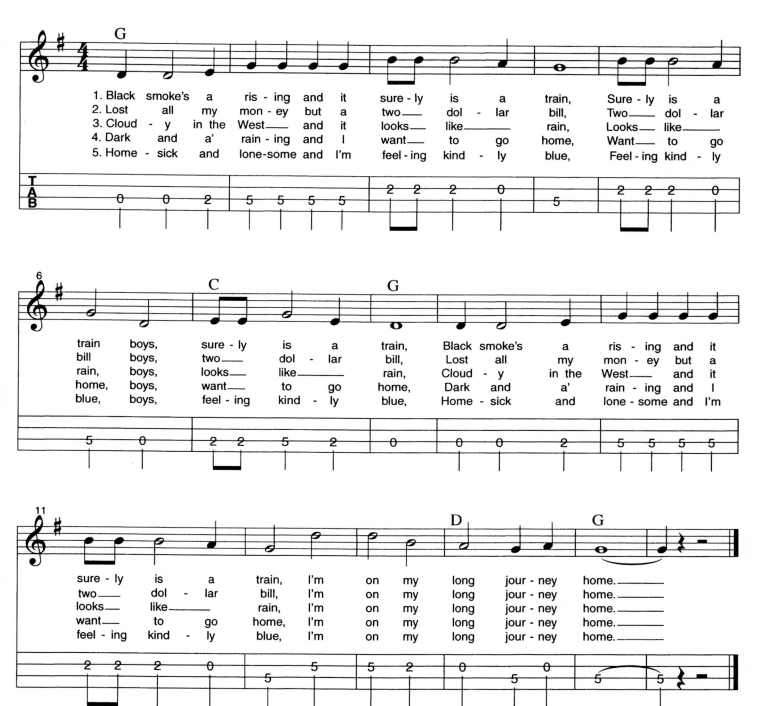

1. Black smoke's a ris-ing and it sure-ly is a train, Sure-ly is a train boys, sure-ly is a train, Black smoke's a ris-ing and it sure-ly is a train, I'm on my long jour-ney home.
2. Lost all my mon-ey but a two dol-lar bill, Two dol-lar bill boys, two dol-lar bill, Lost all my mon-ey but a two dol-lar bill, I'm on my long jour-ney home.
3. Cloud-y in the West and it looks like rain, looks like rain, boys, looks like rain, Cloud-y in the West and it looks like rain, I'm on my long jour-ney home.
4. Dark and a' rain-ing and I want to go home, Want to go home, boys, want to go home, Dark and a' rain-ing and I want to go home, I'm on my long jour-ney home.
5. Home-sick and lone-some and I'm feel-ing kind-ly blue, Feel-ing kind-ly blue, boys, feel-ing kind-ly blue, Home-sick and lone-some and I'm feel-ing kind-ly blue, I'm on my long jour-ney home.

Monroe Bros., Stanley Bros., R. Stanley, D. Watson, D. Grisman, Ken. Colonels, NLCR, Country Gentlemen, Jim & Jesse, John-son Mtn. Boys, L. Sparks, Lilly Bros.

Lord, I'm Coming Home

M: G; F: C or D
CD 2-Track 15

Wm. J. Kirkpatrick, 1892

1. I've wan - dered far a - way__ from God, Now I'm com - ing__
2. I've wast - ed man - y pre - cious years, Now I'm com - ing__
3. I'm tired of sin and stray - ing, Lord, Now I'm com - ing__

home;__ The paths of sin too long__ I've trod, Lord, I'm com - ing__
home;__ I now re - pent with bit - ter tears, Lord, I'm com - ing__
home;__ I'll trust Thy love, be - lieve__ Thy Word, Lord, I'm com - ing__

home.__ Cho: Com - ing__ home, com - ing__ home, Nev - er - more to roam,
home.__
home.__

O - pen wide Thine arms__ of love, Lord, I'm com - ing__ home.__

Stanley Bros., Country Gentlemen, Jim & Jesse, J. Martin, Louvin Bros., Mac Wiseman

```
        G              C       G
4. My soul is sick, my heart is sore,
                D
Now I'm coming home;
     G                    C      G
My strength renew, my hope restore,
            D       G
Lord, I'm coming home.
```

5. My only hope, my only plea,
Now I'm coming home;
That Jesus died, and died for me.
Lord, I'm coming home.

6. I need His cleansing blood, I know,
Now I'm coming home;
O wash me whiter than the snow,
Lord, I'm coming home.

Mama Don't Allow

M: C; F: F or G
CD 2-Track 16

Traditional

Mama don't allow no banjo playing here, etc.
Guitar, mandolin, Dobro, etc.

Man of Constant Sorrow

M: D; F: G or A
CD 2-Track 17

Dick Burnett, ca. 1912

1. I——— am— a man,——— Of con-stant sor-row,——————— I've seen trou-
2. For——— six— long years,——— I've been in trou-ble,——— No pleas-ure here—

ble all— my days.——— I——— bid fare-well,——— To old Ken-
— on earth— I find.——— For——— in this world,——— I'm bound to

tuck - y,——————— The place where I——— was borned— and raised.———
ram - ble,——————— I have no friends——— to help— me now.———

D   G
3. It's fare thee well, my own true lover,
        A   D
I never expect to see again.
                                              G
For I'm bound to ride, that northern railroad,
        A   D
Perhaps I'll die upon this train.

4. You can bury me, in some deep valley,
For many years where I may lay.
Then you may learn, to love another,
While I am sleeping in my grave.

5. Maybe your friends think, I'm just a stranger,
My face you never will see no more.
But there is one promise that is given,
I'll meet you on God's golden shore.

Stanley Bros., R. Stanley, "O Brother" soundtrack, Grisman, Garcia, Rice, Blue Highway, Bluegrass Band, Dillards, P. Rowan

The Maple on the Hill

M: G; F: C or D
CD 2-Track 18

G.L. Davis, 1880

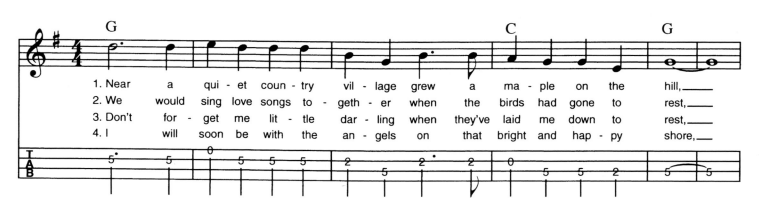

1. Near a qui - et coun - try vil - lage grew a ma - ple on the hill,____
2. We would sing love songs to - geth - er when the birds had gone to rest,____
3. Don't for - get me lit - tle dar - ling when they've laid me down to rest,____
4. I will soon be with the an - gels on that bright and hap - py shore,____

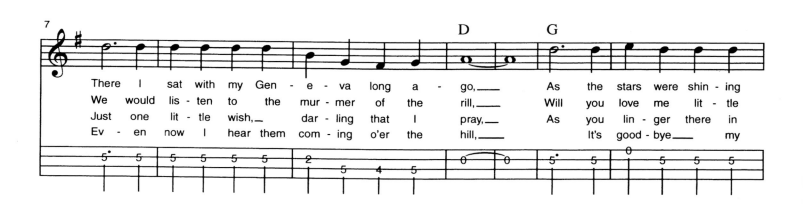

There I sat with my Gen - e - va long a - go,____ As the stars were shin - ing
We would lis - ten to the mur - mer of the rill,____ Will you love me lit - tle
Just one lit - tle wish,__ dar - ling that I pray,__ As you lin - ger there in
Ev - en now I hear them com - ing o'er the hill,____ It's good - bye__ my

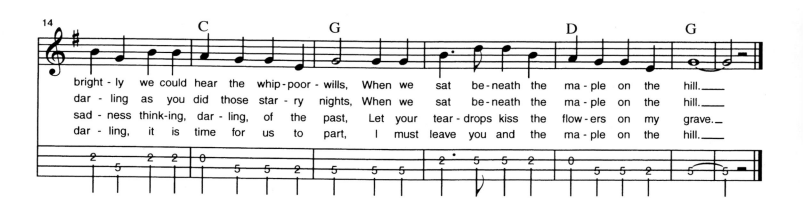

bright - ly we could hear the whip - poor - wills, When we sat be - neath the ma - ple on the hill.____
dar - ling as you did those star - ry nights, When we sat be - neath the ma - ple on the hill.____
sad - ness think-ing, dar - ling, of the past, Let your tear - drops kiss the flow - ers on my grave.____
dar - ling, it is time for us to part, I must leave you and the ma - ple on the hill.____

Stanley Bros., R. Stanley, Dixon Brothers, Mac Wiseman, J.E. Mainer

John Duffy first came to prominence in the late 1950s with The Country Gentlemen. Known as much for his powerful tenor voice as for his mandolin playing, Duffy later co-founded The Seldom Scene and helped forge their wonderful blend of modern bluegrass. This photo is from 1981.

Multi-instrumentalist and singer Mike Seeger, shown here in the early 1980s, has brought American old time music to millions around the world since his early work with The New Lost City Ramblers in the late 1950s.

Methodist Pie

M: D; F: G or A

CD 2-Track 19, medley pt. 1

Traditional

B. Kincaid, Goose Island Ramblers, B. Clifton, Greenbriar Boys

Cho: Oh, lit - tle chil - dren, I___ be - lieve, Oh, lit - tle chil - dren,

I___ be - lieve, Oh, lit - tle chil - dren, I be - lieve, I'm a

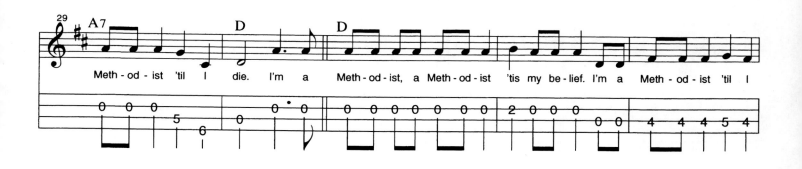

Meth - od - ist 'til I die. I'm a Meth - od - ist, a Meth - od - ist 'tis my be - lief. I'm a Meth - od - ist 'til I

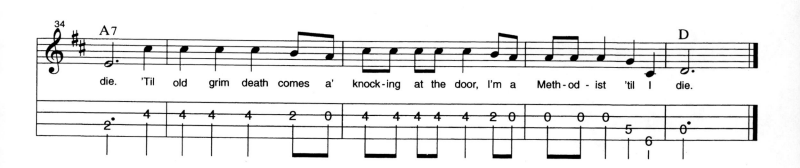

die. 'Til old grim death comes a' knock - ing at the door, I'm a Meth - od - ist 'til I die.

Midnight on the Stormy Deep

M: D; F: G or A
CD 2-Track 19, medley pt. 2

Traditional

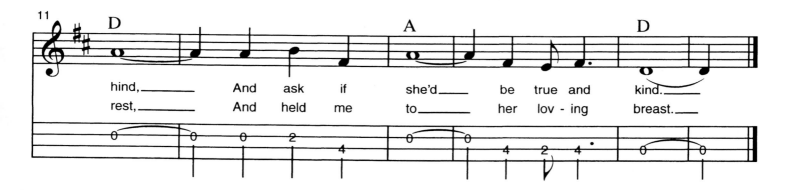

D

3. Oh Willy don't go back to sea,
There's other girls as good as me,
      G   **D**
But none can love you true as I,
      A   **D**
Pray don't go where the bullets fly.

4. The deep, deep sea may us divide,
And I may be some other's bride,
But still my thoughts will oft times stray,
To thee when thou are far away.

5. I never have proved false to thee,
The love I gave is true and kind,
But you have proved untrue to me,
I can no longer call thee mine.

6. Then fare thee well, I'd rather make,
My home upon some icy lake,
Where the southern sun refuses to shine,
Then to trust a love so false as thine.

Milwaukee Blues

M: C; F: F or G
CD 2-Track 20

Traditional

1. One Tues-day morn-ing and it looked like rain, 'Round the curve come a pas-sen-ger train, On the blind__ sat__

old Bill Jones, He's a good old ho - bo and he's trying to get home. He's a' trying to get home,___ He's

trying to get home,_____ He's a good old ho - bo and he's trying to get home.___

C
2. Way down in Georgia on a tramp,
   G
The roads are getting muddy and the leaves are
        getting damp,
C   **F**
Got to catch a freight train, leave this town
            C   **G**   **C**
Cause they don't 'low no hoboes a' hanging around.
         F   **C**
Hanging around, hanging around,
                    G   **C**
They don't 'low no hoboes a' hanging around.

3. Left Atlanta one morning 'fore day,
The brakeman said, "You'll have to pay."
Had no money so I pawned my shoes,
I want to go west, I've got the Milwaukee blues.
Got the Milwaukee blues, got the Milwaukee blues,
I want to go west, I got the Milwaukee blues.

4. Old Bill Jones said before he died,
"Fix the road so the 'boes can ride.
When they ride, they will ride the rods,
Put all their trust in the hands of God.
In the hands of God, in the hands of God,
Put all their trust in the hands of God."

5. Old Bill Jones said before he died,
There's two more roads he'd like to ride.
Fireman said, "What can it be?"
"The Southern Pacific and the Santa Fe.
Santa Fe, yes, the Santa Fe,
The Southern Pacific and the Santa Fe."

Molly and Tenbrooks

M: G; F: C or D
CD 2-Track 21

Traditional

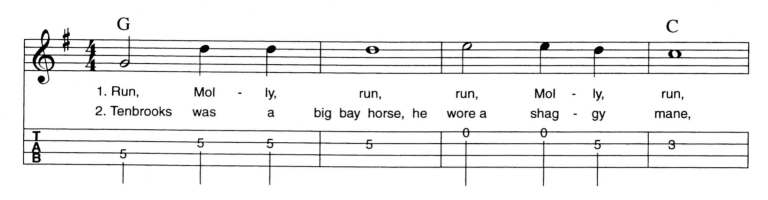

1. Run, Mol - ly, run, run, Mol - ly, run,
2. Tenbrooks was a big bay horse, he wore a shag - gy mane,

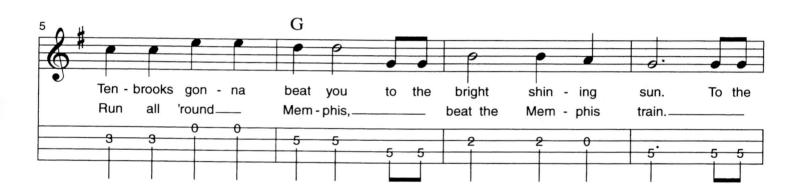

Ten - brooks gon - na beat you to the bright shin - ing sun. To the
Run all 'round Mem - phis, beat the Mem - phis train.

bright shin - ing sun, oh, Lord, To the bright shin - ing sun.
Beat the Mem - phis train, oh Lord, Beat the Mem - phis train.

B. Monroe, Stanley Bros., J.D. Crowe, Country Gentlemen, E. Taylor, Bluegrass Band, Country Gazette, Jimmy Martin, J. Val, Osborne Bros., Bluegrass Album Band, Seldom Scene, D. Grisman Carter Fam., Bluegrass Album Band, D. Watson, K. Kallick

```
              G                                              C
3. Tenbrooks said to Molly, "What makes your head so red?"
                            G              D          G
"Running in the hot sun with a fever in my head.
                                  D            G
Fever in my head, oh Lord, fever in my head."
```

4. Molly said to Tenbrooks, "You're looking mighty squirrel,"
Tenbrooks said to Molly, "I'm leaving this old world." (etc.)

5. Out in California where Molly done as she pleased,
She come back to old Kentucky, got beat with all ease. (etc.)

6. The women's all a' laughing, the children all a' crying,
Men folks all a' hollering, old Tenbrooks a' flying. (etc.)

7. Kuyper, Kuyper, you're not riding right,
Molly's a beatin' old Tenbrooks clear out of sight. (etc.)

8. Kuyper, Kuyper, Kuyper, my son,
Give Tenbrooks the bridle and let old Tenbrooks run. (etc.)

9. Go and catch old Tenbrooks and hitch him in the shade,
We're gonna bury old Molly in a coffin ready made. (etc.)

My Home's Across the Blue Ridge Mountains

M: D; F: G or A

CD 2-Track 22

Traditional

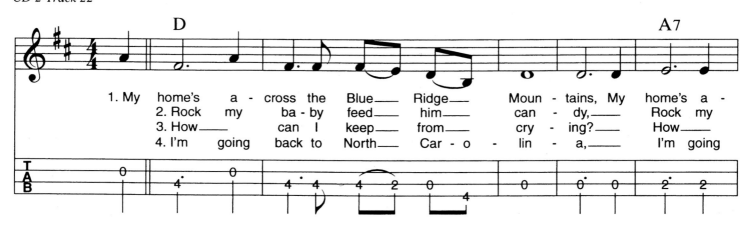

1. My home's a - cross the Blue —— Ridge —— Moun - tains, My home's a -
2. Rock my ba - by feed —— him —— can - dy, —— Rock my
3. How —— can I keep —— from —— cry - ing? —— How ——
4. I'm going back to North —— Car - o - lin - a, —— I'm going

cross the Blue Ridge Moun - tains, My home's a - cross the Blue —— Ridge ——
ba - by feed him can - dy, —— Rock my ba - by feed —— him ——
can I keep from cry - ing? —— How —— can I keep —— from ——
back to North Caro - lin - a, —— I'm going back to North —— Car - o -

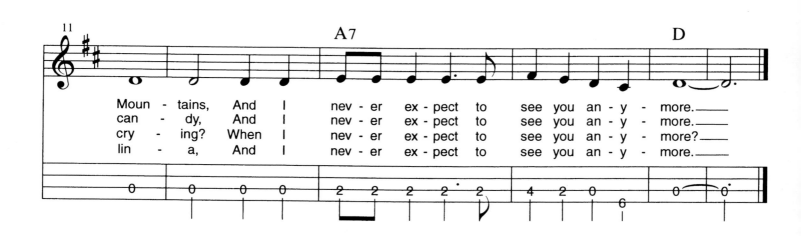

Moun - tains, And I nev - er ex - pect to see you an - y - more. ——
can - dy, And I nev - er ex - pect to see you an - y - more. ——
cry - ing? When I nev - er ex - pect to see you an - y - more? ——
lin - a, And I nev - er ex - pect to see you an - y - more. ——

Carter Fam., Bluegrass Album Band, D. Watson, K. Kallick

You're never too young or too old to start jamming!

My Little Georgia Rose

M: G ; F: C or D
CD 2-Track 23

Bill Monroe

180   B. Monroe, Seldom Scene, D. Grisman

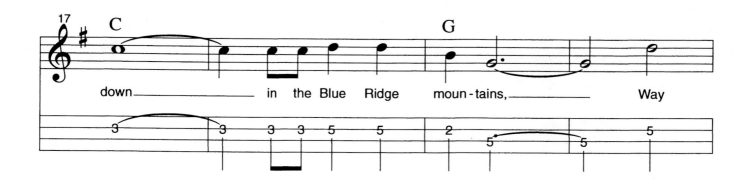

down_____ in the Blue Ridge moun-tains,_____ Way

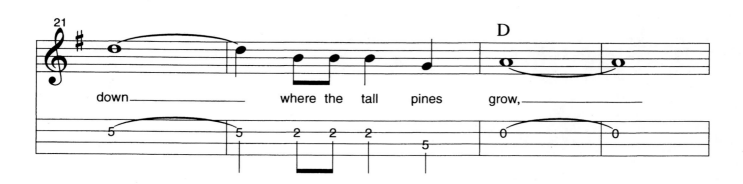

down_____ where the tall pines grow,_____

Lives my sweet-heart of the moun-tains,_____

She's my lit-tle Geor-gia rose._____

New River Train

M: G; F: C or D
CD 2-Track 24, medley pt. 1

Traditional

Cho: I'm rid - ing on that New Riv - er Train,
1. Dar - ling_____ you can't love_____ one,

Rid - ing on that New Riv - er Train, That same old train that
Dar - ling_____ you can't love_____ one, You can't love one and

brought me here, Gon - na car - ry me a - way a - gain.
have any fun, Oh,_____ dar - ling,_____ you can't love one.

G
2. Darling, you can't love two,
          D
Darling, you can't love two,
  G   **C**
You can't love two and your little heart be true,
  D   **G**
Oh, darling, you can't love two.

3. Darling, you can't love three, (2X)
You can't love three and still love me,
Oh, darling, you can't love three.

4. Darling, you can't love four, (2X)
You can't love four and love me anymore,
Oh, darling, you can't love four.

Nine Pound Hammer

M: G; F: C or D
CD 2-Track 24, medley pt. 2

Traditional

1. Well the nine pound ham-mer_____ is a lit-tle too hea-vy,_____ Bud-dy, for my
2. I'm go-in' on the moun-tain,_____ Just to see___ my ba-by,_____ And I ain't coming

size,_____ Bud-dy, for my size.___ Cho: So roll on bud-dy,_____ Don't you roll so
back,_____ Lord I ain't coming back.___

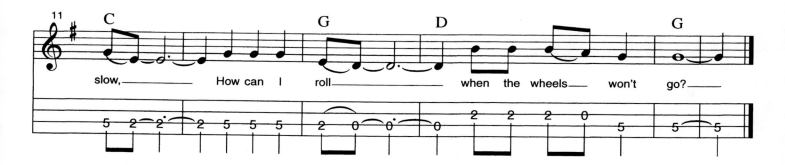

slow,_____ How can I roll_____ when the wheels___ won't go?_____

          G   C
3. There ain't no hammer, in this tunnel,
               G   D   G
That can ring like mine, that can ring like mine.

4. This nine pound hammer, it killed John Henry,
But it won't kill me, no it won't kill me.

5. It's a long way to Harlan, it's a long way to Hazard,
Just to get a little brew, just to get a little brew.

6. I'm working all day, down under ground,
Black as night, it's black as night.

Monroe Bros., B. Monroe, Flatt & Scruggs, Stanley Bros., R. Stanley, Osborne Bros., T. Rice, D. Watson, R. Allen & F. Wake-field, D. Grisman, Ken. Colonels, C. White, Blue Sky Boys, Jim & Jesse   **183**

Nobody's Business

M: G; F: C or D
CD 2-Track 25

Traditional

1. There's where my mon - ey goes, Buy - ing my ba - by clothes,— No - bod - y's
2. She drives a Ford mach - ine, I buy the gas - o - line,— No - bod - y's

bus - iness if I do._____ Cho: No - bod - y's bus - iness,
bus - iness if I do._____

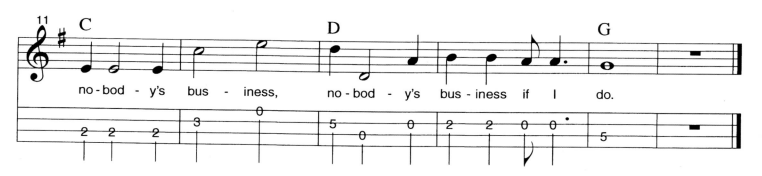

no - bod - y's bus - iness, no - bod - y's bus - iness if I do.

G
3. She's worth her weight in gold,
C
She likes to rock & roll,
D   **G**
Nobody's business if I do,

Chorus:
G   **C**
Nobody's business, Nobody's business,
D   **G**
Nobody's business if I do,

4. My wife's from Alabam,
Way out in no man's land,
Nobody's business if I do, (etc.)

5. Sliced ham and pickled feet,
Ham and eggs and sausage meat,
Nobody's business if I do, (etc.)

6. She rides the limousine,
I crank the old machine,
Nobody's business if I do, (etc.)

Oh Death

M: Em; F: Am or Bm
CD 2-Track 26

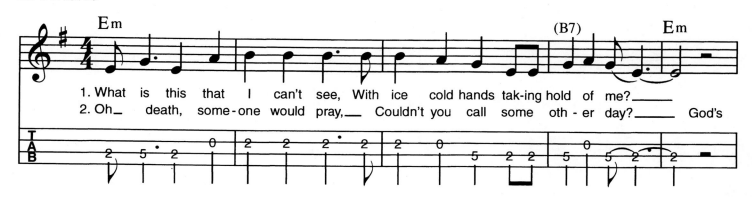

1. What is this that I can't see, With ice cold hands tak-ing hold of me?_____
2. Oh_ death, some-one would pray,_ Couldn't you call some oth-er day?_____ God's

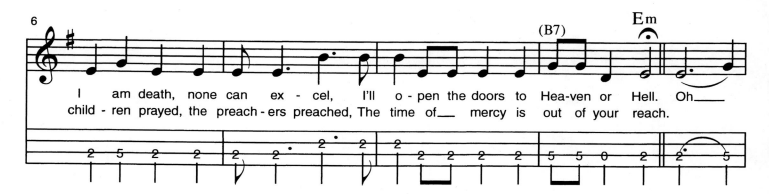

I am death, none can ex-cel, I'll o-pen the doors to Hea-ven or Hell. Oh_____
child-ren prayed, the preach-ers preached, The time of_ mercy is out of your reach.

death,_ Oh_ death,_ won't you spare me o-ver 'til an-oth-er year?_____

Em

3. I'll fix your feet so you can't walk,
        B7   **Em**
I'll lock your jaws so you can't talk,
I'll close your eyes so you can't see,
        B7   **Em**
This very hour come go with me. *(Repeat chorus)*

4. Death, I come to take the soul,
Leave the body and leave it cold,
To drop the flesh off of the frame,
The earth and worms both have a claim.

5. My mother come to my bed,
Place a cold towel upon my head,
My head is warm, my feet are cold,
Death is moving upon my soul.

6. Oh death, how you treat me,
You close my eyes so I can't see.
You hurt my body, you make me cold,
You've run the life right out of my soul.

7. Oh death, please consider my age,
Please don't take me at this stage,
My wealth is all at your command,
If you will move your icy hand.

8. Old, the young, the rich or poor,
All alike with me, you know,
No wealth, no land, no silver, no gold,
Nothing satisfies me but your soul.

Stanley Bros., R. Stanley, "O Brother" soundtrack, NLCR, Carter Fam. **185**

Oh! Didn't He Ramble

M: G; F: C or D
CD 2-Track 27, medley pt. 1

Will Handy, 1902

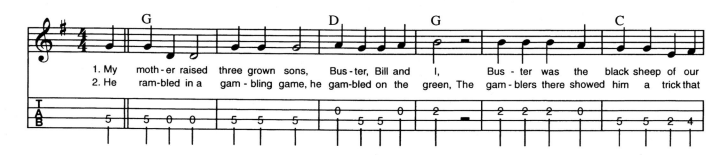

1. My moth-er raised three grown sons, Bus-ter, Bill and I, Bus-ter was the black sheep of our
2. He ram-bled in a gam-bling game, he gam-bled on the green, The gam-blers there showed him a trick that

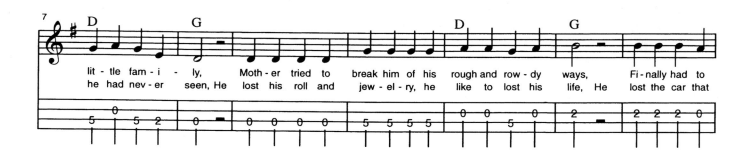

lit-tle fam-i-ly, Moth-er tried to break him of his rough and row-dy ways, Fi-nally had to
he had nev-er seen, He lost his roll and jew-el-ry, he like to lost his life, He lost the car that

get the judge to give him nine-ty days. Cho: And did-n't he ram - ble, ram - ble, He ram-bled all a - round,
carried him there and some-body stole his wife.

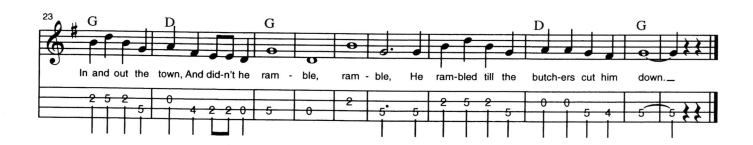

In and out the town, And did-n't he ram - ble, ram - ble, He ram-bled till the butch-ers cut him down.

```
     G                            D        G
3. He rambled in a swell hotel, his appetite was stout,
                   C                 D              G
And when he refused to pay the bill, the landlord kicked him out.
                                        D              G
He reached a brick to smack him with, and when he went to stop,
                   C                D        G
The landlord kicked him over the fence, right in a barrel of slop.
```

(Repeat chorus after each verse)

4. He rambled through the tunnel once, on board a moving train.
Another train came rumbling in, and rammed him out again.
It rammed him just a block, and then, they caught him on the fly,
And with a ton of dynamite, they rammed him to the sky.

5. He rambled to an Irish wake, on one St. Patrick's night.
They asked him what he'd like to drink, they meant to treat him right.
But like the old Kilkenny cats, their backs began to arch.
When he called for orange phosphate, on the seventeenth of March.

6. He rambled to the races, to make a gallery bet.
He backed a horse named Hydrant, and Hydrant's running yet.
He would have had to walk back home, his friends all from him hid.
By luck he met old George Sedam, it's a damn good thing he did.

Old Dan Tucker

M: G; F: C or D
CD 2-Track 27, medley pt. 2

Traditional

1. Old Dan Tuck-er was a migh-ty man, He washed his face in a fry-ing pan, He
2. Old Dan Tuck-er, he__ come to town,__ Riding a billy goat,_ leading a hound,_
3. Old Dan Tuck-er_____ he got drunk,_ Fell in the fire and_ kicked up a chunk,_

combed his hair with a wag-on wheel, Died with a tooth-ache in his heel.
Hound dog bark and the billy goat jump, Landed Dan_ Tucker on top of the stump._
Red hot coal got_ in his shoe, And oh my_ Lord how the ash-es flew.___

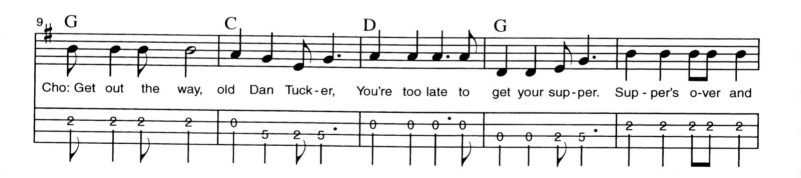

Cho: Get out the way, old Dan Tuck-er, You're too late to get your sup-per. Sup-per's o-ver and

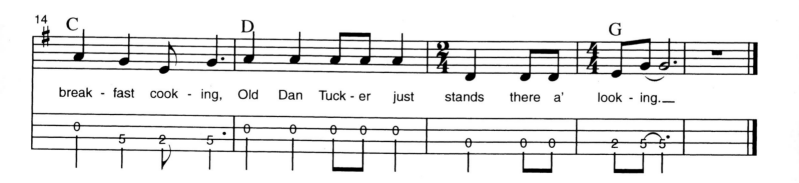

break-fast cook-ing, Old Dan Tuck-er just stands there a' look-ing.__

Ralph Stanley began his professional music career with his brother Carter as The Stanley Brothers. Apart from Bill Monroe, the Stanley sound is probably the most influential in bluegrass and old time music.

Old Home Place

M: G; F: C or D
CD 2-Track 28

Webb & Jayne

1. It's been ten long years since I left my home, In the
2. I fell in love with a girl from the town,
3. The girl ran off with some-bod-y else, The
4. Now the geese fly south and the cold wind blows, As

hol - low where I was born,   Where the
I   thought that she'd be true,   Then
tav - erns took all my pay,   And
I   stand here and hang my head,   I've

cool   fall nights   make the wood smoke   rise,   And the
I   ran a - way   to   Char - lottes - ville,   And
here   I   stand   where the old home   stood,   Be -
lost   my   love,   I've lost my   home,   And

fox   hun - ter   blows   his   horn.
worked   in a   saw - mill   crew.
fore   they   took it   a - way.
now   I   wish that I   was dead.

Cho: What have they done to the old home place?

Why did they tear it down? And

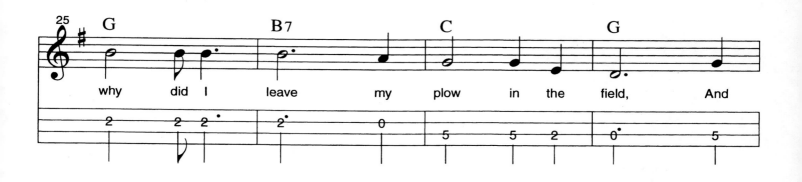

why did I leave my plow in the field, And

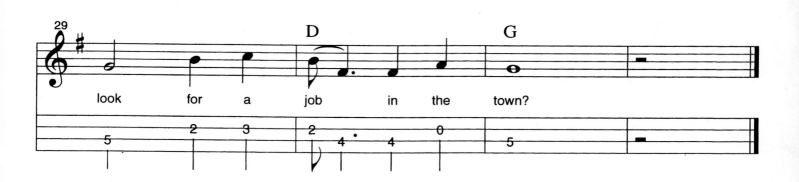

look for a job in the town?

Old Joe Clark

M: D; F: G or A
CD 2-Track 29

Traditional

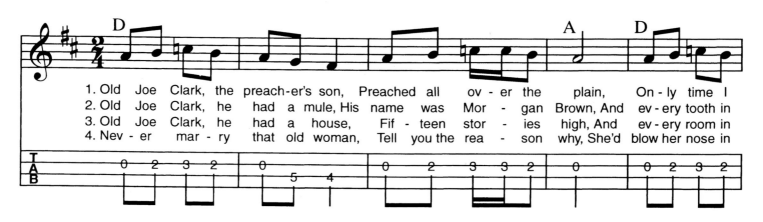

1. Old Joe Clark, the preach-er's son, Preached all ov - er the plain, On - ly time I
2. Old Joe Clark, he had a mule, His name was Mor - gan Brown, And ev - ery tooth in
3. Old Joe Clark, he had a house, Fif - teen stor - ies high, And ev - ery room in
4. Nev - er mar - ry that old woman, Tell you the rea - son why, She'd blow her nose in

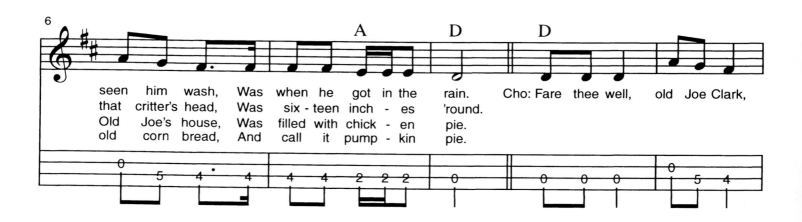

seen him wash, Was when he got in the rain. Cho: Fare thee well, old Joe Clark,
that critter's head, Was six - teen inch - es 'round.
Old Joe's house, Was filled with chick - en pie.
old corn bread, And call it pump - kin pie.

Fare thee well I say, Fare thee well, old Joe Clark, Bound to go a - way.

Flatt & Scruggs, B. Monroe, Goose Island Ramblers, Ken. Colonels, C. White, Skillet Lickers, Red Allen, D. Dillard, T. Adams, T. Trischka, A. Munde

Old Man at the Mill

M: G; F: C or D
CD 2-Track 30

Traditional

Dillards, D. Watson, NLCR   193

Old Paint

M: G; F: C or D
CD 2-Track 31

Traditional

1. I ride an old paint, I lead an old Dan, I'm going to Mon-
2. Old___ Bill Jones had a daugh-ter and a son,___ One___ went to
3. When___ I die, take my sad-dle from the wall,___ Put it on my

tan - a to throw a Hool-i-han. They feed 'em in the coul-ees, they wa-ter in the
Den - ver and the oth-er we-nt wrong. His wife___ she___ died___ in a pool___ room___
po - ny and lead him from his stall. Tie my bones___ to his back, turn our fac-es to the

draw, Their tails are all mat-ted, their backs are all raw. Cho: Ride a-round lit-tle
fight, but still he keeps sing-ing from morn-ing 'til night.
west, And we'll ride the prair-ie that we love the best.

do - gies, ride arou-nd re-al slow, for the fier-y and the snuf-fy are rar-ing to go.___

The Old Rugged Cross

M: A; F: D or E
CD 2-Track 32

Geo. Bennard, 1913

Old Time Religion

M: G; F: C or D
CD 2-Track 33

Traditional

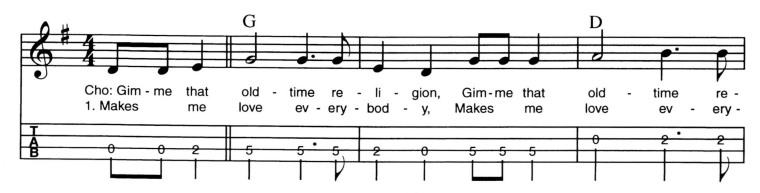

Cho: Gim - me that old - time re - li - gion, Gim-me that old - time re-
1. Makes me love ev - ery - bod - y, Makes me love ev - ery -

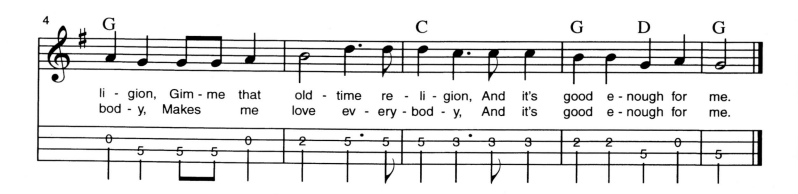

li - gion, Gim - me that old - time re - li - gion, And it's good e - nough for me.
bod - y, Makes me love ev - ery - bod - y, And it's good e - nough for me.

G
2. It was good for our mothers,
    D   **G**
It was good for our mothers,
        C
It was good for our mothers,
     G   **D**   **G**
And it's good enough for me.

3. It has saved all our fathers, (3X, etc.)
4. It will save all our children, (3X, etc.)
5. It was good for Paul and Silas, (3X, etc.)
6. It was good for the Prophet Daniel, (3X, etc.)
7. It was good for the Hebrew children, (3X, etc.)
8. It was tried in the fiery furnace, (3X, etc.)
9. It will do when I'm a'dying, (3X, etc.)
10. It will take us all to heaven, (3X, etc.)

On and On

M: G; F: C or D
CD 2-Track 34

Bill Monroe

Over the Hills to the Poorhouse

M: G; F: C or D
CD 2-Track 35

Traditional

1. Oh how can it be they have driv - en,___ Their fath - er so help - less and old?_
2. Oh heav - en, I'm sad and I'm wear - y,_ See the tears, how they course down my cheek,
3. Long years_ since Mar - y was tak - en,___ My faith - ful, af - fec - tion - ate wife,.
4. Oh me, on the door-step up yon - der,___ I've set with my babes on my knee,
5. I gave them the house they were born in,___ A deed to the farm___ and more,

Oh God, may their crimes be for - giv - en,____ To per - ish out here in the cold. Cho: I'm
This world is so lone - ly and wear - y,____ My heart for re - lief vain - ly seeks.
Since then I'm a - lone and for - sak - en,____ The light has died out of my life._
No fath - er so hap - py or fon - der,____ Than I of my lit - tle ones three.
I gave them the place that they lived on,____ And now I am turned from its door.

old, I'm help - less and fee - ble,____ And the days of my youth have gone by,____ And

o - ver the hills to the poor house,___ I must wan - der a - lone there to die.___

Pass Me Not

M: G; F: C or D
CD 2-Track 36

Crosby & Doan, ca.1870

1. Pass   me   not, oh gen - tle Sav-ior, Hear my hum-ble cry;   While   on oth-ers Thou art
2. Let   me   at Thy throne of mer-cy, Find a sweet re - lief,   Kneel - ing there in deep con-
3. Trust - ing on - ly in Thy mer - it, Would I seek Thy face;   Heal   my wound-ed, bro-ken
4. Thou   the Spring of all my com-fort, More than life to me,   Whom   have I on earth be-

call - ing,   Do   not pass me   by.   Cho: Sav - ior,   Sav - ior,
tri - tion;   Help   my un - be - lief.
spir - it,   Save   me by Thy   grace.
side Thee?   Whom   in heaven but   Thee?

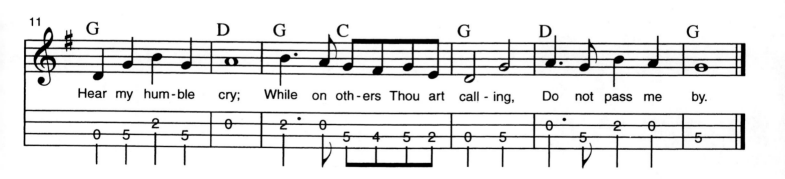

Hear my hum-ble   cry;   While   on oth-ers Thou art call-ing,   Do   not pass me   by.

B. Monroe, Stanley Bros., R. Stanley, K. Baker 199

Paul and Silas

M: G; F: C or D
CD 2-Track 37

Traditional

1. Paul and Si - las bound in jail, all night long,— Paul and Si - las
2. Paul and Si - las prayed to God, all night long,— Paul and Si - las
3. That old jail - er locked the door, all night long,— That old jail - er
4. That old jail it reeled and rocked, all night long,— That old jail it
5. He - brew children in the burn - ing fire, all night long,— He - brew children in the

bound in jail, all night long,— Paul and Si - las bound in jail,
prayed to God, all night long,— Paul and Si - las prayed to God,
locked the door, all night long,— That old jail - er locked the door,
reeled and rocked, all night long,— That old jail it reeled and rocked,
burn - ing fire, all night long,— He - brew children in the burn - ing fire,

all night long,— Say - ing, "Who shall de - liv - er poor me?"
all night long,— Say - ing, "Who shall de - liv - er poor me?"
all night long,— Say - ing, "Who shall de - liv - er poor me?"
all night long,— Say - ing, "Who shall de - liv - er poor me?"
all night long,— Say - ing, "Who shall de - liv - er poor me?"

Pig in a Pen

M: G; F: C or D
CD 2-Track 38

Traditional

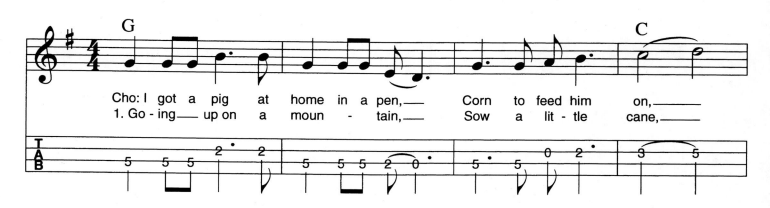

Cho: I got a pig at home in a pen,— Corn to feed him on,—
1. Go-ing— up on a moun - tain,— Sow a lit - tle cane,—

All I need is a pret-ty lit-tle girl, To feed him when I'm gone.
Put that old gray— bon - net— on,— Sweet little Li - za Jane.

G
2. Going up on a mountain,
       C
To sow a little cane,
         G
Raise a barrel of sorghum,
D   G
Sweet little Liza Jane.

3. Black smoke arising,
Surely is a train,
Put that old gray bonnet on,
Little Liza Jane.

4. Bake them biscuits baby,
Bake 'em good and brown,
When you get them biscuits baked,
I'm Alabama bound.

Poor Ellen Smith

M: G; F: C or D
CD 2-Track 39

Traditional

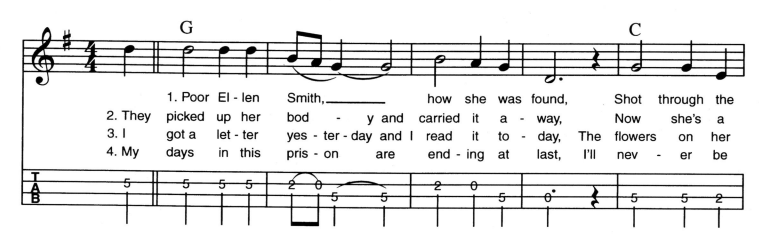

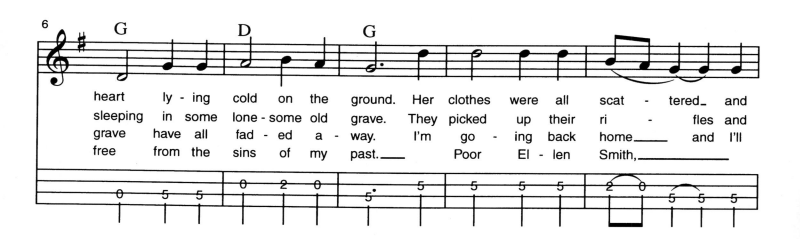

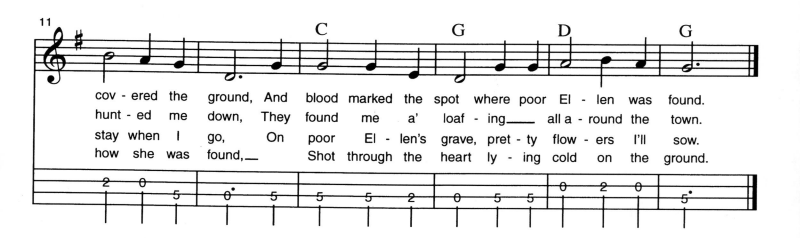

J. Martin, Stanley Bros., Flatt & Scruggs, NLCR, E. Taylor, Country Gentlemen, Reno & Harrell, J. Val, Mac Wiseman, N. Blake, Bluegrass Intentions

Precious Memories

M: G; F: C or D
CD 2-Track 40

J.B.F. Wright

1. Pre - cious mem - ories, un - seen an - gels, Sent from some - where to my soul,_____
2. Pre - cious fa - ther, lov - ing moth - er, Fly a - cross the lone - ly years,_____

How they lin - ger, ev - er near me, And the sac - red past un - fold._____
And old home scenes of my child - hood, In fond mem - o - ry ap - pear._____

Cho: Pre - cious mem - ories, how they lin - ger, How they ev - er flood my soul,_____

In the still - ness, of the mid - night, Pre - cious, sa - cred scenes un - fold._____

G   C   G
3. In the stillness of the midnight,
              D
Echoes from the past I hear;
G   C   G
Old time singing, gladness bringing,
           D   G
From that lovely land somewhere.

4. I remember mother praying,
Father, too on bended knee;
Sun is sinking, shadows falling,
But their prayers still follow me.

5. As I travel on life's pathway,
Know not what the years may hold;
As I ponder, hope grows fonder,
Precious memories flood my soul.

Pretty Polly

M: G; F: C or D
CD 2-Track 41

Traditional

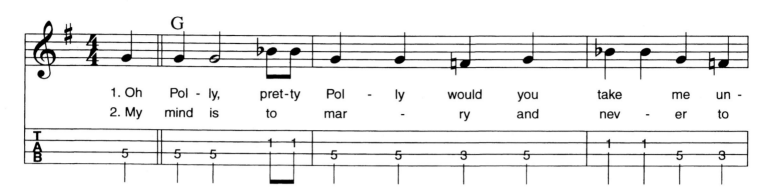

1. Oh Pol - ly, pret-ty Pol - ly would you take me un -
2. My mind is to mar - ry you and nev - er to

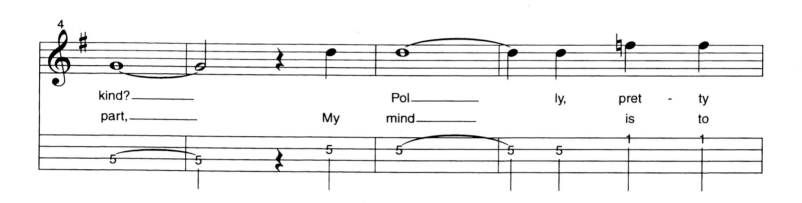

kind?_____ Pol_____ ly, pret - ty
part,_____ My mind_____ is to

Pol - ly would you take me un - kind? For me to sit be -
mar - ry and nev - er to part, The first time I

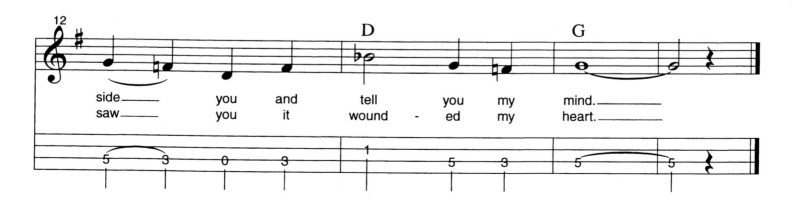

side_____ you and tell you my mind._____
saw_____ you it wound - ed my heart._____

Stanley Bros., R. Stanley, Dillards, C. White, D. Grisman, NLCR, D. Watson, D. Boggs

     G
3. Oh, Polly, pretty Polly, come and go along with me,
Polly, pretty Polly, come and go along with me,
                              D   G
Before we get married some pleasure to see.

4. He led her over mountains and valleys so deep,
He led her over mountains and valleys so deep,
Polly mistrusted and then began to weep.

5. Saying, "Willie, oh Willie, I'm afraid of your ways,
"Willie, oh Willie, I'm afraid of your ways,
The way you've been rambling, you'll lead me astray."

6. Well Polly, pretty Polly, your guess is about right,
Polly, pretty Polly, your guess is about right,
I dug on your grave the best part of last night.

7. Then he led her a little farther and what did they spy?
Led her a little farther and what did they spy?
A new-dug grave with a spade lying by.

8. She knelt down before him a' pleading for her life,
Knelt before him a' pleading for her life,
"Let me be a single girl if I can't be your wife."

9. Now Polly, pretty Polly, that never can be,
Polly, pretty Polly, that never can be,
Your past reputation's been trouble to me.

10. He stabbed her in the heart and her blood it did flow,
He stabbed her in the heart and her blood it did flow,
And into the grave pretty Polly did go.

11. Then he went down to the jail house and what did he say?
He went to the jail house and what did he say?
"I've killed pretty Polly and tried to get away."

12. Now gentlemen and ladies, I bid you farewell,
Gentlemen and ladies, I bid you farewell,
For killing pretty Polly my soul must go to hell.

Put My Little Shoes Away

M: G; F: C or D
CD 2-Track 42

Mitchell & Pratt, 1873

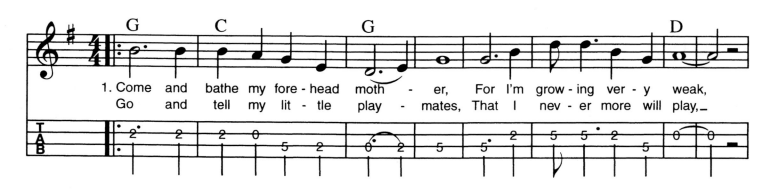

1. Come and bathe my fore-head moth - er, For I'm grow-ing ver-y weak,
Go and tell my lit-tle play - mates, That I nev-er more will play,_

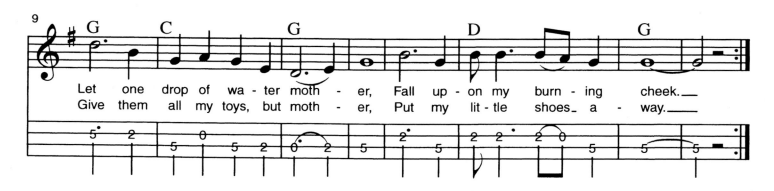

Let one drop of wa-ter moth - er, Fall up-on my burn-ing cheek._
Give them all my toys, but moth - er, Put my lit-tle shoes_ a - way._

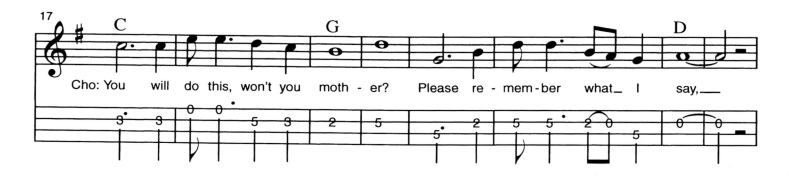

Cho: You will do this, won't you moth - er? Please re-mem-ber what_ I say,_

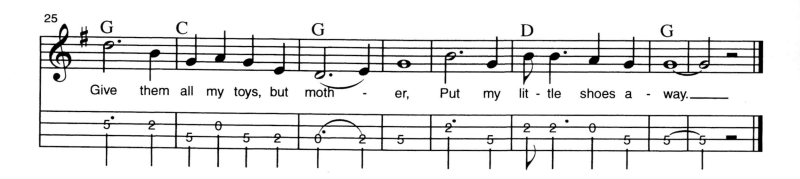

Give them all my toys, but moth - er, Put my lit-tle shoes a - way._

```
     G      C                         G
3. Santa Claus, he brought them to me,
                       D
With a lot of other things,
G      C                        G
And I think he brought an angel,
            D            G
With a pair of golden wings.
          C            G
I will be an angel, Mother,
                      D
By perhaps another day,
G      C            G
You will do this for me, Mother,
         D       G
Put my little shoes away.
```

```
4. Soon the baby will be larger,
Then they'll fit his little feet,
Won't he look so nice and cunning,
When he walks upon the street?
I'm going to leave you, Mother,
So remember what I say,
You will do this for me, Mother,
Put my little shoes away.
```

```
5. Now I'm growing tired, dear Mother,
Soon I'll say to you "Good Day,"
Always remember what I told you,
Put my little shoes away.
I'm about to leave you, Mother,
So remember what I say,
You will do this for me, Mother,
Put my little shoes away.
```

Railroad Bill

M: C; F: F or G
CD 2-Track 43

Traditional

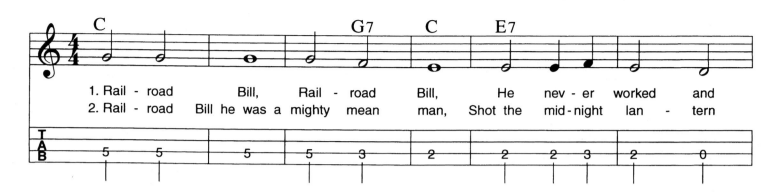

1. Rail - road Bill, Rail - road Bill, He nev - er worked and
2. Rail - road Bill he was a mighty mean man, Shot the mid-night lan - tern

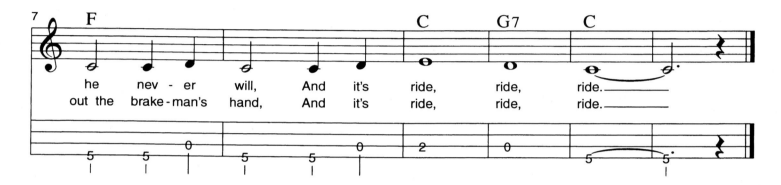

he nev - er will, And it's ride, ride, ride.
out the brake-man's hand, And it's ride, ride, ride.

      C   G7 C
3. Railroad Bill took my wife,
E7   F
Said if I didn't like it, he would take my life,
        C   G7 C
And it's ride, ride, ride.

4. Going on a mountain, going way out west,
Thirty-eight special sticking out of my vest,
And it's ride, ride, ride.

5. Gonna buy me a pistol, long as my arm,
Kill everybody that's ever done me harm,
And it's ride, ride, ride.

6. I've got a thirty-eight special on a forty-five frame,
How can I miss him when I got dead aim,
And it's ride, ride, ride.

7. Honey, babe, do you think that I'm a fool,
Think that I'd quit you with the weather still so cool,
And it's ride, ride, ride.

D. Bruce & J. Nunally, D. Watson, E. Baker, Skillet Lickers

Rain and Snow

M: Am dorian; F: Dm or Em dorian
CD 2-Track 44

Traditional

1. I mar-ried me a wife,— she give me trou-ble all of my life, She ran me
2. She came— down the stairs,— comb-ing back— her yel-low hair, And her
3. I done all I can do,— to try to get a - long with you, And I'm
4. She came in-to the room,— where she— met— her fa-tal doom, And I'm

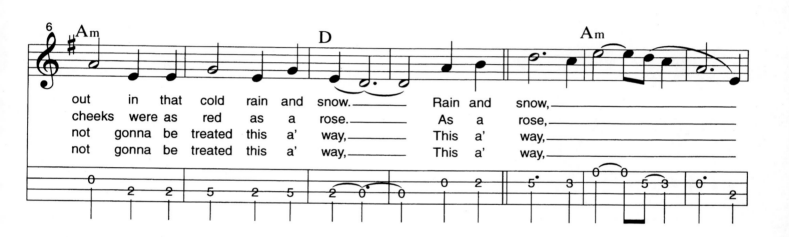

out in that cold rain and snow.———— Rain and snow,———
cheeks were as red as a rose.———— As a rose,———
not gonna be treated this a' way,———— This a' way,———
not gonna be treated this a' way,———— This a' way,———

Lord,———— She ran me out in that cold rain and snow.————
Lord,———— And her cheeks were as red as a rose.————
Lord,———— And I'm not gonna be treated this a' way,————
Lord,———— And I'm not gonna be treated this a' way,————

Rank Strangers to Me

M: G; F: C or D
CD 2-Track 45

Albert E. Brumley

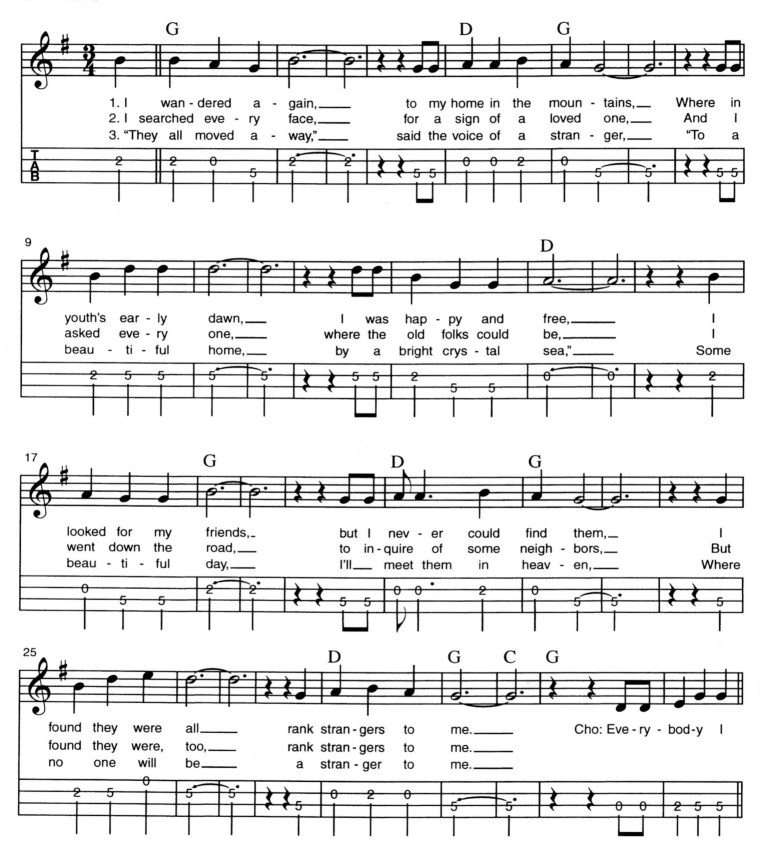

1. I wan-dered a-gain,____ to my home in the moun-tains,__ Where in
2. I searched eve-ry face,____ for a sign of a loved one,__ And I
3. "They all moved a-way,"____ said the voice of a stran-ger, "To a

youth's ear-ly dawn,____ I was hap-py and free,_____ I
asked eve-ry one,____ where the old folks could be,_____ I
beau-ti-ful home,__ by a bright crys-tal sea,"_____ Some

looked for my friends,_ but I nev-er could find them,__ I
went down the road,____ to in-quire of some neigh-bors,__ But
beau-ti-ful day,____ I'll__ meet them in heav-en,____ Where

found they were all_____ rank stran-gers to me.____ Cho: Eve-ry-bod-y I
found they were, too,____ rank stran-gers to me.____
no one will be_____ a stran-ger to me.____

Stanley Bros., R. Stanley, Hot Rize, D. Watson, Osborne Bros., Country Gentlemen

met,_____ seemed to be a rank stran-ger,_____ No

moth-er or dad,____ not a friend could I see,____ They

knew not my name,____ and I knew not their fac-es,_____ I

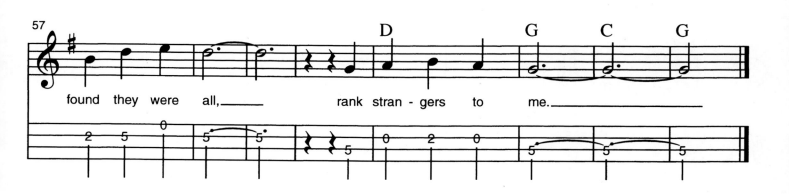

found they were all,_____ rank stran-gers to me._____

Red Rocking Chair

M: *G*; F: *C or D*
CD 2-Track 46

Traditional

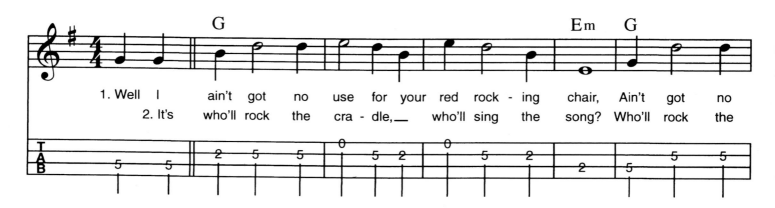

G   Em
3. I'll rock the cradle, I'll sing the song,
G   Em
I'll rock the cradle when you're gone, Lord, Lord,
D   G
I'll rock the cradle when you're gone.

4. It's all I can do, all I can say,
Ain't gonna be treated this a' way, Lord, Lord,
Ain't gonna be treated this a' way.

5. It's all I can do, all I can say,
Sing it to you mama next pay day, Lord, Lord,
Sing it to you mama next pay day.

C. Monroe, Country Gentlemen, D. Watson, Reno & Harrell, Dry Branch Fire Squad, J.D. Crowe, Mac Wiseman, Muleskinner, Kruger Bros.

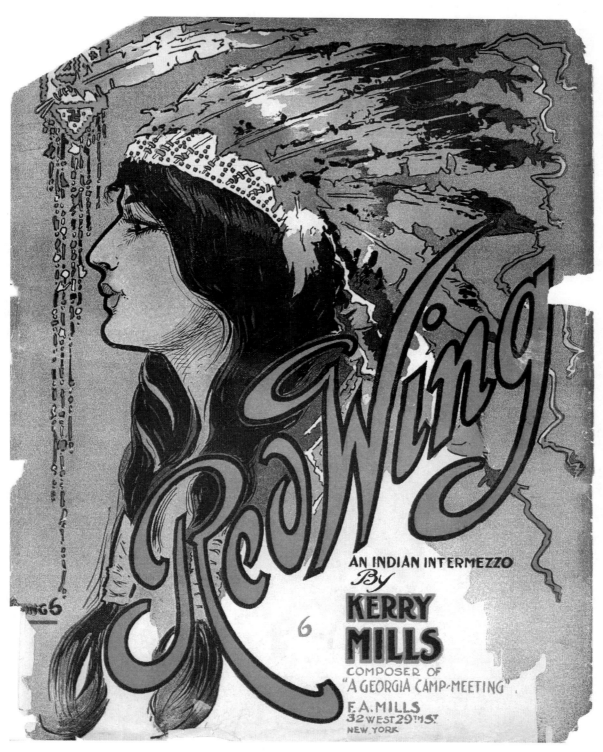

"Red Wing" is one of those songs that everyone seems to recognize. It's been a hit since 1907.

Red Wing

M: C; F: F or G
CD 2-Track 47

Chattaway & Mills, 1907

1. There once lived an In - dian maid, A shy lit - tle prair - ie maid, Who
2. She watched for him day and night, She kept all the camp fires bright, And

sang a lay, a love song gay, As on the plain she'd while a - way the day; She
un - der the sky, each night she would lie, And dream a - bout his com - ing by and by, But

loved a war - rior bold, This shy lit - tle maid of old, But
when all the braves re - turned, The heart of___ Red Wing yearned, For

brave and___ gay, he rode one___ day, To bat - tle far___ a - way. Cho: Now, the
far, far a - way, her war - ri - or gay, Fell brave - ly in___ the fray.

214   N. Blake, Osborne Bros., R. Smiley, J. McEuen, A. Munde, L. Flatt & B. Monroe,

Reuben's Train

M: D; F: G or A
CD 2-Track 48

Traditional

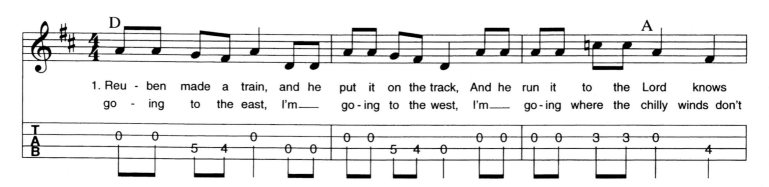

1. Reu - ben made a train, and he put it on the track, And he run it to the Lord knows
go - ing to the east, I'm___ go - ing to the west, I'm___ go - ing where the chilly winds don't

where. Oh me, oh my,___ run it to the Lord knows where. 2. I'm
blow. Oh me, oh my,___ go - ing where the chilly winds don't blow.___

D
3. If that train's running right, see my woman tomorrow night.
          A   **D**
I'm nine hundred miles away from home.
           A   **D**
Oh me, oh my, nine hundred miles away from home.

4. You ought to been uptown, to see that train come down,
You could hear the whistle blow a hundred miles.
Oh me, oh my, hear the whistle blow a hundred miles.

5. Last night I lay in jail, had no money to go my bail,
Lord, how it sleeted and it snowed.
Oh me, oh my, Lord how it sleeted and it snowed.

6. Oh, the train that I ride, is a hundred coaches long,
You can hear the whistle blow a hundred miles.
Oh me, oh my, you can hear the whistle blow a hundred miles.

7. I got myself a blade, laid Reuben in the shade,
I'm starting me a graveyard of my own.
Oh me, oh my, starting me a graveyard of my own.

Rocky Top

M: G; F: C or D
CD 2-Track 49

Beaudleaux & Felice Bryant

1. Wish that I was on old Rock-y Top, Down in the Ten-nes-see hills,
2. Once I had a girl on Rock-y Top, Half bear the oth-er half cat,
3. Once two stran-gers climbed old Rock-y Top, Look-ing for a moon-shine still,
4. Corn won't grow at all on Rock-y Top, Dirt's too rock-y by far,
5. I've had years of cramped up ci-ty life, Trapped like a duck in a pen,

Ain't no smog-gy smoke on Rock-y Top, Ain't no tel-e-phone bills.
Wild as a mink, but sweet as so-da pop, I still dream a-bout that.
Stran-gers ain't come down from Rock-y Top, Reck-on they nev-er will.
That's why all the folks on Rock-y Top, Get their corn from a jar.
All I know is it's a pit-y life, Can't be sim-ple a-gain.

Chorus: Rock-y Top, you'll al-ways be, Home sweet home to me,

Good old Rock-y Top, Rock-y Top, Ten-nes-see, Rock-y Top, Ten-nes-see.

Roll in My Sweet Baby's Arms

M: A; F: D or E
CD 2-Track 50

Traditional

1. I ain't gon-na work on the rail-road,___ I ain't gon-na work on the farm,___ I'll
2. Now where were__ you last__ Fri - day night,_ While I__ was ly - ing in jail?____ Out

lay a-round the shack 'til the mail train gets back, And I'll roll in my sweet ba - by's arms.___
walk - ing__ the streets with an - oth - er___ man,____ Wouldn't even go__ my bail.___

Cho: Roll in my sweet ba-by's arms, ___ Roll in my sweet ba - by's arms,____ Lay a-round the

shack 'til the mail train gets back, And I'll roll in my sweet ba - by's arms.___

A
3. I know your parents don't like me,
                            E7
They drove me away from your door,
  A   A7   D
If I had my life to live over,
  E7   A
I'd never go there any more.

4. Mama's a beauty operator,
Sister can weave and spin,
Pappa's got an interest in an old cotton mill,
My, how the money rolls in!

5. Sometimes there's a change in the weather,
Sometimes there's a change in the sea,
Sometimes there's a change in my own true love,
But there's never a change in me.

Roll on Buddy

M: G; F: C or D
CD 2-Track 51

Traditional

1. I'm go - ing to that East Cai - ro, I'm go - ing to that East Cai - ro, I'm go - ing to the east, I'm go - ing to the west, I'm go - ing to the one that I love best.

Cho: Roll on, buddy, roll on, Roll on, buddy, roll on, You would-n't roll so slow if you knew what I know, So roll on bud - dy, roll on.

2. I've got a good woman just the same, I've got a good woman just the same, Got a wo - man just the same, says she's gon - na change her name, I've got a good wo - man just the same.

3. My home is down in Ten - nes - see, My home is down in Ten - nes - see, In Ten - nes - see, that's where I long to be, Way down in sun - ny Ten - nes - see.

Monroe Bros., B. Monroe, R. Stanley, Ken. Colonels, V. Williams, D. Watson, D. McCoury

Roving Gambler

M: G; F: C or D
CD 2-Track 52

Traditional

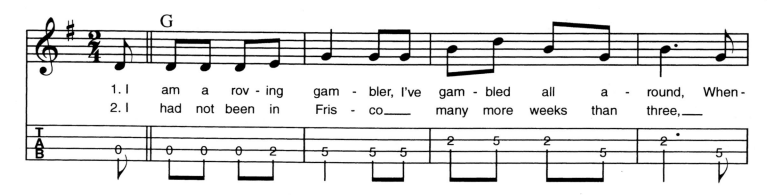

1. I am a rov - ing gam - bler, I've gam - bled all a - round, When-
2. I had not been in Fris - co___ many more weeks than three,___

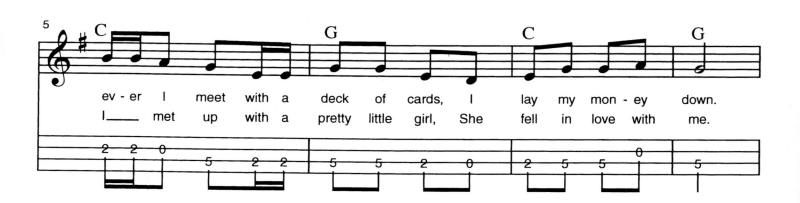

ev - er I meet with a deck of cards, I lay my mon - ey down.
I___ met up with a pretty little girl, She fell in love with me.

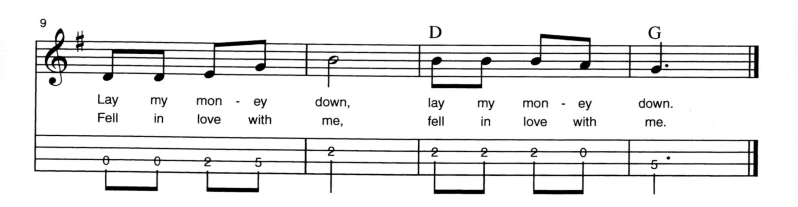

Lay my mon - ey down, lay my mon - ey down.
Fell in love with me, fell in love with me.

Stanley Bros., Country Gentlemen, P. Rowan, D. Watson, B. Clifton, Mac Wiseman

      G
3. She took me in her parlor, she cooled me with her fan,
    C   G
She whispered low in her mother's ear,
 C   G
"I love this gambling man.
                     D   G
Love this gambling man, love this gambling man."

4. Oh daughter, oh dear daughter, how can you treat me so?
Leave your dear old mother,
And with a gambler go,
With a gambler go, with a gambler go?

5. Oh mother, oh dear mother, you cannot understand,
If you ever see me a'coming back,
I'll be with the gambling man,
With the gambling man, with the gambling man.

6. I left her in Frisco and I ended up in Maine,
I met up with a gambling man,
We got in a poker game,
Got in a poker game, got in a poker game.

7. We put our money in the pot and dealt the cards around,
I saw him deal from the bottom of the deck,
So I shot that gambler down,
Shot the gambler down, shot the gambler down.

8. Now I'm up in prison, got a number for my name,
Jailer said as he locked the door,
"You've gambled your last game,
Gambled your last game, gambled your last game."

Sailor on the Deep Blue Sea

M: D; F: G or A
CD 2-Track 53

Traditional

1. It was on one sum - mer's eve - ning,— Just a-
2. Oh, he prom - ised to write me a let - ter,— He—
3. Oh, my moth - er's dead and bur - ied,— My—
4. Oh— cap - tain, can you tell me— Where.
5. Fare - well to friends and re - la - tions,— It's the

bout the hour of three, When my dar - ling start - ed to
said he'd write to me, But I've not heard from my—
pa's for - sak - en me, And I have no one for to
can my sail - or be, Oh— yes, my lit - tle—
last you'll see of me, For I'm go - ing to end my

leave me,— For to sail up - on the deep . blue sea.
dar - ling,— Who is sail - ing on the deep blue sea.
love me,— But the sail - or on the deep blue sea.
maid - en,— He is drown - ded in the deep blue sea.
trou - bles,— By— drown - ing in the deep blue sea.

Sally Goodin

M: A; F: D or E
CD 2-Track 54

Traditional

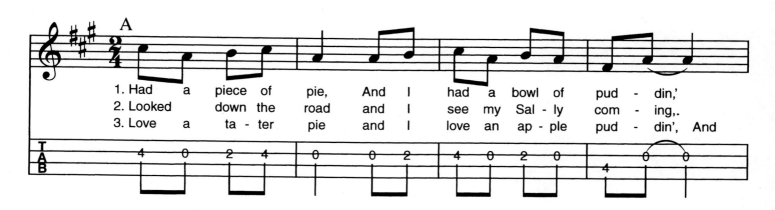

1. Had a piece of pie, And I had a bowl of pud - din,'
2. Looked down the road and I see my Sal - ly com - ing,.
3. Love a ta - ter pie and I love an ap - ple pud - din', And

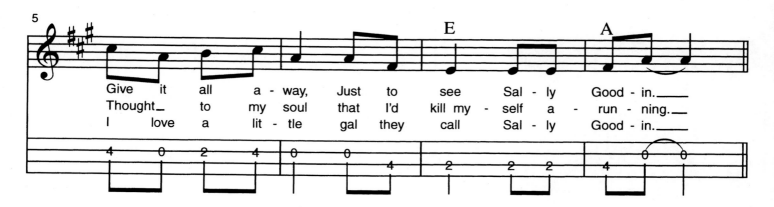

Give it all a - way, Just to see Sal - ly Good - in._____
Thought_ to my soul that I'd kill my - self a - run - ning._
I love a lit - tle gal they call Sal - ly Good - in.____

Part 2 for instrumental

G
4. I dropped the tater pie and I left the apple puddin',
                             D   **G**
Went across the mountain to see my Sally Goodin.

5. Sally is my dooxy and Sally is my daisy,
When Sally says she hates me I think I'm going crazy.

6. Little dog'll bark and the big dog'll bite you,
Little gal'll court you and a big gal'll fight you.

7. Raining and a' pouring and the creek's running muddy,
I'm so drunk I can't stand steady.

8. I'm goin up the mountain and marry little Sally,
Raise corn on the hillside and the devil in the valley.

Shady Grove

Bluegrass style

M: C; F: F or G
CD 2-Track 55

Cho: Sha - dy   Grove,   my   lit - tle   miss,   Sha - dy   Grove,   my   dar - ling,
1. If   you   see   my   lit - tle   miss,   If   you   see   my   dar - ling,
2. Eve - ry   time I   walk this___ road,   Al - ways   dark   and   cloud - y,

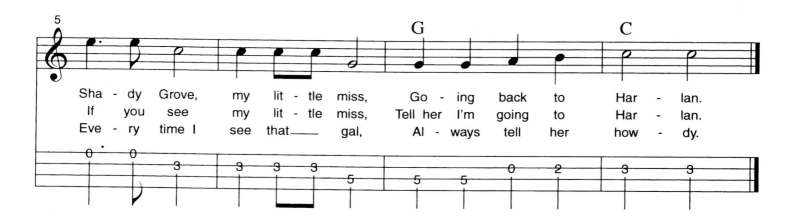

Sha - dy   Grove,   my   lit - tle   miss,   Go - ing   back   to   Har - lan.
If   you   see   my   lit - tle   miss,   Tell her   I'm   going   to   Har - lan.
Eve - ry   time I   see   that___ gal,   Al - ways   tell   her   how - dy.

C

4. Fly around, my pretty little dove,
Fly around, my daisy,
Fly around, my pretty little love,
G   **C**
Bound to drive me crazy.

5. Wish I was in Shady Grove,
Sitting in a rocking chair,
And if those blues would bother me,
I'd rock away from there.

6. All I want is a pig in a pen,
Corn to feed him on,
Pretty little girl to stay at home,
Feed him when I'm gone.

7. Wish I had a banjo string,
Made of golden twine,
Every tune I'd play on it,
I wish that girl was mine.

8. Wish I had a needle and thread,
Fine as I could sew,
I'd sew that pretty girl to my side,
And down the road I'd go.

9. Some come here to fiddle and dance,
Some come here to tarry,
Some here to fiddle and dance,
I come here to marry.

224   *B. Monroe, Garcia & Grisman, Ken. Colonels, Hot Rize, D. Watson, Grisman, Garcia, Rice*

Shady Grove

Old Time style

M: *Em modal;* **F:** *Am or Bm modal*
CD 2-Track 56

Traditional

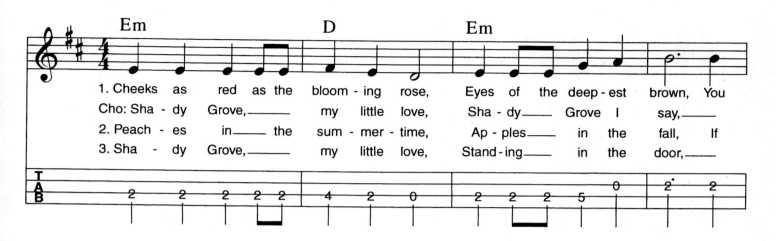

1. Cheeks as red as the bloom - ing rose, Eyes of the deep - est brown, You
Cho: Sha - dy Grove,_____ my little love, Sha - dy_____ Grove I say,_____
2. Peach - es in_____ the sum - mer - time, Ap - ples_____ in the fall, If
3. Sha - dy Grove,_____ my little love, Stand - ing_____ in the door,_____

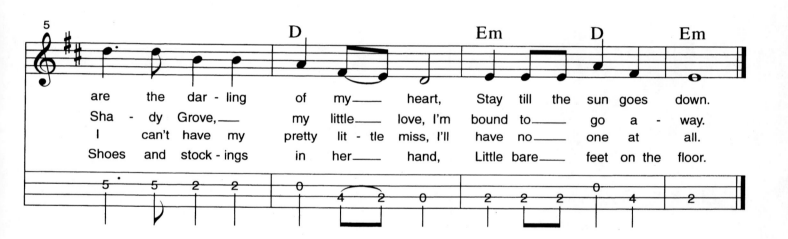

are the dar - ling of my_____ heart, Stay till the sun goes down.
Sha - dy Grove,_____ my little_____ love, I'm bound to_____ go a - way.
I can't have my pretty lit - tle miss, I'll have no_____ one at all.
Shoes and stock - ings in her_____ hand, Little bare_____ feet on the floor.

Shall We Gather at the River

M: C; F: F or G
CD 2-Track 57

Robert Lowry

1. Shall we gath-er at the riv-er, Where bright an-gel feet have trod,____
2. On the bos-om of the riv-er, Wash-ing up its sil-ver spray,____

With its crys-tal tide for-ev-er, Flow-ing by the____throne of____ God?
We will talk and wor-ship ev-er, All the hap-py____gold-en____ day.____

Cho: Yes, we'll gath-er at the riv-er, The beau-ti-ful, the beau-ti-ful____ riv-er;

Gath-er with the saints____ at the riv-er, That flows by the throne of____ God.

C
3. 'Ere we reach the shining river,
G7
Lay we every burden down;
C
Grace our spirits will deliver,
       G7   C
And provide a robe and crown.

4. At the smiling of the river,
Mirror of the Savior's face,
Saints, whom death will never sever,
Lift their songs of saving grace.

5. Soon we'll reach the shining river,
Soon our pilgrimage will cease;
Soon our happy hearts will quiver,
With the melody of peace.

A Short Life of Trouble

M: C; F: F or G
CD 2-Track 58

Traditional

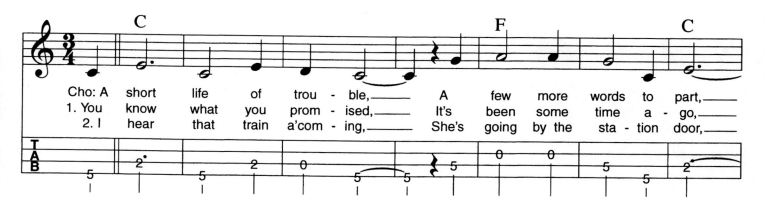

Cho: A short life of trou - ble,_____ A few more words to part,_____
1. You know what you prom - ised,_____ It's been some time a - go,_____
2. I hear that train a'com - ing,_____ She's going by the sta - tion door,_____

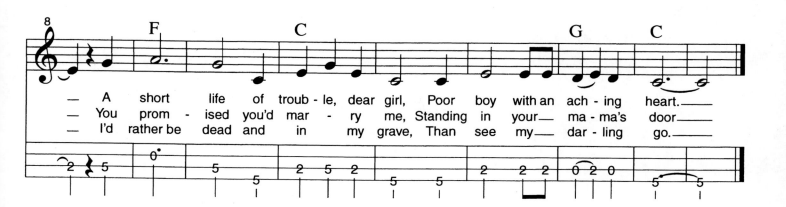

— A short life of troub - le, dear girl, Poor boy with an ach - ing heart._____
— You prom - ised you'd mar - ry me, Standing in your__ ma - ma's door_____
— I'd rather be dead and in my grave, Than see my__ dar - ling go._____

C
3. Now you've broken your promise,
    F   **C**
Go marry whom you may,
F   **C**
For this old world's so big and so wide,
      G   **C**
I'll ramble back some day.

4. Now you've gone and left me,
I don't know what I'll do,
I'd give the world and half of my life,
Just to be married to you.

5. I see my coffin coming,
My shroud and all is on,
To take me to some lonesome graveyard,
And let the grave be my home.

6. And when my days have ended,
Will you come sow some flowers,
To show to the people 'round you,
The heart you've broken lies there.

D. Watson, R. Stanley, Grayson & Whitter, Burnett & Rutherford, Blue Sky Boys, E. Taylor, Mac Wiseman 227

Shortenin' Bread

M: D; F: G or A
CD 2-Track 59

Traditional

Silver Threads Among the Gold

M: G; F: C or D
CD 2-Track 60

Rexford & Danks, 1901

G   D7   G

3. Love can never more grow old,

D7   G

Locks may lose their brown and gold,

G   D7   G

Cheeks may fade and hollow grow,

D7   G

But the hearts that love will know.

D7   G

Never, never, winter's frost and chill,

D   A7   D7

Summer warmth is in them still;

G   D7   G

Never winter's frost and chill,

D7   G

Summer warmth is in them still.

4. Love is always young and fair,
What to us is silver hair?
Faded cheeks or steps grown slow,
To the heart that beats below?
Since I kissed you, mine alone, alone,
You have never older grown;
Since I kissed you, mine alone,
You have never older grown.

Sitting on Top of the World

M: G; F: C or D
CD 2-Track 61

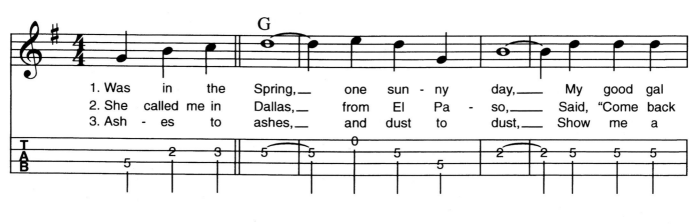

1. Was in the Spring, one sun-ny day, My good gal
2. She called me in Dallas, from El Pa-so, Said, "Come back
3. Ash-es to ashes, and dust to dust, Show me a

left me, she went a-way. Cho: And now she's gone, and I don't
Dad-dy, Lord I need you so."
wom-an, any man can trust.

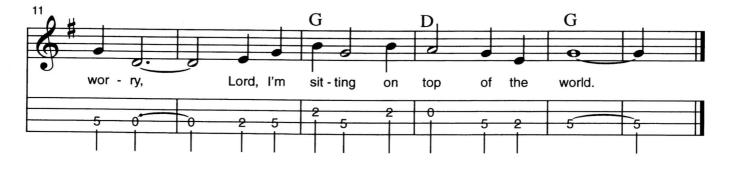

wor-ry, Lord, I'm sit-ting on top of the world.

G
4. Mississippi River, long, deep and wide,
       C   **G**
The woman I'm loving's, on the other side.
Chorus: But now she's gone, and I don't worry,
              D   **G**
Lord, I'm sitting on top of the world.

5. You don't like my peaches, don't you shake my tree,
Get out of my orchard, let my peaches be. (Chorus)

6. Don't you come here running, poking out your hand,
I'll get me a woman, like you got your man. (Chorus)

B. Monroe, R. Stanley, D. Watson, F. Wakefield, D. Bruce & J. Nunally, Nitty Gritty Dirt Band

Softly and Tenderly

M: G; F: C or D
CD 2-Track 62

W.L. Thompson

1. Soft - ly and ten - der - ly Je - sus is call - ing, Call - ing for you and for me.____
2. Why should we tar - ry when Je - sus is plead - ing, Plead - ing for you and for me?____
3. Time is now fleet - ing, the mo - ments are pass - ing, Pass - ing from you and from me;____
4. O, for the won - der - ful love He has prom - ised, Prom - ised for you and for me!____

See, on the por - tals He's wait - ing and watch - ing, Watch - ing for you and for me. Cho: Come
Why should we lin - ger and heed not His mer - cies, Mer - cies for you and for me?
Sha - dows are gath - er - ing, death - beds are com - ing, Com - ing for you and for me.
Though we have sinned, He has mer - cy and par - don, Par - don for you and for me.

home,____ Come home,____ You who are wear - y come home____

Ear - nest - ly, ten - der - ly Je - sus is call - ing, Call - ing "O sin - ner come home!"____

Stanley Bros.   231

Somebody Touched Me

M: G; F: C or D
CD 2-Track 63

Traditional

G

2. While I was preaching, somebody touched me,
C   G
While I was preaching, somebody touched me,
While I was preaching, somebody touched me,
                                 D   G
It must have been the hand of our Lord.

3. While I was singing, somebody touched me, etc.

B. Monroe, Stanley Bros., R. Stanley, Dillards, D. Watson

Standing in the Need of Prayer

M: G; F: C or D
CD 2-Track 64

Traditional

Sugar Hill

M: G; F: C or D
CD 2-Track 65

Traditional

Sweet By and By

M: G; F: C or D
CD 2-Track 66

Bennett & Webster

Sweet Sunny South

M: G; F: C or D
CD 2-Track 67

W.L. Bloomfield, 1853

1. Take me back to the place where I first saw the light,____ To the sweet sun - ny
2. I____ think with re - gret of the dear ones I left,____ Of the warm hearts that
3. Take me back to the place where the orange trees__ grow,____ To my cot in the

south take me home,____ Where the mock - ing - birds sing me to
shel - tered me then,____ Of____ wife and of dear ones of
ev - er - green shade,____ Where the flowers from the riv - er's green

sleep ev - ery night,____ Oh, why was I tempt - ed to roam?____
whom I'm be - reft,____ I long for the old place a - gain.____
mar - gins may blow,____ They are sweet on the banks where we played.____

G   D7
4. The path to our cottage they say has grown green,
        G   C
And the place is quite lonely around,
 G   C   G   D7
I know that the smiles and the forms I have seen,
      G   D7   G
Now lie deep in the soft mossy ground.

5. Take me back, let me see what is left that I know,
Could it be that the old house is gone?
The dear friends of my childhood indeed must be few,
And I must lament all alone.

6. But yet I'll return to the place of my birth,
Where my children have played 'round the door,
Where they pulled the white blossoms that gar-
         nished the earth,
Which will echo their footsteps no more.

7. Take me back to the place where my little ones
         sleep,
Where poor massa lies buried close by,
O'er the graves of my loved ones, I long to weep,
And among them to rest when I die.

236   *C. Poole, Grisman, Garcia, Rice, K. Hall, Bluegrass Album Band, T. O'Brien*

Swing Low, Sweet Chariot

M: G; F: C or D
CD 2-Track 68

Traditional

B. Monroe, Stanley Bros., R. Allen & F. Wakefield, Louvin Bros.   237

Take This Hammer

M: G; F: C or D
CD 2-Track 69

Traditional

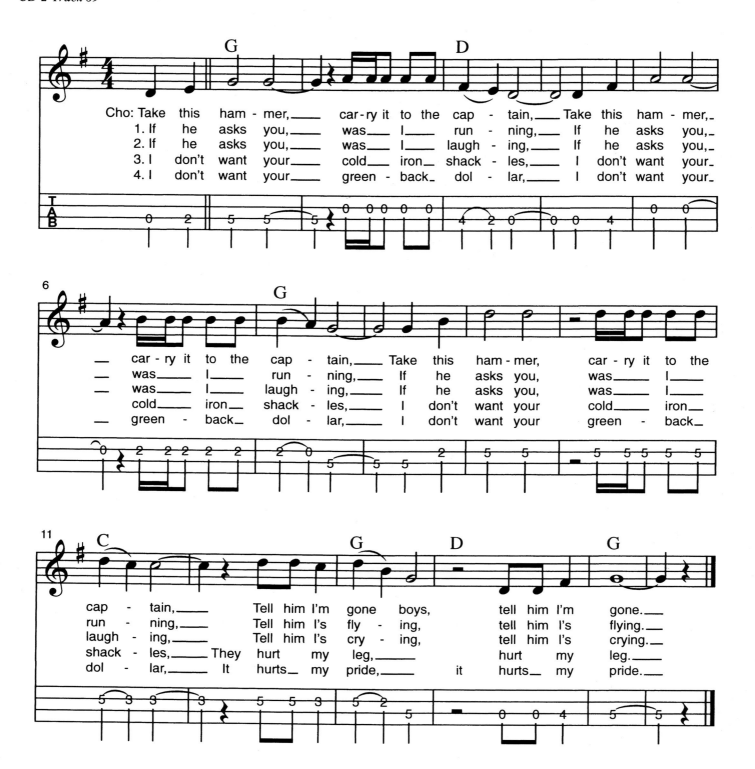

Flatt & Scruggs, C. White, J.D. Crowe, Country Gentlemen, Osborne Bros.

Talk About Sufferin'

M: Em; F: Am or Bm
CD 2-Track 70

Traditional

1. Talk a-bout suf-fer-in' here be-low___ and let's keep a' fol-low-in' Je-sus,
2. Talk a-bout suf-fer-in' here be-low___ and let's keep a' lov-in'___ Je-sus.

Talk a-bout suf-fer-in' here be-low___ and let's keep a' fol-low-in' Je-sus,
Talk a-bout suf-fer-in' here be-low___ and let's keep a' fol-low-in' Je-sus.

The___ Gos-pel train is com-ing, Now don't you want to go?
Oh,___ can't you hear it, fath-ers, And don't you want to go?

And___ leave this world of sor-row and trou-bles here___ be-low?
And___ leave this world of tri-als and trou-bles here___ be-low?

Oh, can't you hear it mothers, sisters, etc.

There's More Pretty Girls Than One

M: C; F: F or G

CD 2-Track 71

Traditional

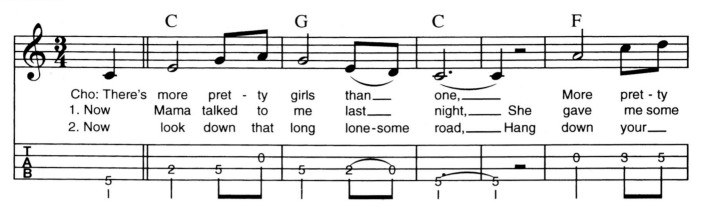

Cho: There's more pret - ty girls than____ one,_____ More pret - ty
1. Now Mama talked to me last____ night,____ She gave me some
2. Now look down that long lone-some road,____ Hang down your____

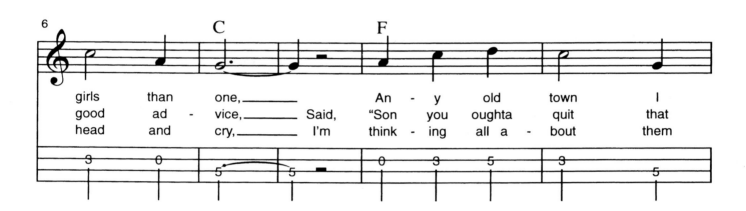

girls than one,_____ An - y old town I
good ad - vice,_____ Said, "Son you oughta quit that
head and cry,_____ I'm think - ing all a - bout them

ram - ble a - round,__ There's more pret - ty girls than__ one.____
old ram - bling 'round,__ And marry you a sweet lov - ing wife."____
pretty lit - tle girls,__ And hoping that__ I'll nev - er die.____

"They Gotta Quit Kickin' My Dawg Aroun'" dates from 1912.

They Gotta Quit Kickin' My Dawg Aroun'

M: G; F: C or D
CD 2-Track 72

Oungst &
Perkins,1912

1. Once me and Lem Briggs and old Bill Brown, Took a load of corn to town.
we— passed by Sam John - son's store, A passel of yapes came out the door.

Old Jim Dawg, that orn - ery cuss, He just nat - ur' - ly foll - owed us. As—
Lem's dog stopped to smell a box, They threw at him— a bunch of rocks.—

Cho: Ev - ery time I go to town, The boys keep kick - in' my dawg a - roun'.

Makes no differ - ence if he is a hound, You got - ta quit kick - in' my dawg a - roun'.

```
     G              C
2. They tied a tin can to his tail,
D                  G
Drove him past the county jail.
                   C
That plum natur'ly made me sore,
D                  G
Lem, he cussed and Bill he swore.
G                        C
Me and Lem Briggs and old Bill Brown,
D          G
Lost no time in jumping down.
                         C
We whipped those guys upon the ground,
    D                 G
For kickin' that old hound dog aroun'.
```

3. Well, they say that a dog can't hold no grudge,
Once when I got too much budge,
Those town ducks tried to do me up,
But, they didn't count on old Lem's pup.
He saw his duty there and then,
He lit into those gentlemen,
He sure messed up the courthouse square,
With rags and meat and hunks of hair.

This Little Light of Mine

This Train

M: G; F: C or D
CD 2-Track 74

Traditional

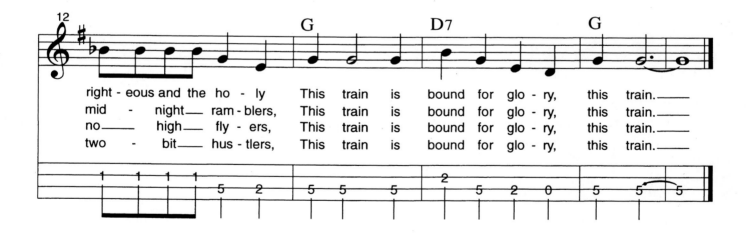

This World is Not My Home

M: G; F: C or D
CD 2-Track 75

Traditional

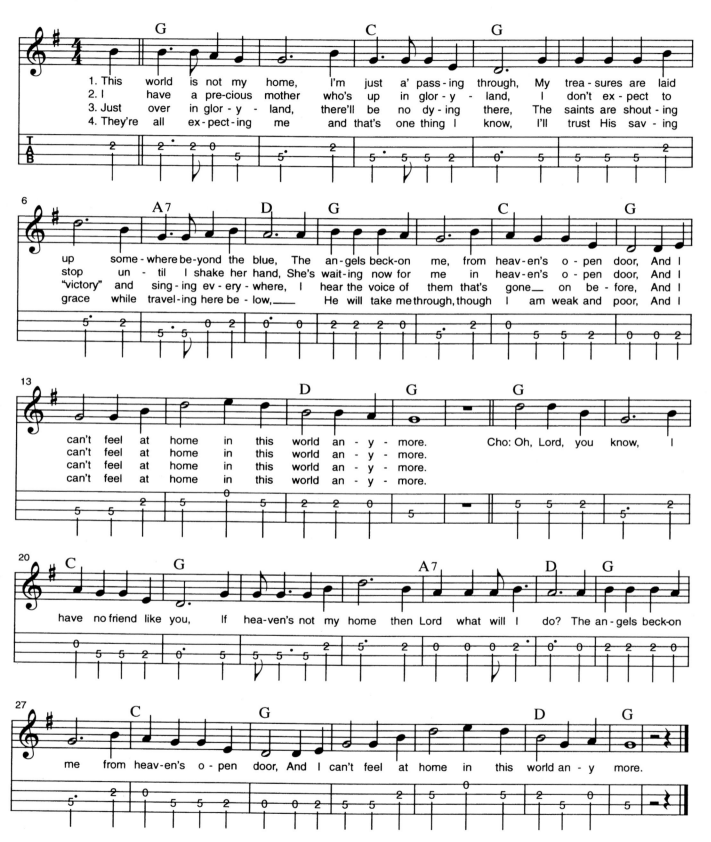

Monroe Bros., B. Monroe, Stanley Bros., Jimmy Martin, Blue Highway, NLCR

Train, Train, Train

M: G; F: C or D
CD 2-Track 76

by Dix Bruce

Cho: My ba - by's leav - ing on the train, train, train, She's gon - na run a - way and
1. She's pack - ing up her lit - tle pink suit - case, She's got her tick - ets and her
2. She asked po - lite - ly for me not to call, Not in the Sum - mer, Win - ter,
3. I guess I could have been a better man, Could have lis - tened to and

change her name, My life is nev - er gon - na be the same,
train's at 8:00, Gon - na dis - ap - pear and leave no trace,
Spring or Fall, I think she does - n't want to see me at all,
held her hand, But then a - gain a man is just a man,

My ba - by's leav - ing on the train,

train, She said she's leav - ing on the train.

The Train That Carried My Girl From Town

M: D ; F: G or A
CD 2-Track 77

Traditional

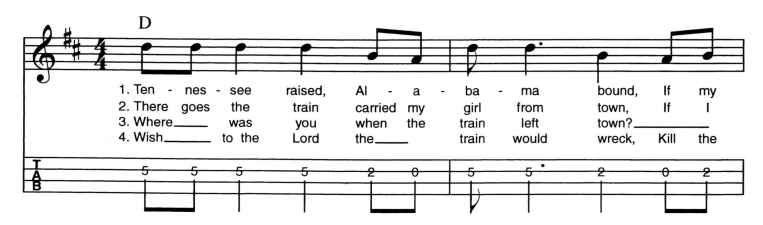

1. Ten - nes - see raised, Al - a - ba - ma bound, If my
2. There goes the train carried my girl from town, If I
3. Where____ was you when the train left town?____
4. Wish____ to the Lord the____ train would wreck, Kill the

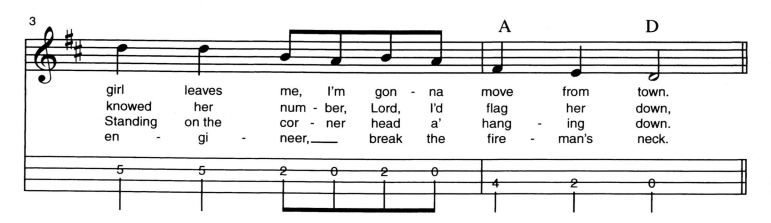

girl leaves me, I'm gon - na move from town.
knowed her num - ber, Lord, I'd flag her down,
Standing on the cor - ner head a' hang - ing down.
en - gi - neer,____ break the fire - man's neck.

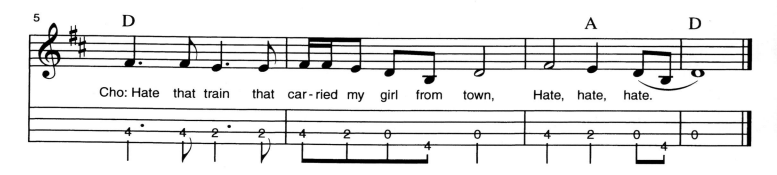

Cho: Hate that train that car - ried my girl from town, Hate, hate, hate.

D

5. Hello central, give me 6-0-9,
             A   **D**
Just wanna talk to that brown of mine.
Cho: Hate that train that carried my girl from town,
    A **D**
Hate, hate, hate. (Repeat chorus after each verse)

6. Rations on the table, coffee's getting cold,
Some old rounder stole my jelly roll.

7. If I had a gun I'd let the hammer down,
Lord, I'd shoot that rounder took my girl from town.

8. There goes my girl, somebody call her back,
She put her hands in my money sack.

9. Ashes to ashes and dust to dust,
Show me a woman a man can trust.

The Unclouded Day

M: G ; F: C or D
CD 2-Track 78

J.K. Alwood, 1890

Wabash Cannonball

M: G; F: C or D
CD 2-Track 79

Traditional

3. Our eastern states are dandy, so the people always say,
    D   **G**
From New York to St. Louis, and Chicago by the way,
                                  C
From the hills of Minnesota, where the rippling waters fall,
    D   **G**
No changes can be taken, on the Wabash Cannonball.

4. Here's to Daddy Claxton, may his name forever stand,
And always be remembered in the courts thoughout the land,
His earthly race is over and the curtains 'round him fall,
We'll carry him home to victory on the Wabash Cannonball.

5. I have rode the I.C. Limited, also the Royal Blue,
Across the eastern countries on mail car number two,
I have rode those highball trains from coast to coast that's all,
But I have found no equal to the Wabash Cannonball.

Carter Fam., R. Acuff, Flatt & Scruggs, B. Monroe, Mac Wiseman, Louvin Bros., Osborne Bros., Claire Lynch,
250 *Nitty Gritty Dirt Band*

John Reischman cut his bluegrass teeth in The Good Ole Persons in the 1970s. He later played with The Tony Rice Unit and currently fronts his own band, John Reischman and the Jaybirds. He's shown here in 1990 recording session for my BackUP TRAX: Old Time & Fiddle Tunes, Vol. 2.

Lorraine Duisit performed a unique mix of old time and original music with the eclectic acoustic band Trapezoid. I photographed her playing her mandolin in 1984.

Walk in Jerusalem Just Like John

M: F; F: Bb or C
CD 2-Track 80

Traditional

1. Oh John, oh John, now what did you say?— Walk in Je-ru-sa-lem just like John, That I'll be there at the crown-ing day,— Walk in Je-ru-sa-lem just like John. Cho: I want to be read-y, I want— to be read-y, I want— to be read-y, Lord To walk in Je-ru-sa-lem just like John.

2. Oh, some come crippled and some come— lame,— Walk in Je-ru-sa-lem just like John, Gonna meet you walking in— Je-sus' name,— Walk in Je-ru-sa-lem just like John.

3. Oh, John said the city was just four— square,— Walk in Je-ru-sa-lem just like John, And he de-clared he'd— meet me there,— Walk in Je-ru-sa-lem just like John.

```
              F
4. When Peter was preaching at the Pentacost,
                    C        F
Walk in Jerusalem just like John,
He was endowed with the Holy Ghost,
                    C        F
Walk in Jerusalem just like John.
F                      Bb            F
Cho: I want to be ready, I want to be ready,
                           Dm
I want to be ready, Lord
   F              C        F
To walk in Jerusalem just like John.
```

5. If you get there before I do,
Walk in Jerusalem just like John,
Tell all my friends I'm a'coming too,
Walk in Jerusalem just like John.

Walking in My Sleep

M: C; F: F or G
CD 2-Track 81

Traditional

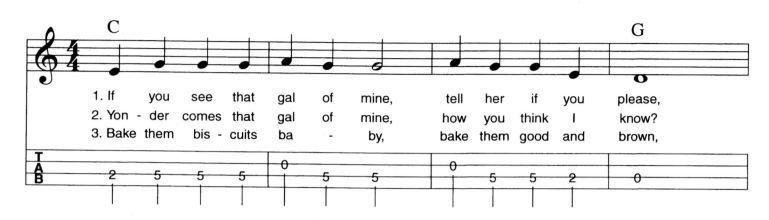

1. If you see that gal of mine, tell her if you please,
2. Yon - der comes that gal of mine, how you think I know?
3. Bake them bis - cuits ba - by, bake them good and brown,

'Fore she goes to make my bread to roll up her dir - ty sleeves.
Tell___ by her a - pron strings___ hang - ing down___ so low.
When you get them bis - cuits, baked I'm Al - a - bam - y bound.

Cho: Walk - ing in my sleep babe, walk - ing in my sleep.

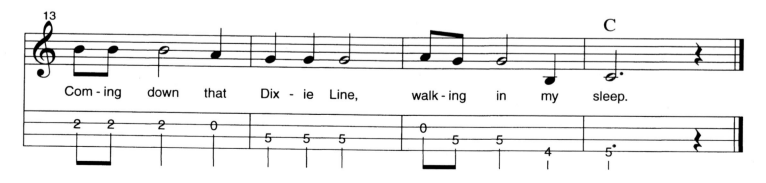

Com - ing down that Dix - ie Line, walk - ing in my sleep.

B. Clifton, H. Dickens & A. Gerrard

The Wayfaring Stranger

M: Dm; F: Gm or Am
CD 2-Track 82

Traditional

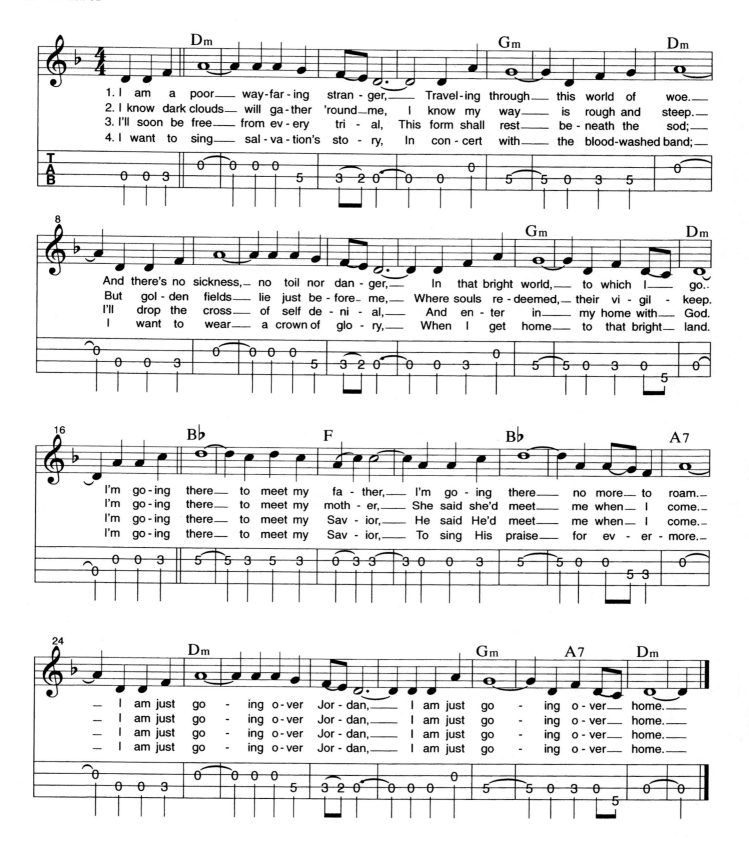

1. I am a poor wayfaring stranger, Traveling through this world of woe. And there's no sickness, no toil nor danger, In that bright world, to which I go. I'm going there to meet my father, I'm going there no more to roam. I am just going over Jordan, I am just going over home.

2. I know dark clouds will gather 'round me, I know my way is rough and steep. But golden fields lie just before me, Where souls redeemed, their vigil keep. I'm going there to meet my mother, She said she'd meet me when I come. I am just going over Jordan, I am just going over home.

3. I'll soon be free from every trial, This form shall rest beneath the sod; I'll drop the cross of self denial, And enter in my home with God. I'm going there to meet my Savior, He said He'd meet me when I come. I am just going over Jordan, I am just going over home.

4. I want to sing salvation's story, In concert with the blood-washed band; I want to wear a crown of glory, When I get home to that bright land. I'm going there to meet my Savior, To sing His praise for evermore. I am just going over Jordan, I am just going over home.

B. Monroe, D. Watson, T. Rice, E.L. Harris, Bluegrass Alliance, D. Parton, R. Ickes   255

Were You There When They Crucified My Lord?

M: G; F: C or D

CD 2-Track 83, medley pt. 1

Traditional

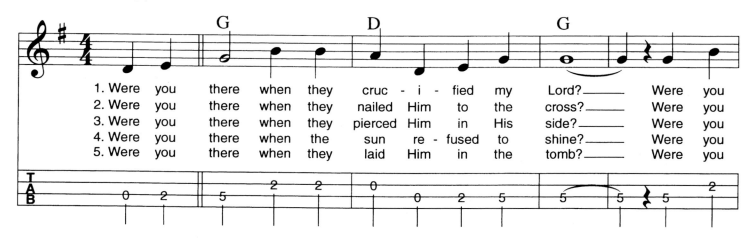

1. Were you there when they cruc - i - fied my Lord?_____ Were you
2. Were you there when they nailed Him to the cross?_____ Were you
3. Were you there when they pierced Him in His side?_____ Were you
4. Were you there when the sun re - fused to shine?_____ Were you
5. Were you there when they laid Him in the tomb?_____ Were you

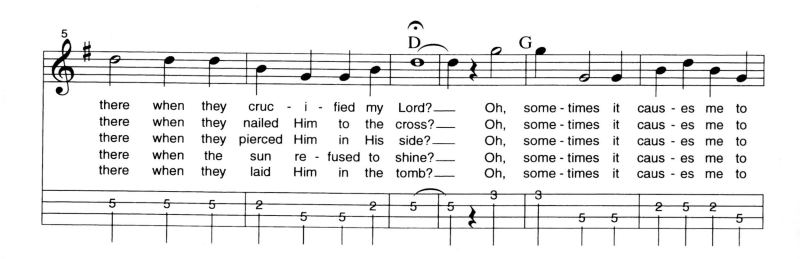

there when they cruc - i - fied my Lord?____ Oh, some - times it caus - es me to
there when they nailed Him to the cross?____ Oh, some - times it caus - es me to
there when they pierced Him in His side?____ Oh, some - times it caus - es me to
there when the sun re - fused to shine?____ Oh, some - times it caus - es me to
there when they laid Him in the tomb?____ Oh, some - times it caus - es me to

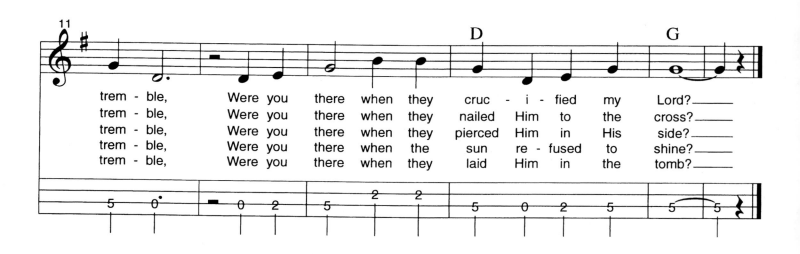

trem - ble, Were you there when they cruc - i - fied my Lord?_____
trem - ble, Were you there when they nailed Him to the cross?_____
trem - ble, Were you there when they pierced Him in His side?_____
trem - ble, Were you there when the sun re - fused to shine?_____
trem - ble, Were you there when they laid Him in the tomb?_____

What a Friend We Have in Jesus

M: G; F: C or D
CD 2-Track 83, medley pt. 2

Converse & Scriven, ca. 1868

Stanley Bros., Osborne Bros., D. Bruce, D. Parton, M. Wiseman

When I Die

M: G; F: C or D
CD 2-Track 84

Dix Bruce

3. Will I roam through the fields down the mountains, cross the land?
    G   C   G
Wade the rivers down to the ocean sand?
                  D
C G   C   G
Will I touch trusted friends in a whisper of the wind?
               D   G
When I die, when I die.

4. Can I be with my family, can I visit with my friends?
As they spend the short time they were lent?
Will they quietly know that I really did not go?
When I die, when I die.

5. Will the ones that I love someday join me up above?
Will we laugh, will we sing, will we cry?
Together will we be through all eternity?
When I die, when I die.

6. Will I grow in the hearts of those I have known?
Will they think of me fondly now and then?
Will I live on and on when my life on earth is done?
When I die, when I die.

When I Lay My Burden Down

M: *G;* **F:** *C or D*
CD 2-Track 85

Traditional

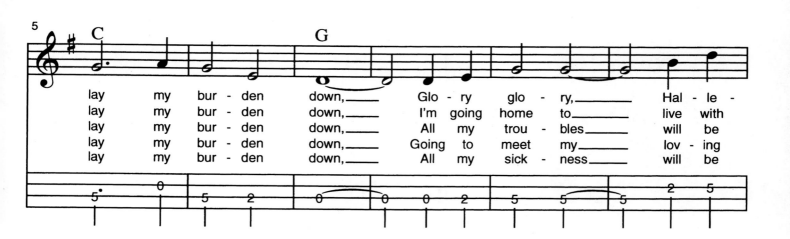

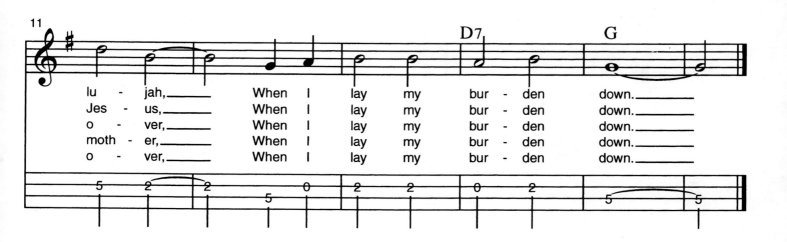

When My Race is Run

M: G ; F: C or D
CD 2-Track 86

Dix Bruce

1. When my race is run, when I'm ly-ing still, Don't you come a-round,
2. When my sun sinks down, be-low shad-owed hills, When the world grows dark

when they read my will. Don't send me flowers and keep from my grave,
and the trees grow still. Then say a prayer, no one will hear,

— It would break your heart to see me this way. Cho: I've known the pain
— To one who's gone, who loves you dear.

that some-day you'll feel, That emp-ti-ness in-side and tears so real. Then think of

me, a life un-ful-filled, A-cross the years, I'll love you still.

Vern Williams, California's master of traditional bluegrass, jamming in the mid-1970s.

Photo by Dix Bruce

When the Roll is Called Up Yonder

M: G; F: C or D
CD 2-Track 87, medley pt. 1

J.M. Black, 1893

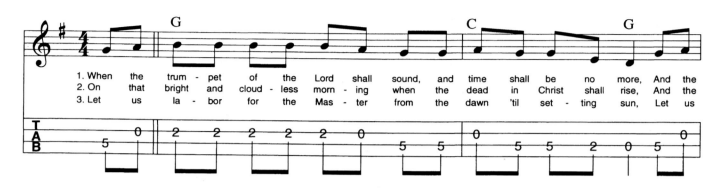

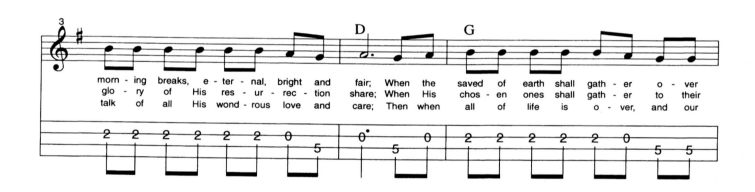

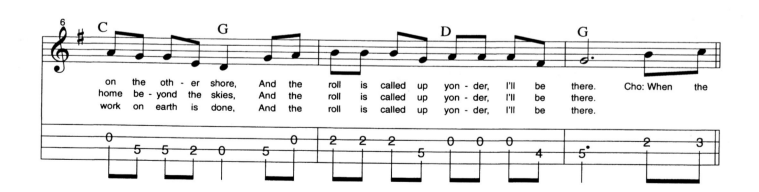

roll,——— is called up yon - der, When the roll,——— is called up

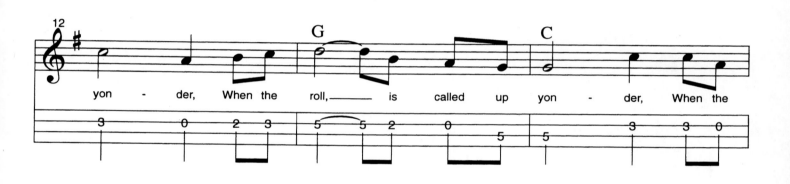

yon - der, When the roll,——— is called up yon - der, When the

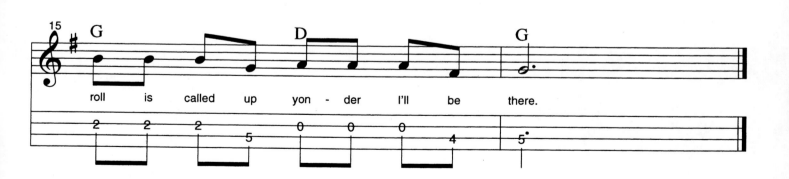

roll is called up yon - der I'll be there.

When the Saints Go Marching In

M: G; F: C or D
CD 2-Track 87, medley pt. 2

Traditional

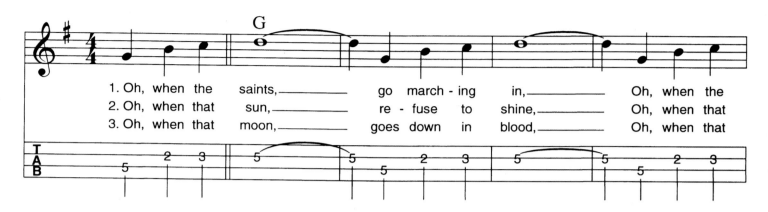

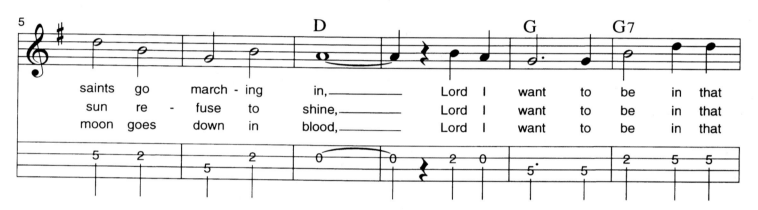

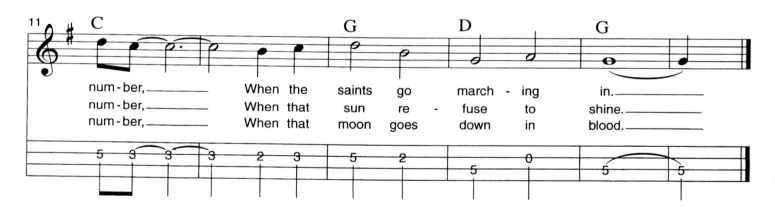

G

4. Oh, when they crown Him King of kings,

               D

Oh, when they crown Him King of kings,

  G   G7   C

Lord I want to be in that number,

        G   D   G

When they crown Him King of kings.

5. Oh, when they gather 'round the throne, (etc.)

6. Oh, while the happy ages roll, (etc.)

The author, right, trading licks with Frank Wakefield in 1980.

In the late 1970s I played in Frank Wakefield's band, The Good Old Boys. The three singers are, left to right, Tom Stern, Frank, and me.

When the Work's All Done This Fall

M: C; F: F or G
CD 2-Track 88

Traditional

1. A group of jol-ly cow-boys dis-cuss-ing plans at ease, Says one, "I'll tell you some-thing, boys, if you will lis-ten please, I am an old cow punch-er al-though I'm dressed in rags, I used to be a tough one and go on great big jags."

2. "When I left my hap-py home, boys,— Moth-er for me cried, She begged me not to leave her,— for me she would have died, Moth-er's heart is bro-ken for a wand-ering boy, that's all, With God's help I'll see her when the work's all done this fall."

D. Watson, Goose Island Ramblers, B. Clifton, N. Blake, M. Wiseman

```
        C                           F
3. "Well, after the roundup's over, and the shipping's done,
   G                                         C
I'm going right home boys, before my money's gone,
                                    F
I have changed my ways, boys, no more will the temptors call,
   G                                         C
I want to see my mother, when the work's all done this fall."
```

4. That very night the cowboy, went out to stand his guard,
The night was dark and cloudy, and storming very hard,
The cattle all got freightened, and rushed in wild stampede,
The cowboy tried to head them, while riding at full speed.

5. While riding in the darkness, so wildly did he shout,
He tried his best to turn them, and head the herd about,
His saddle pony stumbled, and on the boy did fall,
He won't see his mother, when the work's all done this fall.

6. His body was so mangled, the boys all thought him dead,
They picked him up so gently, and laid him on the bed,
He opened wide his blue eyes, and looking all around
He motioned for his comrades, to sit near him on the ground.

7. "Well, send my mother my wages, the wages that I've earned,
I won't live to see her, the last steer I have turned,
I'm going to a new range, I've heard the Master's call,
And I won't see my mother, when the work's all done this fall."

8. "Hey George, you take my pistol, Jack you take my bed,
Jim you take my saddle, after I am dead,
Boys, speak of me kindly, when you look upon them all,
For I won't see my mother, when the work's all done this fall."

9. Well, Charlie was buried at daybreak, no tombstone at his head,
Nothing but a little board, and this is what it said,
"Charlie died at daybreak, and he died from the fall,
He won't see his mother, when the work's all done this fall."

When You And I Were Young Maggie

M: F ; F: Bb or C
CD 2-Track 89

Johnson &
Butterfield, ca. 1866

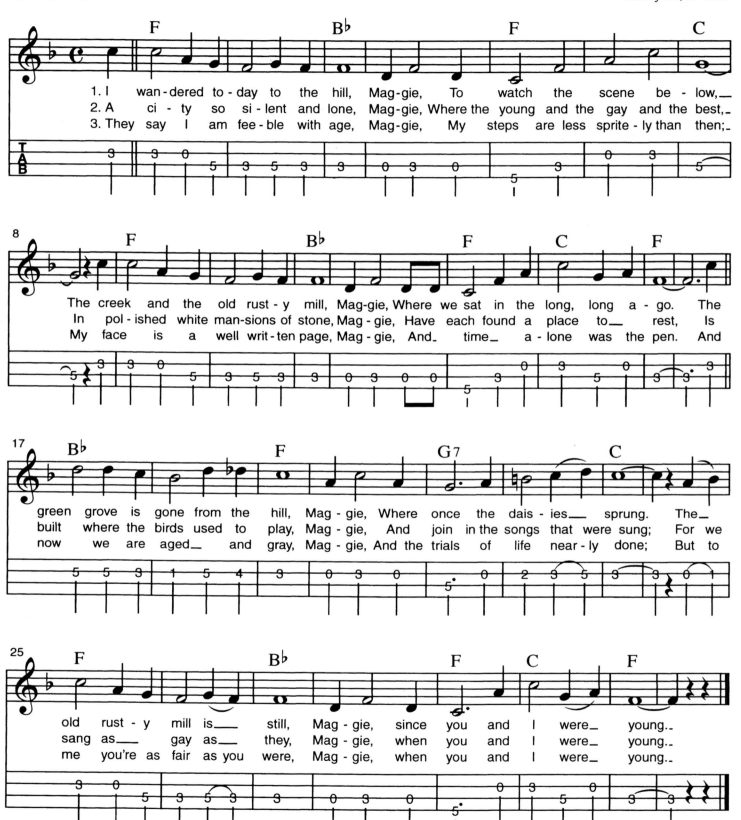

Stanley Bros., Reno & Smiley, Fiddlin' John Carson, Mac Wiseman, D. Grisman, B. Waller

Where the Soul Never Dies

M: E; F: A or B
CD 2-Track 90

Wm. Golden

Tablature on page following.

Where the Soul Never Dies

Whitehouse Blues

M: G; F: C or D
CD 2-Track 91, medley pt. 1

Traditional

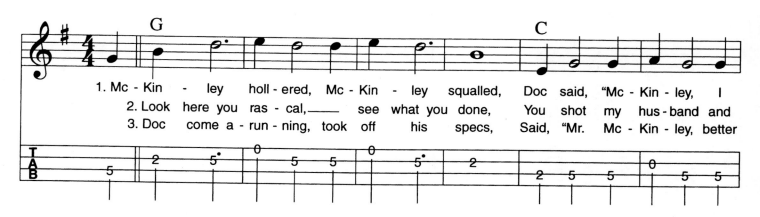

1. Mc - Kin - ley holl - ered, Mc - Kin - ley squalled, Doc said, "Mc - Kin - ley, I
2. Look here you ras - cal,____ see what you done, You shot my hus - band and
3. Doc come a - run - ning, took off his specs, Said, "Mr. Mc - Kin - ley, better

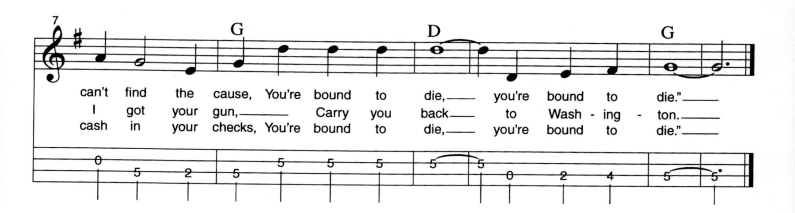

can't find the cause, You're bound to die,____ you're bound to die."____
I got your gun,____ Carry you back____ to Wash - ing - ton.____
cash in your checks, You're bound to die,____ you're bound to die."____

G
4. Roosevelt's in the White House, doing his best,
C   **G**
McKinley's in the graveyard taking his rest,
           D   **G**
He's long gone, long gone.

5. Roosevelt's in the White House, drinking out
    of a silver cup,
McKinley's in the graveyard, he's never gonna wake up,
He's long gone, long gone.

6. Hush up little children, now don't you fret,
You're bound to draw a pension from your papa's death,
He's long gone, long gone.

7. Jumped on a horse, he threw down his reins,
He said to the horse, "You gotta outrun the train,
From Buffalo to Washington."

8. Nixon's in the Whitehouse, making a mess,
Johnson's in the graveyard, taking his rest,
He's long gone, long gone.

B. Monroe, D. Watson, Greenbriar Boys, Muleskinner, D. McCoury, Dillards, Reno & Harrell   271

Who Broke the Lock?

M: G; F: C or D

CD 2-Track 91, medley pt. 2

Traditional

The Goose Island Ramblers and me in 1999:
left to right: Wendy Whitford, George Gilbertsen, Dix Bruce, Bruce Bollerud

Left to right: Kathy Kallick, Bill Monroe, Julia LaBella, me.
San Francisco, late 1970s.

Who Will Sing for Me?

M: A; F: D or E
CD 2-Track 92

Traditional

Flatt & Scruggs, Stanley Bros., R. Stanley, Scruggs/Watson/Skaggs, Jimmy Martin, E.L. Harris

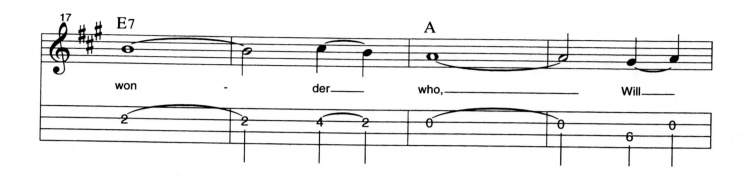

won - der___ who,_____ Will___

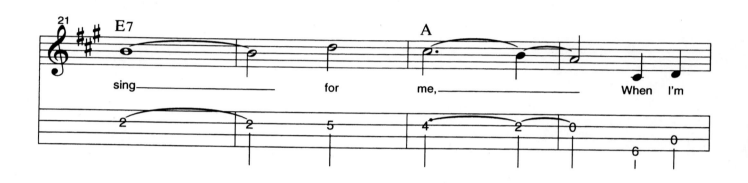

sing_____ for me,_____ When I'm

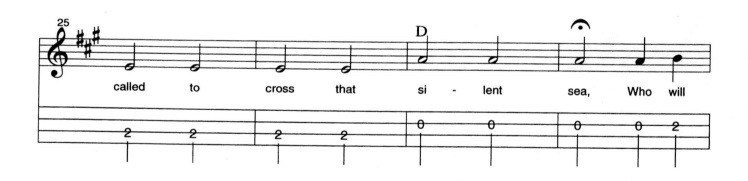

called to cross that si - lent sea, Who will

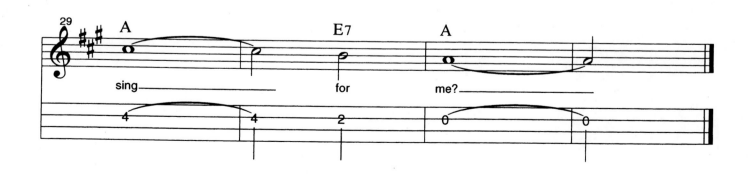

sing_____ for me?_____

Wild Bill Jones

M: G; F: C or D
CD 2-Track 93

Traditional

Wildwood Flower

M: C; F: F or G
CD 2-Track 94

Traditional

Carter Fam., Stanley Bros., Flatt & Scruggs, D. Grisman, C. White, Ken. Colonels, Lilly Bros., D. Bruce & J. Nunally 277

Will the Circle Be Unbroken?

M: G; F: C or D
CD 2-Track 95, medley pt. 1

Traditional

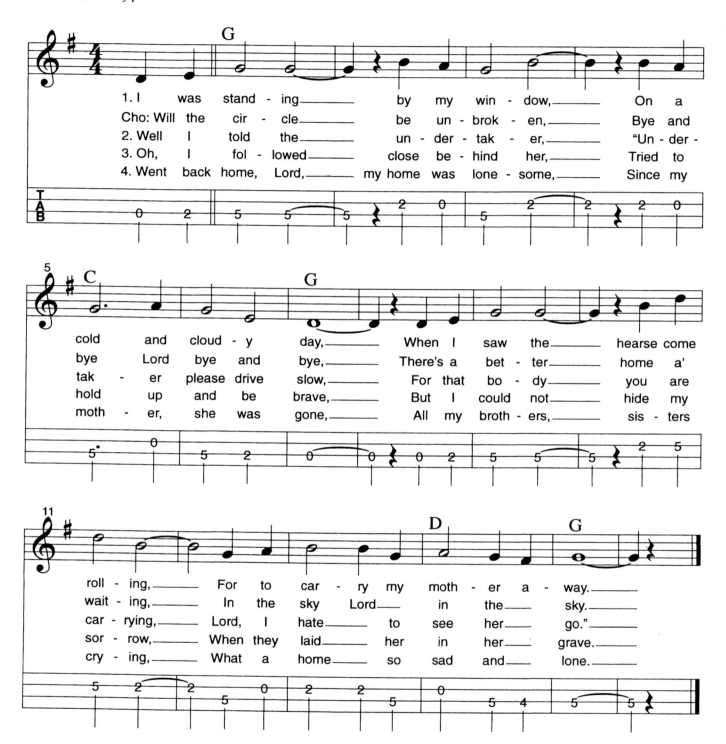

Carter Fam., Monroe Bros., D. Watson, Stanley Bros., Nitty Gritty Dirt Band

Will There Be Any Stars in My Crown?

M: G; F: C or D
CD 2-Track 95, medley pt. 2

Sweney & Hewitt, ca 1897

Willie My Darling

M: G; F: C or D
CD 2-Track 96

Traditional

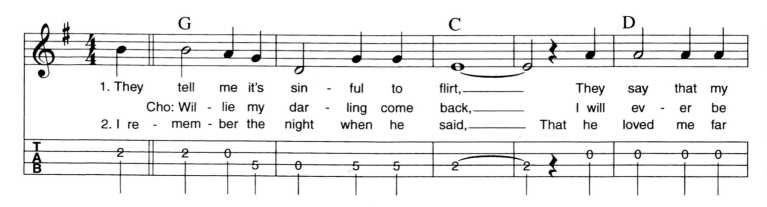

1. They tell me it's sin - ful to flirt,_____ They say that my
Cho: Wil - lie my dar - ling come back,_____ I will ev - er be
2. I re - mem - ber the night when he said,_____ That he loved me far

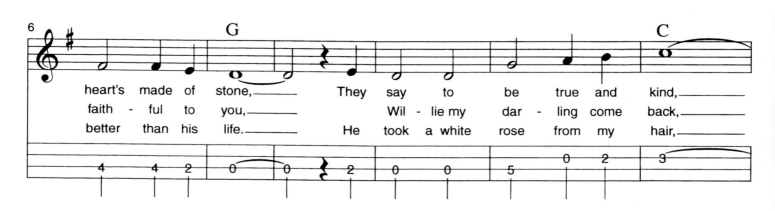

heart's made of stone,_____ They say to be true and kind,_____
faith - ful to you,_____ Wil - lie my dar - ling come back,_____
better than his life._____ He took a white rose from my hair,_____

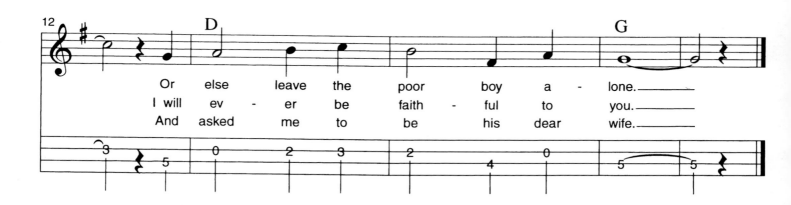

Or else leave the poor boy a - lone._____
I will ev - er be faith - ful to you._____
And asked me to be his dear wife._____

G   C
3. "Well, Willie," I said with a smile,
   D   G
"I'm afraid that I'll have to say no,
                              C
'Cause Papa and Mama aren't willing,"
     D   G
Then he said, "Goodbye, I must go."

4. Next morning poor Willie was found,
He was drowned in the pond by the mill.
In the cold, icy waters so deep,
That flowed from the brink of the hill.

5. His blue eyes forever were closed,
And damp were his curls so fair.
And close to his pale lips he held,
The white rose that he took from my hair.

Worried Man Blues

M: C; F: F or G
CD 2-Track 97, medley pt. 1

Traditional

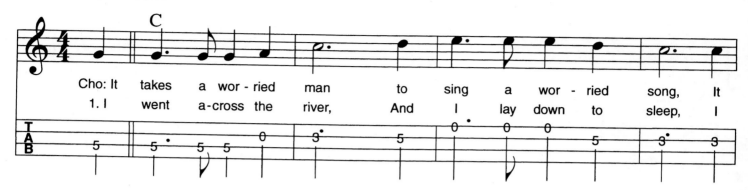

Cho: It takes a wor - ried man to sing a wor - ried song, It
1. I went a-cross the river, And I lay down to sleep, I

takes a wor - ried man to sing a wor - ried song, I'm wor - ried
went a - cross the river, And I lay down to sleep, when I a -

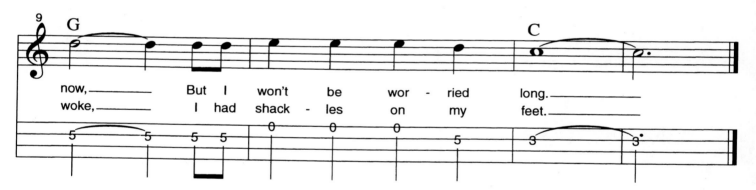

now,_____ But I won't be wor - ried long._____
woke,_____ I had shack - les on my feet._____

C
2. Twenty nine links of chain around my leg,
F   **C**
Twenty nine links of chain around my leg,
          G   **C**
And on each link an initial of my name.

3. I asked the judge, what might be my fine,
I asked the judge, what might be my fine,
Twenty one years on the R.C. Mountain Line.

4. If anyone should ask you, who composed this song
If anyone should ask you, who composed this song,
Tell them 'twas I, and I sing it all day long.

5. I looked down the track, as far as I could see,
I looked down the track, as far as I could see,
A little hand was waving after me.

Carter Fam., Flatt & Scruggs, Stanley Bros., NLCR, Blue Sky Boys, Reno & Harrell, Jim & Jesse, Osborne Bros.,
W. Guthrie **281**

The Wreck of the Old 97

M: C; F: F or G
CD 2-Track 97, medley pt. 2

Traditional

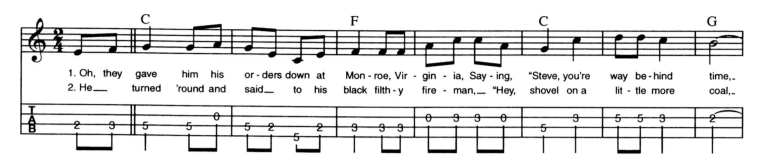

1. Oh, they gave him his or-ders down at Mon-roe, Vir - gin - ia, Say - ing, "Steve, you're way be - hind time,.
2. He__ turned 'round and said__ to his black filth-y fire - man,__ "Hey, shovel on a lit - tle more coal,.

__ This is not Thir-ty - Eight, but it's old Nine-ty - Sev - en, You must put her in - to Spen-cer on time."__
__ And__ when we__ cross that__ white oak__ moun - tain, Just__ watch old Nine - ty - Sev - en roll."__

     C   F
3. It's a mighty rough road from Lynchburg to Danville,
     C   G
And lying on a three mile grade,
      C   F
It was on that grade that he lost his average,
     C   G   C
You see what a jump he made.

4. He was going down the grade making ninety miles an hour,
When his whistle broke into a scream,
He was found in the wreck with his hand on the throttle,
And scalded to death by the steam.

5. Well, a telegram came to Washington City,
And this is how it read:
"The brave engineer that run old Ninety-Seven,
Is lying in old Danville dead."

6. Now all you ladies, heed, take warning,
From this time on and learn,
Never speak harsh words to your true loving husband,
He may leave you and never return.

You're a Flower Blooming in the Wildwood

M: G; F: C or D
CD 2-Track 98

Traditional

1. On an even-ing long a - go, when the sun was sink - ing low, My dar-ling went to
2. Well, the let - ter came to me, from a cap - tain on the sea, That told__ me my
3. He's__ gone for - ev - er more, he can - not come back to shore, He's drown - ded__

sail a - cross the sea.__ It was in the month of June, when the ros - es were in bloom, He
dar - ling was dead.__ Oh the shock and great sur - prise, put the tear-drops in my eyes, When I
down be - low, you see. When it's in the month of June, and the ros - es are in bloom, It

took me in his arms and said to me:___ Cho: "You're a flow-er bloom-ing in the wild -
thought a - bout the last words that he said:___
seems to me I hear my dar - ling say:___

wood, You're a flow - er bloom - ing there for me,___ Sweet-er than the morn - ing

dew, and I'll soon re - turn to you, You're a flow - er bloom-ing there for me."__

D. McCoury, Goose Island Ramblers   283

Mandolin Chords

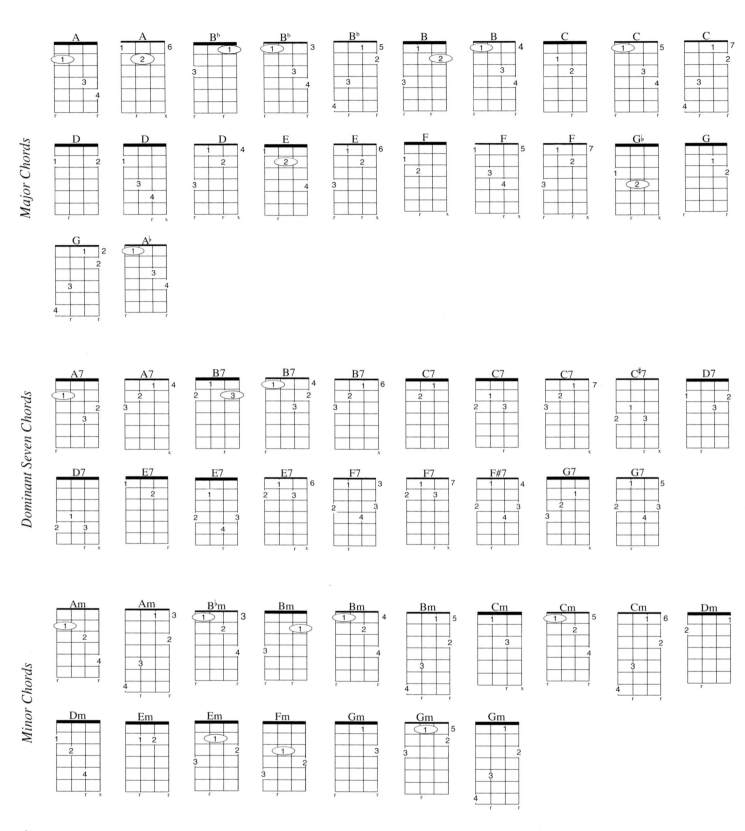

Major Chords

Dominant Seven Chords

Minor Chords

Diminished Chords

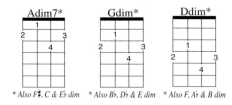

* Also F#, C & Eb dim   * Also Bb, Db & E dim   * Also F, Ab & B dim

Note: Closed position chords, or chords with no open stringed notes, like the first two A chords at top left, the first two A7s, the first two A minors, the diminished chords etc., are moveable up and down the fingerboard. Move either of the Am chords down one fret in pitch (toward the nut) and the new chord will be an Abm or G#m chord. Move either of the A7 chords up one fret in pitch (toward the bridge) and you'll have an A#7 or Bb7 chord. If you keep this in mind, you'll find it much easier to transpose songs from one key to another. If you can't find a specific chord listed here, just move one up or down to the correct fret. The small "r" under a chord grid indicates a chord's root tone. An "x" means to mute or not play that string.

Notes on Selected Songs
For a complete alphabetical listing of all the songs in this book, see the Table of Contents on page 2.

A

All the Good Times, p. 10: An eloquent description of the despair lost love can bring.

Amazing Grace, p. 11: Probably the greatest hit of spiritual music, it appeals to people with a wide variety of beliefs.

Angel Band, p. 12: I love the comforting message of "Angel Band." Quite a different point of view from "He Will Set Your Fields on Fire." (p. 96)

Angeline, the Baker, p. 13: Probably the source for the instrumental "Angelina Baker." This vocal version is quite happy and peppy considering that the story is about a slave who's sweetheart has "gone away," no doubt sold to another owner. Like many songs of the pre-Civil War period, this one idealized slave and plantation life. "Darling Nellie Gray" (p. 56) has a very similar story but is much more somber in tone.

Angels Rock Me To Sleep, p. 14: Another comforting image of death.

Are You From Dixie? p. 16: One of a vast repertoire of songs that idealize the sunny south including "Sweet Sunny South," (p. 236) "My Old Kentucky Home," "Blue Ridge Mountain Blues" (p. 28). "The Girl I Loved in Sunny Tennessee" (p. 78). These types of songs, some from the mid-1800s, some as recent as the latest pop country hit, have resonated across the US and throughout the world. Of course we're not all from the south but we all have a mother, maybe a sweetheart, or a warm concept of home. That might explain the enduring popularity of these types of songs.

Are You Washed in the Blood of the Lamb? p. 18: This one, along with many other great old time gospel songs, comes from my worn Baptist hymnal "Tabernacle Hymns." You can still find these for a dollar or two or three in used books stores.

Arkansas Traveller, p. 19: You probably sang this as "Bringing Home a Baby Bumble Bee" as a kid. My dream is to play "Arkansas Traveller" for Bill Clinton. It's probably been done.

As I Went Down in the Valley to Pray: See "Down in the Valley to Pray." (p. 67)

Aunt Dinah's Quilting Party, p. 20: Sometimes titled "Seeing Nellie Home."

Away in a Manger, p. 21: One of my favorites since childhood. Peaceful and reassuring. Makes a good bluegrass Christmas song.

B

Banks of the Ohio, p. 22: I love the melody to this grisly but popular murder ballad. There must be hundreds of versions of it with a variety of different lyrics. On some the chorus is, "Only say that you'll be mine/And in no other's arms entwine." In the version in this book the third verse makes little sense. Suddenly we're talking about the sea instead of the Ohio River. No matter, it's still a powerful song and a good example of the "folk process" where lyrics are repeated, misheard, changed, repeated, etc.

Beautiful Life, A, p. 23: Who could argue with the sentiments expressed in this song? It's usually performed in an intricate vocal quartet arrangement. Like several other similar songs, I've simplified the arrangement in this book for clarity and the sake of space. Listen to one of the original recordings to hear the vocal arrangement.

Beautiful Star of Bethlehem, p. 24: One of the prettiest Christmas songs and one often performed by bluegrass bands.

Bile Them Cabbage Down, p. 26: There are several songs with similar verses about one mammal in a tree, the other on the ground imploring him to "shake some 'simmins (persimmons) down." Wendy Whitford of the Goose Island Ramblers always sang "Shake them *cinnamons* down."

Black Eyed Susie, p. 27: Compare this song with "Blue Eyed Verdie" and some of the verses in "Pig in a Pen," among other songs with similar lyrics.

Blue Ridge Mountain Blues, p. 28: This song is unusual in that subsequent choruses have alternate lyrics. Some singers also fit in lyrics that include "Want to see my old dog Trey."

Bluebirds are Singing for Me, p. 29: The: Usually performed with a "call-and-response" chorus with repeated or echoed lines: "There's a bluebird singing" / *"There's a bluebird singing"* / "In the Blue Ridge Mountains" / *"In the Blue Ridge Mountains,"* etc.

Bound to Ride, p. 30: When I hear this song, I imagine a young bachelor riding the train, far away from home and sweetheart, eating saltine crackers because they're so cheap. I remember in my own youth when Kraft Macaroni and Cheese could be had for $.25 a package. Tough to prepare and eat in a moving vehicle though.

Bright Morning Stars, p. 31: Often performed a capella. This arrangement is shown with accompanying chords.

Bring Back to Me My Wandering Boy, p. 32: Bill Monroe's version of this song is called "Out in the Cold World."

Buffalo Gals, p. 33: Another one we sang as kids. Of course that was during "The Enlightenment" when most public schools had art and music classes.

Bully of the Town, The, p. 34: A great song then and now! We've still got bullies coming out of the woodwork and heroes ready to take 'em on. A G diminished chord can be substituted for the Gb chord.

Bury Me Beneath the Willow, p. 36: One of the first folk or old time songs players learn. A "must know."

C

C-H-I-C-K-E-N, p. 38: Originally a pop song from 1902.

Can't You Hear Me Callin'?, p. 40: Also the title of a comprehensive biography of Monroe, *Can't You Hear Me Callin': The Life of Bill Monroe, Father of Bluegrass* by Richard D. Smith (Warner Books). The chorus is often sung as "I loved you best," but "Bess" was Monroe's long time companion and bass player Bessie Lee Mauldin. You decide how to sing it.

Careless Love, p. 41: A standard in the folk, bluegrass, and jazz repertoires. I first heard the "in the family way" lyrics when I discovered them while doing research for this book. The song makes much more sense in this light.

Children Go Where I Send Thee, p. 42: Reminiscent of "The Twelve Days of Christmas" with the numbers and repetitions of characters. Listen to the CD to hear how the chorus grows upon repetition. Great bluegrass Christmas song.

Church in the Wildwood, The, p. 43: I remember my grandmother Nellie Bruce singing this to us grandkids. The chorus is often performed with multiple parts. My grandmother would crack us up singing the bass part, which was a chant below the melody on the chorus: "Oh come, come, come, come…"

Cindy, p. 44: Another I learned in grade school music class. I was pleasantly surprised to discover it in the bluegrass repertoire.

Cold Jordan: See "Jordan." (p. 134)

Columbus Stockade: See "Columbus Stockade Blues." (p. 45)

Columbus Stockade Blues, p. 45: This one makes a great hard country or rockabilly song.

Come All Ye Fair and Tender Ladies: See "Fair and Tender Ladies." (p. 72)

Coo Coo, The: See "Cuckoo, The" (p. 51)

Cotton-Eyed Joe, p. 46: A standard for fiddlers in all types of country and old time music.

Crawdad Song, The, p. 48: Makes a wonderful kids' bluegrass song.

Cripple Creek, p. 49: Most often played as an instrumental but when it is sung, the lyrics are usually only sung on part one. Also known as "Shootin' Creek."

Cuckoo, The, p. 51: I love the verses, melancholy mood, and varied verses of "The Cuckoo," alternately titled "The Coo Coo."

D

Daniel Prayed, p. 52: I'd heard "Daniel Prayed" for years but really got into it when I transcribed a Doc Watson recording with three vocal parts, lead, tenor, and bass, for my Doc Watson and Clarence Ashley book (MB97056) published by Mel Bay. It's a wonderful old time gospel trio arrangement. Check it out. The version in this book is simplified and written with just the lead voice. The book is packed with songs that have become "greatest hits" of old time and bluegrass.

Danny Boy, p. 54: Often played as an instrumental, this song's lyrics are haunting and beautiful. War takes its toll on all those involved in it but surely mothers bear the greatest burden.

Darling Corey, p. 55: Notice the close similarity in lyrics between "Darling Corey" and "Little Maggie." (p. 158) Many of the songs in *The Parking Lot Picker's Songbook*, and indeed in the greater traditional American music repertoire, share lines, whole verses, or themes with other songs. Credit the "folk process" of hearing songs, adding verses, swapping lyrics or melodies, mixing the whole thing up and serving it new as each individual singer adapts a song.

Darling Nellie Gray, p. 56: One of the most powerful songs I've ever heard. When Jim Nunally and I perform it, an older listener invariably comes up to tell us they'd learned the song in grade school, but had never heard verse four. "Darling Nellie Gray" has been a popular song for generations, for obvious reasons, published again and again, but that particular verse, the one that gave the lyric its power and the song its meaning, was censored. Many people mistakenly assume this is a Stephen Foster composition when in fact it was composed by B.R. Hanby. I hear a similarity in the movement and tone of the melody between this and Bob Wills' classic "Faded Love."

Darling Will You Ever Think of Me? p. 58: I wanted to include a few of my own compositions in *The Parking Lot Picker's Songbook*. Here's one that I hope you'll enjoy.

Deep Elem Blues p. 59: I first learned this when I played in Frank Wakefield's band in the late 1970s. It's a comical look at the bad part of town.

Diamonds in the Rough, p. 60: Worth learning for the metaphor alone. Performed in both 4/4 (as written) and 6/8 (on CD).

Didn't He Ramble: See "Oh, Didn't he Ramble." (p. 186)

Do Lord, p. 62: The C♯7 and F♯m chords in measure eleven are enclosed in parenthesis noting that they are optional. In the process of collecting the songs for this book, I consulted several hymnals. To my surprise I found that the harmonies in my old Baptist hymnal often included these somewhat "modern" sounding chords, the three dominant and the six minor.

Don't Let Your Deal Go Down, p. 63: This arrangement combines elements from different old time and more modern bluegrass sources. Compare these lyrics with "Storms are on the Ocean."

Don't You Hear Jerusalem Moan? p. 65: A fun and funny song that's slightly "crooked" with an extra vocal phrase. And, could we ever have enough songs that make fun of preachers and authority in general? Here's another set of lyrics:

1) Well I went to church last Sunday morning/Don't you hear Jerusalem moan?/ Heard all them sinners just a moaning and a groaning/Don't you hear Jerusalem moan?

2) I'm gonna get down on my knees today,
Don't you (etc.)
Let Jesus wash my sins away, (etc.)

3) There's many souls lost here in sin,
Don't you go and talk to them, (etc.)

Down Among the Budded Roses, p. 66: One I learned from Wendy Whitford and the Goose Island Ramblers and a "true" song with a perfect image that says it all: "Down among the budded roses/I am nothing but a stem." As the others are coming into the bloom of life, the singer's own life seems over due to a lost love. Compare with "Wildwood Flower" (p. 277) and "Little Rosewood Casket." (p. 161)

Down in the Valley to Pray, p. 67: This song is performed as "Down to the River to Pray" in the film "O Brother Where Art Thou?"

Down in the Willow Garden, p. 68: I'm not sure what "burglar's wine" is, unless it's a mickey. Some people sing "burgundy wine."

Down the Road, p. 69: The Greenbriar Boys and Country Gazette performed this with an added chorus: "Down the road, down the road, Got a little pretty girl down the road." Flatt & Scruggs left the chorus out. You can fill in your own name in the lyric "Old man (or woman) ____ (insert your name here)."

Down to the River to Pray: See "Down in the Valley to Pray." (p. 67)

E

East Virginia Blues, p. 71: This is a truly epic story and there are several versions of it that are sung in old time and bluegrass circles. Compare it with "Katy Dear." (p. 141) The lyrics to "East Virginia Blues" vary according to version. For example, in verse two, some versions have white lilies on her breast and in verse #4, the second and third lines are also sung "Where she lies, a' taking her rest," For in her hand she holds a dagger." The order and number of verses varies widely.

End of My Journey: See "Let Me Rest at the End of My Journey." (p. 148)

F

Fair and Tender Ladies, p. 72: Lots of great songs came to bluegrass from the folk revival of the 1960s. These types of songs were often performed by the more "modern" bluegrass groups like the Osborne Brothers and the Country Gentlemen.

Fathers Have a Home Sweet Home, p. 73: Often performed with lead, tenor, and bass vocal parts.

Feast Here Tonight, p. 74: Sometimes called "Rabbit in a Log," this song is a classic. The definitive version was recorded by the Monroe Brothers.

Footprints in the Snow, p. 76: Bill Monroe's version sets the bluegrass standard for this song.

G

Girl I Left in Sunny Tennessee, The: (see "Girl I Loved in Sunny Tennessee, The") (p. 78)

Girl I Loved in Sunny Tennessee, The, p. 78: The original source of this song is a sentimental pop song from 1899. It's often called "The Girl I *Left* in Sunny Tennessee."

Give Me Oil in My Lamp, p. 80: From the Baptist canon.

Give Me the Roses While I Live, p. 81: A popular theme in several different traditional and old time songs. It's as true today as it was a hundred or more years ago. Don't let someone slip away without them knowing of your love or admiration. It can happen in the blink of an eye.

Going Down This Road Feeling Bad, p. 82: Also known as "Lonesome Road Blues" and the basis of Earl Scruggs' instrumental of the same name. It's sometimes performed with an Em chord in measure twelve over the lyrics "Lord/And I."

Going Up Cripple Creek: See "Cripple Creek." (p. 49)

Going Up Home to Live in Green Pastures: See "Green Pastures." (p. 87)

Grandfather's Clock, p. 84: Long a hit with banjo pickers and guitar fingerpickers, this one also makes a wonderful vocal with its eerie story.

Green Pastures, p. 87: Another Stanley standard with a beautiful, peaceful view of the great beyond.

Groundhog, p. 88: Red Allen repeats the word "groundhog" twice more as a kind of chorus.

H

Hallelujah! I'm Ready, p. 89: A few of the songs in *The Parking Lot Picker's Songbook* are written with basic two part vocal arrangements. In the case of this "call and response" duet, I've omitted the tablature stems to make it easier to read. You can hear the arrangement on the accompanying CD.

Hand Me Down My Walking Cane, p. 90: Long a favorite among folkies, Norman Blake does a great old time version of this song.

Handsome Molly, p. 91: Every generation updates traditional music. My favorite update of "Handsome Molly" is a kind of Latin-Reggae romp by the Extended Playboys. Try to find that on your iTunes! In one of Doc Watson's earlier versions of "Handsome Molly" he sings "I wish I was in London/or some other *depot* town."

Hard Times, Come Again No More, p. 92: This is still a very popular song among folk singers, especially at group sings.

He Was a Friend of Mine, p. 94: I first heard a version of this on a Byrds' LP where it was rewritten about John F. Kennedy's assassination. Since that time in the mid-1960s, I've heard it performed in several folk contexts including bluegrass and traditional blues.

He Will Set Your Fields on Fire, p. 96: Talk about your fire and brimstone! This one is usually performed with an intricate, multi-voice arrangement.

High on a Mountain, p. 98: One incredible song by Ola Belle Reed. The image, melody, modal chord movement, story, and tone of it all make it a classic and a "must-know" song.

Highway of Sorrow, p. 99: Bill Monroe had a reputation as a gruff, tough and stubborn curmudgeon. When I interviewed him in the early 1980s, I found this to not be the case, exactly. While reserved and private, he also showed a great sense of humor and a playful streak. He was expansive on many subjects from his own legacy to his thoughts about rock and jazz as well as his views on life. It's amazing to me that he revealed himself as much as he did in compositions like "Highway of Sorrow," "It's Mighty Dark to Travel," (p. 124) and "Can't You Hear Me Calling." (p. 40) He was truly a great artist.

Hills of Roane County, p. 100: For me, a cryptic verse like: "Sweet Martha was grave but Corey was better/There's better and worse, although you can see," kicks this song into greatness. It's mysterious, beautiful, unknowable.

His Eye is on the Sparrow, p. 102: From "Tabernacle Hymns." Singer and actress Ethel Waters sang "His Eye is on the Sparrow" beautifully and soulfully as part of the Billy Graham Crusades in the 1950s and 1960s.

Hold Fast to the Right, p. 103: In this case I believe "right" refers to the "correct way" as opposed to any far-flung node in the political spectrum.

Hold to God's Unchanging Hand, p. 104: Soothing words for modern life.

Home Sweet Home, p. 105: This song has been a hit for well over a hundred years. Jim Nunally and I play it quite often and audiences still love it.

Hop High Ladies, p. 108: Often played as an instrumental, this song is also known as "Uncle Joe" and "Mrs. McCleod's Reel," among other titles.

Hot Corn, Cold Corn, p. 110: Wonderful goofy song that seems to have something to do with John Barleycorn.

How Can You Treat Me So? p. 111: I had Bill Monroe's voice in mind as I wrote this one.

I

I am a Man of Constant Sorrow: See "Man of Constant Sorrow." (p. 169)

I Know You Rider, p. 113: Originally a blues, this one has been adapted by rock groups and "modern" bluegrass bands, most notably The Seldom Scene.

I Ride an Old Paint: See "Old Paint" (p. 194)

I Shall Not Be Moved, p. 115: From the gospel repertoire and popular in old time gospel, jazz, bluegrass, and folk circles. It was an important and symbolic marching song during the civil rights movement of the 1950s and 1960s.

I Wonder How the Old Folks Are at Home, p. 116: Good old pop song from 1909. Popularized in bluegrass by Mac Wiseman.

I'll Be All Simes Tonight, p. 118: I first heard this from Wendy Whitford of the Goose Island Ramblers. It's a wonderful take on the woman's point of view of a breakup. It's sung by both men and women. See also "Little Rosewood Casket" (p. 161) and "Wildwood Flower." (p. 277)

I'll Fly Away, p. 120: Everybody's favorite gospel/bluegrass song.

I'm Ready: See "Hallelujah! I'm Ready." (p. 89)

I'm Sitting on Top of the World: See "Sitting on Top of the World." (p. 230)

I'm Standing in the Need of Prayer: See "Standing in the Need of Prayer." (p. 233)

In the Garden, p. 122: From "Tabernacle Hymns."

In the Pines, p. 123: Another great bluesy standard of bluegrass and old time music.

It's Mighty Dark to Travel, p. 124: Bill Monroe overheard the phrase "it's mighty dark to travel" in a barber shop as someone mentioned that they had a long way to travel in the dark of night. Monroe turned the phrase into a bluegrass standard.

J

Jesse James, p. 126: If you're gonna be an outlaw, you'd better have somebody write a sympathetic folk song about you. This song is all about primitive attempts at "spin." Woody Guthrie wrote a similar but politically charged song about "Pretty Boy Floyd."

Jimmie Brown, the Newsboy, p. 128: A sentimental parlor tune from the late 1800s. Like much of their repertoire, the Carter Family adapted it to fit their style in the late 1920s. Flatt & Scruggs version from the early 1950s brought this great song into the bluegrass repertoire.

John Hardy, p. 130: See "Jesse James" (p. 126) above. Hardy didn't get quite the treatment in song that Jesse did. I say, pay the extra few bucks, get a good songwriter.

John Henry, p. 132: There must be over a hundred different versions of "John Henry." It's been so popular over the years because it so dramatically tells the story of automation and human against machine.

Jordan, p. 134: The chorus to "Jordan" is often performed with the bass voice taking the lead on the first clause of each phrase of the chorus. Bass solo: "Now look at that," ensemble joins in "cold Jordan," etc.

Just a Closer Walk with Thee, p. 136: This one is popular in many musical genres from gospel and blues to dixieland and bluegrass.

Just as I Am, p. 137: You mature youngsters may remember this theme from the televised Billy Graham crusades of the 1950s and beyond. Willie Nelson recorded a beautiful instrumental version for his *Red Headed Stranger* LP.

Just Over in the Gloryland, p. 138: Another song whose popularity spans many musical genres from gospel and blues to dixieland and bluegrass.

K

Katy Dear, p. 141: Compare the lyrics of this "Romeo and Juliet"-type tale with "East Virginia Blues" (p. 71) and "Silver Dagger."

Keep on the Sunnyside, p. 142: An old song the Carter Family adopted as their theme song. What better advice for life?

Knoxville Girl, p. 144: A murder ballad similar to "Banks of the Ohio" (p. 22) but perhaps even more gory and disturbing.

L

Late Last Night, p. 146: Also known as "Way Down Town," I first heard this from Doc Watson on the *Will the Circle be Unbroken* project from the early 1970s. That historic three LP set introduced traditional music and traditional and bluegrass musicians to the rock-oriented youth culture of the era.

Leave it There, p. 147: I heard this on a 1920s recording by Washington Phillips and it really grabbed me. Not only is it filled with great sentiment, I realized I recognized it from somewhere. Turns out it was from the old Baptist hymnal "Tabernacle Hymns."

Let Me Rest at the End of My Journey, p. 148: One of many cowboy-themed songs that ended up in the bluegrass repertoire.

Letter Edged in Black, The, p. 149: When I was a callow youth learning this repertoire from the older generation, songs like "The Letter Edged in Black" struck me as overly sentimental and dramatic. I was more drawn to the hot and fast material. I guess it was because I hadn't yet experienced the loss of a parent. Now, as I've gotten older and experienced more, I've come to love these songs and appreciate their eloquence in dealing with the life and death issues that we all face.

Life is Like a Mountain Railway: See "Life's Railway to Heaven. (p. 150)

Life's Railway to Heaven, p. 150: Even if you're not religious, this song is an apt description of the journey of life.

Li'l Liza Jane, p. 152: Another folk song they taught us in grade school.

Little Annie, p. 153: I first heard this great song from Vern Williams, California's most important contribution to old time bluegrass. "Little Annie" marks the beginning of the massive "Little" section, ironically the largest section in this book, which spans the old time musical horizon from "Annie" to "Willie." (One could argue that "Li'L Liza Jane" belongs here as well, but it's in the "Li'l" section, not the "Little.") For size, the "Old" section is a close rival.

Little Bessie, p. 154: As I mentioned above in "The Letter Edged in Black," my perception of these songs has changed with my age. Being the father of a beautiful twenty-one year old daughter (as of 2005), I find it impossible to sing "Little Bessie" without breaking down in tears.

Little Birdie, p. 156: This arrangement is simplified from the way it's typically performed. Singers usually stretch out syllables like the first "birdie..." an extra measure or longer. The band has to pay attention to the singer!

Little Georgia Rose: See "My Little Georgia Rose." (p. 180)

Little Maggie, p. 158: As with "Little Birdie," (p. 156) singers often stretch lyrics beyond their written time values.

Little Old Log Cabin in the Lane, p. 160: If you can find it, listen to Fiddlin' John Carson's version. It was one of the first "country" or "hillbilly" recordings made in the early 1920s. It's just him singing, with his fiddle, and it's haunting.

Little Rosewood Casket, p. 161: Not about what you might think it's about. Compare with "I'll Be All Smiles Tonight" (p. 118) and "Wildwood Flower." (p. 277)

Little Sadie, p. 162: Both this and "Little Willie" (p. 163) are epic story songs where a lot goes on. Both have similarities to "Banks of the Ohio," (p. 22) "Knoxville Girl," (p. 144) and "Pretty Polly." (p. 204) May not be suitable for younger listeners.

Little Willie, p. 163: A brutal and graphic song but a true representation of real events.

Lonesome Reuben: See "Reuben's Train." (p. 216)

Lonesome Road Blues: See "Going Down This Road Feeling Bad." (p. 82)

Long Journey Home, p. 165: Check out the Monroe Brothers definitive version.

Lord, I'm Coming Home, p. 166: After hearing this for years by artists like the Stanley Brothers and loving it, I discovered "Lord, I'm Coming Home" in one of my worn old hymnals.

M

Mama Don't Allow, p. 168: A well-known and loved song that pops up in a variety of musical styles including jazz and country. It's a proven crowd pleaser.

Man of Constant Sorrow, p. 169: The most famous version of this song is from the film "O Brother, Where Art Thou?" sung by the mythical Soggy Bottom Boys. Their version is based on one recorded by the Stanley Brothers which features a repeat of each verse's last line as in "I have no friends to help me now/He has no friends to help him now."

McKinley: See "White House Blues." (p. 271)

Methodist Pie, p. 172: Another tongue-in-cheek look at religion.

Midnight on the Stormy Deep, p. 174: The classic recording of this song is by Bill Monroe in the mid-1960s. Peter Rowan sings it in duet with Monroe.

Milwaukee Blues, p. 175: If you don't know the music of Charlie Poole, run to the store right now and buy one of the new CD box sets. He's one of the true pioneers of old time and bluegrass music with a repertoire and style that influenced all that came after him. Charlie Poole made great, entertaining music. In the last verse, "Santa Fe" rhymes with "be."

Molly and Tenbrooks, p. 176: One of the all-time hits of bluegrass based on much earlier sources.

More Pretty Girls Than One: See "There's More Pretty Girls Than One." (p. 240)

Mrs. McCleod's Reel: See "Hop High Ladies." (p. 108)

My Home's Across the Blue Ridge Mountains, p. 178: Sometimes sung as "My Home's Across the Smoky Mountains."

My Little Georgia Rose, p. 180: The true story behind this Bill Monroe composition can be found in his biography *Can't You Hear Me Callin': The Life of Bill Monroe, Father of Bluegrass* by Richard D. Smith (Warner Books).

My Walking Cane: See "Hand Me Down My Walking Cane." (p. 90)

My Wandering Boy: See "Bring Back to Me My Wandering Boy." (p. 32)

N

Nellie Gray: See "Darling Nellie Gray." (p. 56)

New River Train, p. 182: Another classic from the Monroe Brothers.

Nine Pound Hammer, p. 183: You gotta learn this one! It's one of the ten or twenty songs played by ALL Parking Lot Pickers.

Nobody's Business, p. 184: There are a variety of versions of this basic song in bluegrass, old time, blues, and jazz. It may be even more well-known in blues than in bluegrass. As far as I know, the Stanley Brothers brought it into the bluegrass lexicon.

O

Oh Death, p. 185: Another great song featured in the film "O Brother, Where Art Thou?" It's usually sung unaccompanied, with no instrumental backup, in a *rubato* (loose, drawn out rhythm) style. It's written here with backup chords, so you can hear the tonality, and in standard rhythm. The B7s in parenthesis are optional. Be sure to listen to Ralph Stanley's recording.

Oh! Didn't He Ramble, p. 186: Another old pop song appropriated by Charlie Poole. Also popular with dixieland jazz bands.

Old Dan Tucker, p. 188: One they taught us in grade school.

Old Joe Clark, p. 192: Check out the less than proper lyrics. Good taste is timeless! Fiddlers usually play this in the key of A.

Old Man at the Mill, p. 193: Also known as "Same Old Man," I first heard this old time song in a bluegrass context by the Dillards. The flatted seven chord, in this case an F natural, gives the song it's modal flavor.

Old Paint, (p. 194) : It always gets back to just a cowboy and his horse. See also "Let Me Rest at the End of My Journey." (p. 148)

Old Rugged Cross, The, p. 195: The A diminished chord in measure one is a little unusual in old time and bluegrass music. Though it comes straight out of the hymnal, in practice it's often played as an Ab chord.

On and On, p. 197: Another very popular Monroe-penned classic of life on the road without your sweetheart.

Out in the Cold World: See "Bring Back to Me My Wandering Boy." (p. 32)

Over in the Gloryland, p. 138: You'll hear this song in gospel, blues, and especially in the traditional jazz repertoire. It's interesting that so many songs end up as favorites in a variety of musical styles. I guess it's because so many types of American music share the same roots, often gospel. And, a good song is a good song, no matter where it comes from or who else sings it.

Over the Hills to the Poorhouse, p. 198: A pre-Social Security song that may have renewed resonance in the next few years, especially for baby boomer bluegrass musicians. It's a true song, if slightly dramatic.

P

Pass Me Not, p. 199: Beautiful melody, comforting lyrics.

Pig in a Pen, p. 201: Different versions of this song feature different combinations of the same basic lyrics. And you'll find verses from "Pig in a Pen" in a variety of other songs.

Poor Ellen Smith, p. 202: Sometimes this song is performed with the one line chorus "Nobody knows how I loved Ellen, nobody knows.

Poor Nellie Gray: See "Darling Nellie Gray." (p. 56)

Poor Wayfaring Stranger: See "Wayfaring Stranger." (p. 255)

Precious Memories, p. 203: I love the dreamy imagery and moving poetry of this song. It's often mistaken for a gospel song though there's nothing overtly religious about it.

Pretty Polly, p. 204: Another murder ballad done so well by Ralph Stanley.

Put My Little Shoes Away, p. 206: The lyric "Won't he look so nice and cunning" always confused me. Webster's Dictionary of 1913 explains, "Pretty or pleasing; as, a cunning little boy."

R

Rabbit in a Log: See "Feast Here Tonight." (p. 74)

Railroad Bill, p. 208: I learned this one from my brother-in-law Rick March when he was teaching me to fingerpick.

Rain and Snow, p. 209: This song has a kind of nebulous tonal center rocking between the Am and the D chord. That gives it a modal feel and the unresolved lyrics add to the song's sense of mystery.

Rank Strangers to Me, p. 210: One of the Stanley Brothers all-time hits that's become a bluegrass standard. The chorus is typically performed in a "call and response" format.

Red Rocking Chair, p. 212: Slightly unusual in that it has an Em or six minor chord in it.

Red Wing, p. 214: One of the most widely known tunes in American music. It's a pop tune from the early 1900s, part of a group of songs that idealized native Americans. Because of its popularity, the melody to "Red Wing" has been adapted again and again to other sets of lyrics. An anonymous writer used it as the basis for "Charlie Chaplin," a children's old time song about the famous tramp, and Woody Guthrie used it for his labor song "Union Maid." The main theme of "Red Wing" is based on Schumann's "The Happy Farmer" from 1849.

Reuben's Train, p. 216: This one shows up with many alternate titles including "Train 45," "Lonesome Reuben," and just plain old "Reuben."

Roll in My Sweet Baby's Arms, p. 218: You gotta know this one if you're going to play bluegrass. Especially for bluegrass bakers.

Roll on Buddy, p. 219: Another great one from the Monroe Brothers song bag. By the way, did you get one of the Monroe Brothers CD box sets yet?

Roving Gambler, p. 220: Another from the folk bag that's slipped into the bluegrass repertoire. Listen to the Country Gentlemen's version.

S

Sally Goodin, p. 223: Probably best known as a fiddle tune, "Sally Goodin" also has some funny lyrics, which are usually sung over the first part. The second part is played instrumentally.

Same Old Man: "Old Man at the Mill." (p. 193)

Seeing Nellie Home: See "Aunt Dinah's Quilting Party." (p. 20)

Shady Grove, p. 224, Bluegrass style: "Shady Grove" is performed with a variety of arrangements and lyrics. Here's a version often played by bluegrass bands. An old time version follows. Lyrics are shared between the two and you'll notice one verse that's also in "Pig in a Pen." (p. 201)

Shady Grove, Old Time style: See "Shady Grove, Bluegrass style." (p. 224)

Shall We Gather at the River, p. 226: Learned in church from "Tabernacle Hymns."

She's My Little Georgia Rose: See "My Little Georgia Rose." (p. 180)

Short Life of Trouble, A, p. 227: Kind of a depressed look at life brought on by a failed love. The theme of verse six is common in traditional music: "You broke my heart, it killed me, plant some flowers on my grave so everybody'll know what a rat you are." Like that would happen!

Shortening Bread, p. 228: A very popular traditional song that fits well into the old time/bluegrass format.

Silver Threads Among the Gold, p. 229: A sentimental old parlor song dating from the late 1800s if not earlier. I've collected several different sheet music versions of the song. Similar to "When You and I Were Young, Maggie," (p. 268) "Silver Threads" has beautiful, moving, and poetic lyrics about true love that seem all the more meaningful as I age.

Sitting on Top of the World, p. 230: From the blues repertoire.

Softly and Tenderly, p. 231: This one reminds me a bit of "Just as I Am," (p. 137) "Angel Band," (p. 12) and some of the other songs in this collection that offer a reassuring view of the inevitable.

Somebody Touched Me, p. 232: A great old gospel rouser.

Standing in the Need of Prayer, p. 233: Ditto "Somebody Touched Me." (p. 232)

Sugar Hill, p. 234: I learned this from the Goose Island Ramblers. Guitarist Wendy Whitford usually sang, "Shake them cinnamons down" instead of "Shake them 'simmons down."

Sweet Sunny South, p. 236: One of my absolute favorite songs with its serious and beautiful poetry that any one who's left home can relate to. I found it with a different melody and called "Take Me Home" (attributed to the composer "Raymond") in a book titled *Heart Songs* published in 1909. I also found other sources that credit W.L. Bloomfield, 1853. This is a slave song of sorts ("Where poor massa lies buried close by") but rather than idealize plantation life, it offers a bittersweet and universal portrait of aging and dying.

Swing Low, Sweet Chariot, p. 237: Another popular song that appears in many different genres from gospel to blues to country.

T

Take Me Home: See "Sweet Sunny South." (p. 236)

Take this Hammer, p. 238: Similar in theme to "Nine Pound Hammer" (p. 183) and other mining songs, "Take This Hammer" has the added edge of forced labor and confinement. I love the verse: "If he asks you was I running/Tell him I's flying."

Take Your Burden to the Lord and Leave it There: See "Leave it There." (p. 147)

Talk About Sufferin', p. 239: This is another song that's typically performed a capella. It's written here with accompaniment chords and fermatas.

Tenbrooks and Molly: See "Molly and Tenbrooks." (p. 176)

That's the Way to Spell Chicken: See "C-H-I-C-K-E-N." (p. 38)

There's More Pretty Girls Than One, p. 240: This song is also performed in 4/4. Check out Tony Rice and Ricky Skaggs' version on "Skaggs and

Rice," one of the most beautiful duo recordings ever set to wax.

They Gotta Quit Kickin' My Dawg Aroun', p. 242: Another from the Goose Island Ramblers and a pop song from the early 1900s. I've collected the original sheet music, or at least most of it. The cover of my copy is missing. I borrowed the one shown.

This Little Light of Mine, p. 244: From Sunday school.

This Train, p. 245: Another one learned in grade school.

This World is Not My Home, p. 246: *The Parking Lot Picker's Songbook* includes a lot of songs about death. I guess that's because, like love, it's a universally mysterious subject we all have difficulty dealing with. "This World is Not My Home" speaks to the fact that we're not here for a very long time; we're only passing through.

Train, Train, Train: p. 247. A new song by Dix Bruce. Never recorded by anybody. You could be the first!

Train 45: See "Reuben's Train."

Train That Carried My Girl From Town, The, p. 248: I suppose the singer's hate of the train, its engineer and fireman, is somewhat misplaced, but that's what makes the song interesting.

'Twas Midnight on the Stormy Deep, p. 174: See "Midnight on the Stormy Deep" (p. 174)

Two Dollar Bill: See "Long Journey Home." (p. 165)

U

Unclouded Day, The: This song would not be near as interesting if it had been titled "The Clear Day."

W

Wabash Cannonball, p. 250: This is one of the true classics of American folk music. There must be hundreds of variations. Some singers use the lyrics "rumor and roar" in the chorus. One of my favorite songs loosely based on "Wabash Cannonball" is Chuck Berry's "Promised Land."

Walk in Jerusalem Just Like John, p. 252: You'll notice the similarity of the last verse to one in "Swing Low, Sweet Chariot." (p. 237)

Walking in My Sleep, p. 254: "Walking in My Sleep" is a great old time song with wonderfully entertaining lyrics like verse one: "If you see that gal of mine tell her if you please/'Fore she goes to make my bread to roll up her dirty sleeves." That's art, man!

Way Downtown: See "Late Last Night, p. 146." (p. 146)

Wayfaring Stranger, The, p. 255: A beautiful standard played many different ways in a variety of genres.

What a Friend We Have in Jesus p. 257: Learned in Sunday school from "Tabernacle Hymns."

When I Die, p. 258: Here's one I wrote. I was walking through the woods one day and suddenly felt the presence of my dear departed grandmother, the one who used to sing "The Church in the Wildwood" (p. 43) to me. The song puts words to my thoughts about the incident.

When I Lay My Burden Down p. 259: Note the similarity of this melody to that of "Will the Circle Be Unbroken." (p. 278)

When My Race is Run, p. 260: Another of mine. I'll show her! Wait 'til I'll die!

When Springtime Comes Again: See "Little Annie." (p. 153)

When the Roll is Called Up Yonder, p. 262: One more from the old Baptist hymnal.

When the Saints Go Marching In, p. 264: You're probably most familiar with this as a New Orleans jazz tune.

When the Work's All Done This Fall, p. 266: A cowboy song that's worked its way into the old time and bluegrass repertoire.

When You And I Were Young Maggie, p. 268: Another moving take on love and aging similar to "Silver Thread Among the Gold" (p. 229) and "Sweet Sunny South." (p. 236)

Where the Soul Never Dies, p. 269: I just had to write out both parts to this great duet. On the verses, the tenor sings the same lyrics as the lead adding "of man" into the phrase "Where the soul never dies." On the chorus the voices are in counterpoint to one another. You can hear it on the CD. I split the TAB from the music so each would fit on one page.

Whitehouse Blues, p. 271: Doctors are better now, especially with their bedside manner. The last verse made the rounds in the late 1960s.

Who Broke the Lock? p. 272: Learned from Wendy Whitford of the Goose Island Ramblers.

Who Will Sing for Me? p. 274: Another ponderous song about death.

Wild Bill Jones, p. 276: Another good "bully" song.

Wildwood Flower, p. 277: This song, probably the best known of all guitar melodies, has wonderful and poetic lyrics which so beautifully express the feelings of the composer. Compare the sentiments to "I'll Be All Smiles Tonight," (p. 118) and "Little Rosewood Casket." (p. 161) The Carter Family sings lyrics that are a bit different here and there. They may have "mis-heard" the names of some of the flowers mentioned.

Will the Circle Be Unbroken? p. 278: One of the greatest hits of old time and bluegrass music.

Willie My Darling, p. 280: Beautiful song with bang-up, unexpected tear-jerker-ending. A classic of the "anti-flirting" genre.

Working on a Building, p. 121: See "I'm Working on a Building." (p. 121)

Worried Man Blues, p. 281: You may have heard the hit version of this in the early 1960s. It goes back much further than that, probably to slavery times.

Wreck of the Old 97, The, p. 282: You will need to know several train wreck songs if you intend to play bluegrass. Here's a good one that also happens to be quite popular.

Y

You're a Flower Blooming in the Wildwood, p. 283: Lost love and death. A perfect summation of the main themes of this collection of songs. Not a word about taxes, politics, gas prices, or cell phones. If you ask me, the writers of all these songs knew what was important.

You're Drifting Too Far From the Shore: See "Drifting Too Far From the Shore." (p. 70)

You've Got to Walk That Lonesome Valley: See "Lonesome Valley." (p. 164)

Index by Artist

*Look at that smile of accomplishment! Must be eleven year
old Louie Kubelbeck's G bluegrass chop chord. He's ready for
some parking lot picking!*

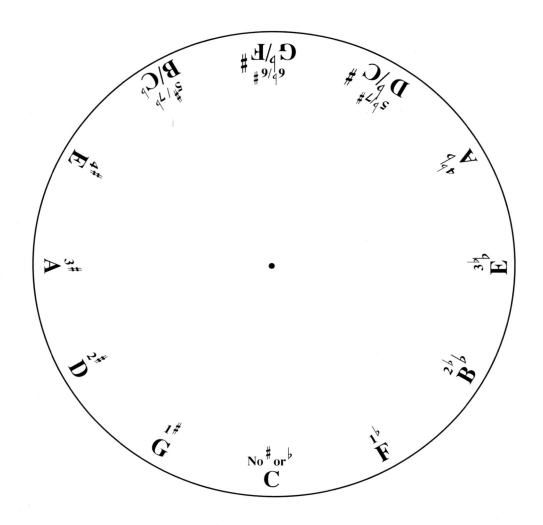

Musix Transposer Wheel

Copy this page onto card stock or download and print it from the "Downloads" section of www.musixnow.com. Carefully cut out both wheels. Punch a small hole at the dot in the middle of each. Attach the smaller wheel to the larger wheel with a paper fastener making sure both wheels can spin independently. To transpose, follow directions on inner wheel.

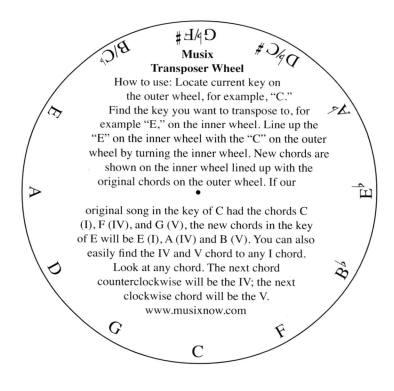

Musix Transposer Wheel
How to use: Locate current key on the outer wheel, for example, "C." Find the key you want to transpose to, for example "E," on the inner wheel. Line up the "E" on the inner wheel with the "C" on the outer wheel by turning the inner wheel. New chords are shown on the inner wheel lined up with the original chords on the outer wheel. If our original song in the key of C had the chords C (I), F (IV), and G (V), the new chords in the key of E will be E (I), A (IV) and B (V). You can also easily find the IV and V chord to any I chord. Look at any chord. The next chord counterclockwise will be the IV; the next clockwise chord will be the V.
www.musixnow.com

Audio Track Listing

1. Late Last Night :38
2. Leave it There :51
3. Let Me Rest at the End of My Journey :47
4. Letter Edged in Black :28
5. Life's Railway to Heaven 1:00
6. Li'l Liza Jane :22
7. Little Annie :41
8. Little Bessie :25
9. Little Birdie :22
10. Little Maggie – Little Old Log Cabin in the Lane medley 1:03
11. Little Rosewood Casket :29
12. Little Sadie :28
13. Little Willie :26
14. Lonesome Valley – Long Journey Home medley :45
15. Lord I'm Coming Home 1:01
16. Mama Don't Allow :21
17. Man of Constant Sorrow :35
18. Maple on the Hill :29
19. Methodist Pie – Midnight on the Stormy Deep medley 1:15
20. Milwaukee Blues :26
21. Molly and Tenbrooks :28
22. My Home's Across the Blue Ridge Mountains :23
23. My Little Georgia Rose :38
24. New River Train – Nine Pound Hammer medley 1:01
25. Nobody's Business :23
26. Oh Death :39
27. Oh Didn't He Ramble – Old Dan Tucker medley 1:06
28. Old Home Place :38
29. Old Joe Clark :21
30. Old Man at the Mill :17
31. Old Paint :37
32. Old Rugged Cross 1:10
33. Old Time Religion :24
34. On and On :43
35. Over the Hills to the Poorhouse :39
36. Pass Me Not 1:03
37. Paul and Silas :21
38. Pig in a Pen :21
39. Poor Ellen Smith :24
40. Precious Memories 1:04
41. Pretty Polly :37
42. Put My Little Shoes Away :44
43. Railroad Bill :23
44. Rain and Snow :37
45. Rank Strangers to Me 1:21
46. Red Rocking Chair :29
47. Red Wing :42
48. Reuben's Train :21
49. Rocky Top :41
50. Roll in My Sweet Baby's Arms :38
51. Roll on Buddy :32
52. Roving Gambler :19

53. Sailor on the Deep Blue Sea :26
54. Sally Goodin :27
55. Shady Grove, bluegrass :21
56. Shady Grove, old time :28
57. Shall We Gather at the River :41
58. Short Life of Trouble, A :22
59. Shortening Bread :26
60. Silver Threads Among the Gold :47
61. Sitting on Top of the World :24
62. Softly & Tenderly :58
63. Somebody Touched Me :35
64. Standing in the Need of Prayer :26
65. Sugar Hill :29
66. Sweet By and By :41
67. Sweet Sunny South :25
68. Swing Low, Sweet Chariot :35
69. Take This Hammer :30
70. Talk about Sufferin' :38
71. There's More Pretty Girls Than One :27
72. They Gotta Quit Kickin' My Dawg Aroun' :34
73. This Little Light of Mine :25
74. This Train :22
75. This World is Not My Home :44
76. Train, Train, Train 1:01
77. Train That Carried My Girl From Town, The :32
78. Unclouded Day, The :41
79. Wabash Cannonball :25
80. Walk in Jerusalem Just Like John :29
81. Walking in My Sleep :21
82. Wayfaring Stranger, The 1:06
83. Were You There When They Crucified My Lord? – What a Friend We Have in Jesus medley 1:32
84. When I Die :31
85. When I Lay My Burden Down :28
86. When My Race is Run 1:09
87. When the Roll is Called Up Yonder – When the Saints Go Marching In medley 1:02
88. When the Work's all Done This Fall :28
89. When You and I Were Young, Maggie :52
90. Where the Soul Never Dies :39
91. Whitehouse Blues – Who Broke the Lock? medley :57
92. Who Will Sing for Me? :52
93. Wild Bill Jones :22
94. Wildwood Flower :31
95. Will the Circle Be Unbroken – Will There Be Any Stars in My Crown? medley 1:21
96. Willie My Darling :51
97. Worried Man Blues – Wreck of the Old 97 medley :59
98. You're a Flower Blooming in the Wildwood :41